THE HE[

MYTH/IMAGE/SYMBOL

BOOKS BY OR EDITED BY DOROTHY NORMAN

THE HERO: MYTH/IMAGE/SYMBOL

NEHRU—THE FIRST SIXTY YEARS

ALFRED STIEGLITZ—INTRODUCTION TO AN AMERICAN SEER

THE HEROIC ENCOUNTER

SELECTED WRITINGS OF JOHN MARIN

AMERICA AND ALFRED STIEGLITZ

DUALITIES

THE HERO:

MYTH/IMAGE/SYMBOL

BY DOROTHY NORMAN

ANCHOR BOOKS

DOUBLEDAY

NEW YORK   LONDON   TORONTO   SYDNEY   AUCKLAND

AN ANCHOR BOOK
PUBLISHED BY DOUBLEDAY
a division of Bantam Doubleday Dell Publishing Group, Inc.
666 Fifth Avenue, New York, New York 10103

ANCHOR BOOKS, DOUBLEDAY, and the portrayal of an anchor
are trademarks of Doubleday, a division of Bantam Doubleday
Dell Publishing Group, Inc.

The Hero: Myth/Image/Symbol was originally published in hardcover
by The New American Library, Inc., in association with The World
Publishing Company, in 1969. The Anchor Books edition is published
by arrangement with the author.

Library of Congress Cataloging-in-Publication Data
Norman, Dorothy, 1905–
    The hero: myth, image, symbol / by Dorothy Norman.
        p. cm.
    Reprint. Originally published: New York:
New American Library, 1969.
    Includes index.
    1. Heroes—Mythology.   2. Heroes—Religious aspects.
3. Heroes—Psychological aspects.   4. Heroes in art.
I. Title.
BL815.H47N67   1990   90-36705
291.2'13—dc20   CIP
ISBN 0-385-26751-7

TO ANANDA K. COOMARASWAMY

CONTENTS

LIST OF PLATES

All line drawings preceded by * are by Mark Hasselriis.

ix

X

AUTHOR'S NOTE

This volume is dedicated to the late Ananda K. Coomaraswamy, because of my own profound regard for him, and his unique contribution to the world at large. The manner in which he illuminated the most subtle meanings of Indian iconography and philosophy served to cast significant light upon the traditions of other civilizations. It has been most aptly said of him that through what he expressed about the East, he helped the West to understand itself. (Which is by no means to underestimate his vast knowledge of Western culture.)

I am deeply grateful to Dr. Coomaraswamy, and to his wife, Dona Luisa, for the many enlightening conversations I have had with each of them—with Dr. Coomaraswamy from 1928, to the year of his death, 1947. I should like further to thank Mrs. Coomaraswamy for her generous cooperation on any number of occasions while I have been working on this volume.

I appreciate, in particular, the invaluable talks I have had with Stella Kramrisch, and her many kindnesses. Exchanges with others, whose work is cited throughout these pages, have been additionally helpful.

I wish to express my special gratitude to Mark Hasselriis for his extraordinary care in making the line drawings for this book, and for the numerous discussions we have had, especially with respect to ancient Egyptian art and philosophy. (Asterisks have been placed before titles of line drawings.)

My heartfelt thanks to Dr. Kramrisch, Alfonso Ossorio, Mr. Hasselriis, Jessie Fraser, and Mary Lescaze for having read my manuscript in its entirety. Their suggestions were invariably perceptive and rewarding, as were those of Richard Ettinghausen of the Freer Gallery; Fong Chow, Aschwin Lippe, and Virginia Burton at the Metropolitan Museum of Art; John Plummer and Richard Priest of the Pierpont Morgan Library; Donald Hansen of the New York University Institute of Fine Arts, who graciously aided me in checking a variety of passages. I am also indebted to Pupul Jayakar for her many courtesies.

Although I have conferred about certain points touched upon in this volume with those cited above, no one other than myself must bear responsibility for what is herewith presented.

Every effort has been made to give proper acknowledgments; to identify the names of all painters, sculptors, and photographers; to provide correct dates and provenance of works of art reproduced.

Whenever ascertainable—except in the case of certain brief passages—sources of quotations from books, poems, and articles, as well as names of translators, are cited in footnotes. Since, at times, I had copied fragments that interested me before I began to write this volume, it has not always been feasible to rediscover where I originally found them. All Biblical texts quoted are from a single edition of the King James Version of the Old and New Testaments, published by the American Bible Society, New York, 1964.

As for further acknowledgments, I should like to express my profound thanks to St.-John Perse for his kind permission to utilize the quotations in Chapters 11, 18, and 24 from "Dante," translated by Robert Fitzgerald, and "On Poetry," translated by W. H. Auden (*Two Addresses,* Bollingen Series LXXXVI, New York: Pantheon Books, 1966). Special mention should be made, also, that the lines from Virgil's *Aeneid* in the quotations preceding Chapter 1, and in Chapter 13 were translated by Rolfe Humphries (New York: Charles Scribner's Sons, 1951); those from the *Bhagavad Gita* in Chapters 14 and 19 by Franklin Edgerton (Cambridge: Harvard University Press, 1952, Vol. I). The lines from Angelus Silesius in Chapter 20 were translated by Willard R. Trask (*The Cherubinic Wanderer,* New York: Pantheon Books, 1953). All of the selections from Martin Buber were translated by Olga Marx.

I wish to acknowledge my gratitude for permission to reproduce the following photographs: Plates 1, 45, 137: Art Reference Bureau, Ancram, New York. Plate 2: National Museum, Copenhagen. Plate 8: Musée Guimet, Paris. Plate 10, from *Monuments of Romanesque Art,* Hanns Swarzenski, Chicago: University of Chicago Press, 1954, and London: Faber and Faber. Plate 11, from *Romische Bronzen, Kirchenturer im mittelalterlichen Europa,* Zurich: Europa Verlag, 1957. Plate 14, from *The Glory of Romanesque Art,* Joseph Gantner and Marcel Pobé, New York: The Vanguard Press, 1956, and London: Thames and Hudson. Plates 15, 29, 63, 64, 96, 121: The Pierpont Morgan Library, New York. Plates 16, 75: Lessing Rosenwald, Jenkintown, Pennsylvania. Plate 17: The Tate Gallery, London. Plates 19, 126: The Metropolitan Museum of Art, New York. Plate 28: Eliot Elisofon, New York. Plate 49: Capitoline Museums, Rome. Plate 58: Museum of Fine Arts, Boston. Plates 62, 76, 95: Philadelphia Museum of Art. Plate 65: Staatsbibliothek der Stiftung Preussischer Kulturbesitz (formerly Preussische Staatsbibliothek), Berlin. Plate 66: Allen Atwell, New York. Plate 70: National Museum, Athens. Plates 71, 80, 134: Cleveland Museum of Art. Plate 72: Willard Gallery, New York. Plate 77: The New York Public Library, Spenser Collection. Plate 78: Kunstmuseum, Basel. Plates 85, 86: Smithsonian Institution, Freer Gallery of Art, Washington, D.C. Plate 88: Dr. Dmitrij Tschizewskij, Heidelberg. Plate 91: Bibliothèque Nationale, Paris. Plate 97: Saul Steinberg; Harper and Row, New York; *The New Yorker.* Plates 98, 100, 102: The Museum of Modern Art, New York. Plate 99: The Solomon R. Guggenheim Museum, New York. Plate 101: Henri Cartier-Bresson, Paris. Plate 104: Alfonso Ossorio, East Hampton, New York. Plate 105: Jean Dubuffet, Paris. Plates 108-117, from *Manual of Zen Buddhism,* Daisetz Teitaro Suzuki, London: Rider and Company, 1956, and New York: Grove Press, Inc. Plate 118: The Detroit Institute of Arts. Plate 119: Dr. Stella Kramrisch, Philadelphia. Plate 123: Contini Collection, Florence. Plate 124: Hofbibliothek, Aschaffenburg. Plate 127: Bayerisches Nationalmuseum, Munich. Plate 128: Musées de la Ville de Strasbourg (painting destroyed by fire, 1947). Plate 129: Museo San Marco, Florence. Plate 135: Mme. Gunvor Moitessier, St. Rémy l'Honoré.

The following line drawings that I have had made especially for this volume are included by the gracious courtesy of those listed below: Plate 3: Museum of Navaho Ceremonial Art, Santa Fe; Plates 4, 26, 69: Musée du Louvre, Paris; Plate 5: Glyptothek und Museum antiker Kleinkunst, Munich; Plate 6: The New York Times Company, New York; Plate 7: The Dean and Chapter of Winchester Cathedral; Plates 20, 25, 35, 36, 125: The British Museum, London; Plate 31: *Archaeology,* Columbia, Missouri; Plate 38: Martin von Wagner-Museum der Universität Würzburg; Plates 40, 41, 42, 83, 87, 122: The Pierpont Morgan Library, New York; Plates 43, 44, 47, 93: Bibliothèque Nationale, Paris; Plates 61, 67: Museo Nazionale, Naples; Plate 82: Cincinnati Art Museum; Plates 84, 92: The Metropolitan Museum of Art, New York; Plate 90: The Bodleian Library, Oxford; Plate 136: Monumenti Musei e Gallerie Pontificie, Vatican City.

I am indebted to the publishers and others listed below who have generously granted permission to reprint passages from the following volumes: *The Gods of the Greeks,* C. Kerényi, translated by Norman Cameron, New York: Vanguard Press, and London: Thames and Hudson. *The Art of Indian Asia,* Heinrich Zimmer, edited by Joseph Campbell, New York: Bollingen Foundation. "The Man with the Blue Guitar," from *Collected Poems,* Wallace Stevens, New York: Alfred A. Knopf, and London: Faber and Faber. *The Golden Legend,* Jacobus de Voragine, translated by Granger Ryan and Helmut Ripperger. *Ten Rungs,* Martin Buber, translated by Olga Marx, New York: Schocken Books. *Hinduism and Buddhism,* Ananda K. Coomaraswamy, New

York: Philosophical Library. *Myth and Ritual in Christianity,* Alan Watts, New York: Vanguard Press, and London: Thames and Hudson. "The Iconography of Dürer's 'Knots' and Leonardo's 'Concatenation,'" Ananda K. Coomaraswamy, in *The Art Quarterly,* Detroit: The Detroit Institute of Arts. *Black Boy,* Richard Wright, New York: Harper and Row, and Paul R. Reynolds, Inc. *Manual of Zen Buddhism,* Daisetz T. Suzuki, London: Rider and Company, and New York: Grove Press. "Ithaca," from *The Complete Poems of Cavafy,* translated by Rae Dalven, New York: Harcourt, Brace and World, Inc., and London: The Hogarth Press. *Ancient Near Eastern Texts,* edited by James B. Pritchard, Princeton: Princeton University Press. *Zen in the Art of Archery,* Eugen Herrigel, translated by R. F. C. Hull, New York: Random House, Inc., Alfred A. Knopf, Inc., and London: Routledge and Kegan Paul Ltd.

In the interest of typographical conformity and readability, diacritical and similar marks or accents have been eliminated — a custom increasingly followed by publishers. (West European accents have been retained.)

Even though certain words in picture headings, titles of books, quotations, and other passages are not spelled identically, no attempt has been made to regularize them, due to the many different sources from which they have been taken. It will be noted that, with regard to proper names, among other examples, Mithras is also spelled Mithra; Jonah, Jonas; Seth, Set; Medousa, Medusa; Dionysus, Dionysos; Huwawa, Humbaba; Cadmus, Kadmos; Daedelus, Dedalus; Heracles, Herakles, Hercules; Shiva, Saiva (which, with a diacritical mark, is Śiva); Shah-Namah, Shah-namah.

My warmest appreciation must be expressed to Elinor Weis, not only for her most valuable suggestions, and superb secretarial work, but for her skill with regard to proofreading, and related editorial matters; to Janet Dowd for her excellent secretarial assistance, and her many perceptive comments; to Lucy Lippard for her aid in checking certain images and texts when I first began to work on this book. I wish to express my gratitude to The New American Library for its imaginative cooperation; in particular to Robert Gutwillig, Wendy Weil, Lea G. Forsman, Estelle Silbermann, Lina Mainiero, Lee Hochman, William Gregory, Frank Kozelek, Paul Bacon, Ony Ryzuk, and Jay Tower.

A word of warning about scholarship: Even the most distinguished authorities often differ with respect to dates and interpretation. In addition to which it is no more possible to assess the nature of dominant beliefs prevalent in civilizations of other eras, with absolute accuracy, than totally to comprehend events in one's own century. Yet, to be alive is to seek, and to share one's findings as best one can, in the hope that they are true in spirit both to what occurred long ago and is happening now — above all, to what does, or could, take place within each of us.

Whereas, initially, the approach of this book may seem more relevant to the ancient, than the contemporary world, preoccupation with the heroic principle in life is eternally compelling. Moreover, material pertaining to cultures other than our own is presented not so that we may attempt blindly to imitate what is described, but in order to open our minds and hearts: to widen the scope of our awareness, to expose ourselves to the greatest possible range of challenge.

New York City
Winter, 1967

"Sometimes a fool, sometimes a sage, sometimes possessed of regal splendor; sometimes wandering, sometimes as motionless as a python, sometimes wearing a benignant expression; sometimes honored, sometimes insulted."

SHANKARACHARYA

"He who would not sacrifice his own soul to save the whole world, is, as it seems to me, illogical in all his inferences, collectively."

CHARLES PEIRCE

"The place or . . . medium of realization is neither mind nor matter, but that intermediate realm of subtle reality which can only be adequately expressed by the symbol. The symbol is neither abstract nor concrete, neither rational nor irrational, neither real nor unreal."

CARL G. JUNG

"In a dark tree there hides
A bough, all golden, leaf and pliant stem,
Sacred to Proserpine. This all the grove
Protects, and shadows cover it with darkness.
Until this bough, this bloom of light, is found,
No one receives his passport to the darkness
Whose queen requires this tribute. In succession,
After the bough is plucked, another grows,
Gold-green with the same metal. Raise the eyes,
Look up, reach up the hand."

VIRGIL

"In dealing with symbols and myths from far away we are
really conversing . . . with ourselves — with a part of
ourselves, however, which is as unfamiliar to our conscious
being as the interior of the earth to the students of geology.
Hence the mythical tradition provides us with a sort of
map for exploring and ascertaining contents of our own
inner being to which we consciously feel only scantily
related."

HEINRICH ZIMMER

"Symbolism does not appertain especially to dreams, but rather to the unconscious imagination, and particularly to that of the people, and it is to be found in a more developed condition in folklore, myths, legends."

SIGMUND FREUD

"We are betrayed by what is false within."

GEORGE MEREDITH

"For as God uses the help of our reason to illuminate us, so should we likewise turn it every way, that we may be more capable of understanding His mysteries; provided only that the mind be enlarged, according to its capacity, to the grandeur of the mysteries, and not the mysteries contracted to the narrowness of the mind."

FRANCIS BACON

"Then will I also confess unto thee that thine own right hand can save thee."

JOB 40:14

"It is better to resist at the beginning than at the end."

LEONARDO DA VINCI

"To know that what is impenetrable to us really exists,
manifesting itself as the highest wisdom and the most
radiant beauty."

ALBERT EINSTEIN

"Every account of a mythology — unless it reproduces its sources in the original text and in their fragmentary condition . . . must be an interpretation. And every interpretation is conditioned by the degree of receptivity of the contemporary presenter of the material. . . . The subjective factor cannot be eliminated, but it must be compensated for by the vigilance of the interpreter and by his faithfulness to his material. . . . The original story-tellers of Greek mythology justified their variations simply with the act of narration, each in his own fashion, of the story. In mythology, to *tell* is to justify. The words: 'It was told' . . . are not intended to compensate for the fact that the tones of the original story-teller, and often, alas, the original narrative itself, are now extinct. They are intended to concentrate the reader's attention on the only thing that matters — namely, *what* was told. This, however it was shaped, was essentially and in all its forms, developments and variations the same permanent and unmistakable basic story. The *words* of the basic story have disappeared, and all that we have are the variations. But behind the variations can be recognised something that is common to them all: a story that was told in many fashions, yet remained the same." [1]

C. KERÉNYI

---

1. THE GODS OF THE GREEKS, translated by Norman Cameron, New York: Grove Press, 1960, pp. 8–9.

THE HERO:
MYTH/IMAGE/SYMBOL

1   INTRODUCTION

Consider the myths of the hero afresh. They convey to us today, as always, subtle yet urgent messages to which we must pay attention. However, in the early years of this century, interest in myth waned. Scientific or realistic data were of primary importance. Mythology was relegated to distant lands and the past. Slowly this attitude has been changing. In my own case, in 1929, meeting A. K. Coomaraswamy, one of the foremost writers on East Indian art and tradition, brought myth and symbol vividly to my undivided attention. I began to realize that the exploits of the most enduring heroes take on special significance because their fundamental content pertains to the release of creative energies in man.

Our perennial preoccupation with the hero's quest concerns the quality of life to be lived, as well as the insatiable search to become more fully integrated which has been mirrored in multiple forms in diverse cultures and eras. Heroes do not represent definable human figures, but rather mythological ideals to be achieved. They appear in numberless guises, one of the most important of which reflects the effort we make — the effort to reach our most creative potential.

The basic intent of this volume is to suggest some of the manifold ways in which this heroic principle in life operates; to present, by means of word and image, variations on the method by which we attain release at crucial turning points; how our transformations occur; the price to be paid for them; and toward what end.

The hero in man must plumb the terrifying depths in order to scale the heights in consonance with a precept, doubtless of Eastern origin but by now universally affirmed: In order *to find the path, follow the path, be the path*, we must discover for ourselves the inner meaning of the *heroic principle in life*. The more relentlessly we expose ourselves to the myths of the hero — ancient or contemporary — the more intensely we will be able to identify with and penetrate their significance. Our concentration, openness, and absorption lead us along the road to self-knowledge, if only we have neither self-deluding preconceptions nor pride because we feel we have comprehended even the slightest fragment of eternally challenging mysteries.

We comprehend only partially at any given moment in our evolution and at different phases of our development the entire scope of the myth of the hero. Symbols that have satisfied for centuries may quite suddenly appear devoid of meaning; those images most lacking in the power to move us can, to our surprise, possess the greatest import when rediscovered at crucial moments or in fresh garb. To make a fetish of the significance of any given concept is to risk becoming enmeshed in distortion. To depend on any extremity or decadence of dogma and doctrine is to court disaster.

When myths function in a life-enhancing manner, they fulfill a deep human need, whether they are projected as a result of overwhelming crisis or positive revelation, by way of art or any other creative act.

The majority of illustrations and texts referred to throughout these pages may at first seem to mystify instead of swiftly to clarify. Yet any oversimplification must becloud the issues or with equal danger expose the sacred to possible profanation.

Since the ways in which myths of the heroes are presented change constantly, they provide both miraculous bridges between one era and another and unexpectedly clear markings that distinguish disparate epochs. They are acts of faith associated by analogy with assurance of the coming of the new day, the successive seasons, the cycle of the year and finally the entire cosmic order. For this reason the heroes are so often looked upon as symbolical mediators between heaven and earth or as dominating the seasons. They are also enlightened warnings to us to make the most of life, despite our limitations and in the face of every catastrophe.

The need persists in man to know that the succession of sun and moon, day and night, the seasons, is fixed, predictable, ordered. He desires to penetrate the mystery of the waxing and waning of the moon, its three-day disappearance, the bewildering phenomenon of the eclipse. He experiences terror before drought and flood, feels deeply the fear of death and the surge toward life: fertility, abundance, survival.

The hero personifies the hardihood to undergo most difficult rites of passage, or initiation into phases equated with the mysterious and frightening unknown; the discipline of arduous labors; the ability to survive both the symbolical night and winter through possessing the fortitude to confront their rigors. Yet whatever inner power the hero attains, he must develop beyond the necessity either to depend upon it or even willfully to utilize it; for example, Arthur's effortless raising of the sword from the rock or, in Hindu mythology, Rama's similar lifting of the bow. Both deeds show how heroic feats of critical importance are enacted at moments when a clear dividing line between will and act no longer exists; when, beyond all necessity to proceed according to any attitude or intended motivation, performer and performance are one; when the hero himself is not even conscious that his act is heroic. Although unaware, he alone can have achieved his task. When Lancelot crosses the perilous sword bridge on his journey to Guinevere, he is the personification of the hero as love.

In ancient civilizations the hero was often seen as the lion or the bull. The two regal beasts themselves represent the two great luminaries, sun and moon, the lion standing for energy, strength, fearlessness; the bull, for wisdom, majesty, the generative power in the universe.

When the hero has conquered the lion or the bull, he has won the right to wear its skin. With each succeeding victory he may sit or stand on the beast; finally, he may carry it.

These ever-recurring symbols within the myth of the hero possess outer and inner meanings, positive and negative powers, material and spiritual aspects that are both creative and destructive. Images that mirror outer phenomena and inner vision — event and dream — merge. Levels shift, conflict, are interdependent. One role of the hero in man is to encounter and transform the negative powers of the lion or the bull inside himself; thus the hero appears as pathfinder, confronted by opposing yet always complementary forces. The seed of the Yin is eternally in the Yang and therefore the opposite is also true. Opposition does not frighten him; he accepts the perennial necessity to resolve the tension of antithetical forces, while accepting conflict as inherent within the universe. The hero in man realizes that through the interplay and clash of polarities, life energy is released. Therefore he battles always in favor of the creative as against the destructive; he intuitively secedes from death-dealing in favor of re-vitalizing action.

This book alludes to birth, to renewal, to dawn and spring, to the depth of night and winter; to the mysteriously creative source and power of revivification within the individual, the collectivity, the universe. It speaks of transformation, of health and wholeness.

Like the gods of creations whom he resembles and emulates, the hero of myth brings forth a most subtle aspect of inner order out of chaos, light rather than torment and doubt. He attains such ends only as part of a mystery, as though he were ever wrapped in an invisible cloak, sacredly, in silence. The line between shadow and revelation hovers delicately about the edges of that intangible carrier of insight, named art. The hero, himself the artist, remains always the prophet, possessed both of the faculty to see before others and the courage to confront the darkness he finds in himself and in the world. Through the process of penetrating darkness — by way of perception itself — light is attained, the life-giving power of illumination. The ground of darkness is pierced.

The hero of myth must abandon all and be abandoned. He enters the pit, the labyrinth, the cavern, the ark, the wilderness, the symbolical netherworld or tomb, as when Heracles combats the Nemean Lion in the cave without weapons or help of any kind. All such tests must themselves be without consequence unless they lead to more profound experience; unless they liberate from the hitherto dreaded; from mistaken dependence upon qualities that should be outgrown.

No attempt has been made to interpret what is touched upon as stemming from any single point of view, or any specific religious, historical, psychological, archeological, ethnological, or anthropological tradition, to the exclusion of others. Unless some other point is illuminated thereby, no special emphasis has been placed upon whether a symbol has migrated, has emerged from one particular source, or been secondarily diffused only in limited areas. Neither have such questions been argued as whether a myth has originated in an archaic, prehistoric, hunting, agricultural, or technological society; in the East or the West; as a result of patriarchy or matriarchy, individual repression, an overarching unconscious — or conscience; because of primitive, totemistic, sophisticated, compensatory, or any other isolated factor.

No debate has been entered upon with respect to whether myth derives — to mention but a few categories — from prescientific concepts, from ancient drama, from cult worship and practice, or from early initiation rites (the latter having to do with such basic phenomena as birth, puberty, marriage, death). No effort has been made to define the hero solely as king, priest, saint, rishi, guru, shaman, yogi, or initiator; as savior, or performer of an act of truth; as asker of the right questions, or object of sectarian reverence; as overthrower of a human tyrant, or symbolical contestant with such beasts as lion and bull. For surely the heroic principle in life pertains to all such poetic images, as well as to many additional ones: to artist, seer, sage, in whatever context; to enlightener or enlightened. Far more crucial is the fact that, irrespective of label, or how often a particular theme may emerge, disappear, and then reappear — whether in seemingly logical, or quite unexpected fashion — what is of primary interest is that total risk and dedication are inevitably involved. Of ultimate significance is the need to become aware of at least a few of the clues that can reveal to us, beyond the confines of any superficially constructed diagram, one of the great basic myths — that of the hero — touching, as it does, upon a major aspect of human endeavor.

Whereas man perennially trembles in the face of Paradise Lost — of chaos, uncertainty, destruction, alienation, night and death — but also of overwhelming ecstasy, life and day, what is of highest concern is the possibility that a heroic vision may dawn within each of us, to be assimilated — beyond theory or intellectualization — into our everyday lives. Only if we gain a sense of integration can we become capable of transfiguring what is narrowly self-serving into what may benefit others. Yet we must ever know that such a phenomenon cannot occur save at the right time, and because of a classic procedure, difficult not merely to describe but, even more important, to endure. The process is impossible to hasten, since it involves both self-discovery and the being transported into harmony with others — as with the very axis of the universe — the most meaningful of all goals.

And now we shall experience at least some of the ways in which the heroic process unfolds. Just as it must, of necessity, evolve only gradually, so we cannot possibly observe all of it at a single glance.

Even though the heroic quest is never totally realized, the very envisioning of it — like our every attempt to embark upon it — comprises one of man's most noble acts of imagination and faith.

2 PRELUDE:
MOVEMENT TOWARD DAWN

1. OFFERING TO THE DIOSKOUROI
Section of votive relief. Hellenistic. 1st century B.C.
Musée du Louvre, Paris. Alinari photograph.

Often referred to as twins in Greek myth or epic, the Dioskouroi — Kastor and Polydeukes (better known in the Western world as Castor and Pollux) — have been spoken of as spending alternate days in the heavens and the netherworld. As with various pairs of legendary brothers, one of the two — in this instance Pollux — is viewed as immortal, the other as mortal. Thus, while Pollux may be looked upon as the divine potential within each of us, Castor typifies the earth force we dare not deny, but must eternally encounter and transform. Without the dual forces — symbolically represented by the zodiacal sign Gemini — there would be no life.

Mounted on their majestic steeds, the Dioskouroi — antithetical, yet complementary — resemble the Aswins of India's Rig Veda, twin offspring of sky or sun, luminous harbingers of dawn. The Aswins, representing heaven and earth; day and night, past and future; the tension of the opposites, or inseparable dualities, mirror — at the point of their dynamic transition from darkness to light — the path that the hero must, of necessity, tread. A way inexorably identified with the traditional and dangerous night journey — a journey, in truth, extending far beyond such brief duration — into the deepest reaches of ourselves: our most dire and tormented netherpoint of despair. So that, as a result of what we confront, experience and must transcend, a fresh level of awareness or rebirth is achieved, as at the horizon of a new day; each battle waged by the hero, in his manifold manifestations, but leading to the next.

"And from that dawn of freshness, as from a very pure fall of dew, they keep, in our midst, something of the dream of creation." [1]

ST.-JOHN PERSE

---

1. BIRDS, as translated by Wallace Fowlie in *Portfolio*, No. 7, Winter 1963, p. 120.

3 BIRTH OF THE CREATIVE PROCESS IN MAN

2. SCULPTOR CARVING A HERM
Detail from vase painting by Epiktetos. Greek.
c. 500 B.C. National Museum, Copenhagen.

In ancient Greece, pillars of Hermes stood by the wayside upon heaps of stones. Hence the name Hermes, since there can be little doubt that the word signifies "he of the stone heap." (In later times the phallus remained a characteristic of the stone pillars of Hermes.)

A sculptor chisels a phallic image associated with the resourceful Hermes, son of heaven and light; one of great "brilliance and inexhaustible abundance," [1] messenger or herald of the gods, who in time became equated with ancient primal fertility deities. Man's as yet unformed creative force is being molded: the potential within ourselves and in the world.

And the Lord said, "I have set before you life and death, blessing and cursing: therefore choose life, that both thou and thy seed may live." [2]

Myths of the heroes speak most eloquently of man's quest to *choose life over death*. They have done so since time immemorial, despite every labor and conflict, confusion and struggle.

"The hero," an ancient Rig Vedic hymn proclaims, "in the depth of . . . heaven, yearning for the dawns, [enters] the great sky and the earth." [3] And then a cry is uttered: "Create the light [for] which we long." [4]

---

1. THE HOMERIC GODS, Walter F. Otto, translated by Moses Hadas, New York: Pantheon Books, 1954, p. 106.
2. DEUTERONOMY 30:19.
3. RIG VEDA SANHITA, Max Müller, London: Trübner and Co., 1869, Vol. I, p. 128.
4. Ibid., p. 137.

4 THE MYTH OF THE HERO
AS COSMIC CREATION MYTH
IN MICROCOSM

Although it is generally assumed that symbols pertaining to cosmic creation are to be viewed in metaphysical terms, whereas myths of the hero pertain to our most essential struggle with ourselves, it is nonetheless imperative to establish a fresh correlation between the two levels.

"The southeast quadrant of [a Navajo] sandpainting . . . shows the Fire God, sleeping near his circular hogan [or dwelling], which is protected by a rainbow [at left]. Across the arms and shoulders of the god is a zig-zag pattern which represents the Milky Way. A constellation also appears on [the God's] black mask, and above his head. He holds a firestick in one hand." The jagged line extending upward from the fire (lower right) "is the path taken by Coyote, who stole fire and carried it to [the] First Man and First Woman." [1]

Prometheus is similarly described as having stolen fire from the gods. As will be shown in conjunction with still further portrayals, the gods have, at times, been symbolized both as awakeners of man by way of crisis or the thunderbolt, and opponents of the development of human consciousness or creativity. It is the hero in man who both reacts most sensitively to challenge, and courageously pays the price for performing whatever deed is necessary to his or our evolution.

---

1. NAVAJO CREATION MYTH, Hasteen Klah and Mary C. Wheelwright, Bulletin Number Six, Santa Fe: Museum of Navajo Ceremonial Art, 1960, back cover.

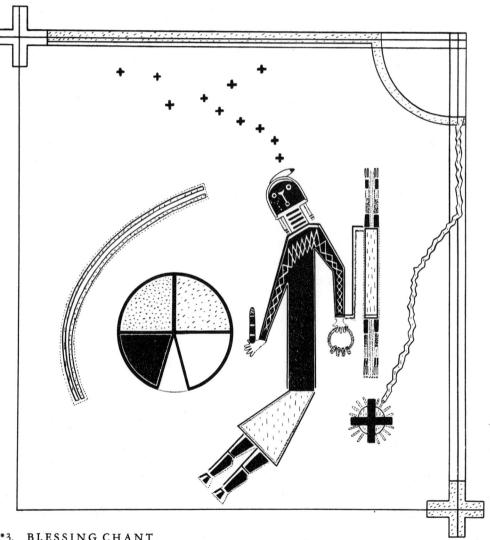

*3. BLESSING CHANT
From sandpainting by Pierre Woodman. 1938.
The Museum of Navajo Ceremonial Art, Santa Fe.

5 FORMS OF AWAKENING

"Shaking the roots & fast foundations of the Earth."

WILLIAM BLAKE

The creative hero-deed of hurling the thunderbolt may be said to mirror, by analogy, the act of the Vedic god Indra who, in order to bring the world into manifestation, struck down the gigantic serpent Vritra, the latter's inhibiting purpose having been to thwart creation: "Indra armed with the thunderbolt broke the way for us, He smote down Vritra, the encloser of the rivers." [1] Whereupon, as a result of Indra's act, the waters poured forth, "eager for their course." [2] "I set the rivers free," quoth the great activator, "for all mankind." [3]

According to the symbolism of ancient Rig Vedic hymns, the release of the waters, affected by the destruction of the serpent Vritra, alludes to "the flood of life and belongs to all. It is the sap of field and forest, the blood coursing in the veins. The monster [Vritra] had appropriated the common benefit, massing his ambitious, selfish hulk between heaven and earth, but now was slain. The juices again were pouring. . . . During the period of the supremacy of the dragon, the majestic mansions of the lofty city of the gods had cracked and crumbled. The first act of Indra was to rebuild them." [4]

"Indra creates existence and . . . destroys the enemies of existence." [5]

STELLA KRAMRISCH

---

1. MYSTERIUM UND MIMUS IM RIG VEDA, Leopold von Schröder, Leipzig: 1908, p. 230.

2. HYMN FROM THE RIG VEDA, 3.33. Quoted in THE INDIAN AND CHRISTIAN MIRACLES OF WALKING ON THE WATER, William Norman Brown, Chicago: The Open Court Publishing Company, 1928, p. 4.

3. Von Schröder, op. cit., p. 105.

4. MYTHS AND SYMBOLS IN INDIAN ART AND CIVILIZATION, Heinrich Zimmer, edited by Joseph Campbell, Bollingen Series VI, New York: Pantheon Books, 1946, p. 3.

5. The god Indra of the ancient Indian Vedas was reverenced in later times in his beneficent character as the bestower of rain in the cause of fertility. He was also feared as ruler of storms—director of lightning and thunder. (The rainbow was his bow.)

*4. ADAD STANDING ON A BULL
From stone relief. Assyrian. Reign of Tiglath-
pileser III, 746–727 B.C. Musée du Louvre, Paris.

Again and again it is the hurling of the thunderbolt, the blinding flash
of lightning, the raging storm, that pierce our hearts, and awaken them:

> *"The Lord . . . thundered in the heavens, and the Highest gave his
> voice. . . . Yea, he sent out his arrows, and scattered them; and he
> shot out lightnings, and discomfited them."* [6]

Adad, god of storm and beneficial rainfall, holds bolts of lightning in
each hand. He is depicted in Plate 4 standing on the bull, his animal attribute, here associated with procreation and fertility.

> *"The Lord . . . maketh lightnings for the rain; he bringeth the
> wind out of his treasuries."*
>
> PSALMS 135:6–7

> *"Longing for help we call as our friend the hero who wields the
> thunderbolt."*
>
> MAX MÜLLER

It is by way of crisis — the fall, the thunderbolt — that we are thrust
into awareness. We become spiritually aroused through bereavement and
reversal. Through the need to make crucial decisions in the face of relentless conflict, challenge, tension, paradox; the agonizingly unforeseen. Our
humanity and compassion are born in myriad ways: at one level through
shock, at another through ecstasy or love.

---

6. PSALMS 18:13–14.

Zeus, like various other ancient gods — Adad, Indra, Yahweh — hurls the thunderbolt that, according to the wisdom of Heraclitus, "steers the course of all things." [7] Receiver of thunder and lightning out of the depths, Zeus — god of the sky — is portrayed in Plate 5 spearing the gigantic Typhon of great strength. The latter, generally called a dragon — half-man, half-beast — is anthropomorphic above and serpentine below. Zeus, gatherer of the clouds that dispense the fertilizing rains, causes sudden storms and tempests to break forth, but then he also calms the elements again, brightening the sky, and sending forth favorable winds.

---

7. It would seem clear that the bolt hurled by Zeus — like similar forms associated with the gods of related traditions — resulted from a combination of "lotus and lightning." Especially so since fire was, at times, regarded as a flower — the sun, in particular, being associated with the lotus in the religion of both ancient Egypt and India. (See ZEUS, A. B. Cook, Cambridge: The University Press, 1940, Vol. 2, pp. 771ff.) The early Greeks, and various other peoples influenced by them — who considered lightning to be made of the same fiery substance as the sun — also created lotiform thunderbolts, as suggested in the image that follows.

A modern Indian parallel, pertaining to the ancient Thunderbolt and Lotus symbol: The hero of Rabindranath Tagore's drama — THE KING OF THE DARK CHAMBER — must remain invisible to his subjects. When a pretender to the throne attempts to delude the latter into thinking he is the true monarch, a character in the play expresses suspicion about the authenticity of the masquerader: "When ever has *our* King set out to dazzle the eyes of the people by pomp and pageantry? . . . If my King chose to make himself shown, your eyes would not have noticed him. He would not stand out like that amongst others — he is one of the people, he mingles with the common populace. . . . *My* King has a thunderbolt within a lotus painted on his flag." (THE KING OF THE DARK CHAMBER, Rabindranath Tagore, London: Macmillan and Co., 1947, pp. 33, 35.)

*5. ZEUS AND TYPHON
From detail of Chalkidian vase. Greek-Italian. Last half 6th century B.C. Glyptothek und Museum antiker Kleinkunst, Munich.

A further illustration of the thunderbolt-lotus theme. (Plate 6.)

*6.   THUNDERBOLT AND LOTUS
From detail of gold coin. Greek. 350–270 B.C.
Unearthed, April, 1966, at Morgantina, Sicily,
by archaeologists from Princeton University,
Princeton, New Jersey.[8]

*7.   THE VISION OF THE PROPHET
EZEKIEL
From manuscript illumination in the style of the
Master of the Morgan Leaf from the Winchester
Bible. English. 12th century. The Cathedral
Library, Winchester.

The Vision of Ezekiel: The friction of the wheels within the wheels
that sets life in motion: "The wheels were lifted up . . . for the spirit of
the living creature was in [them]. . . . And, behold, a whirlwind . . .
a great cloud, and a fire infolding itself, and a brightness was about
it. . . . and their appearance and their work was as it were a wheel in the
middle of a wheel." [9] (Plate 7.)

The god Vishnu "is represented in Hindu myth as the Milky Ocean of
Immortal Life, out of which the transient universe arises and back into
which it again dissolves. This ocean is personified as . . . the primordial
giant serpent of the abyss, who carries the unfolded universe," and is life-

---

8. © 1966 by the New York Times Company. Reprinted by permission from THE NEW YORK TIMES, Tuesday,
May 31, 1966, p. 40.
9. EZEKIEL 1:19, 20, 4, 16.

giving in the depth of space. The serpent is both Vishnu and his support on the surface of the Milky Ocean, the latter again alluding to the god "himself in his elemental form. For this divine being is the primary life-sap or substance, which evolves and nourishes all the shapes of all the living creatures in the universe." [10]

In Plate 8 the gods and titans[11] who are, for once, in harmony, form a chain at either side of the vertical pillar behind the central figure. They pull the giant Cosmic Snake they have grasped. The pillar, representing "the central mountain of the world," is thereby set in motion, as it is twirled around its axis.[12]

Through loss, humiliation — through the piercing of the heart — we are awakened to what it is we must face and sacrifice — make sacred — so that the creative process we name, symbolically, the quest of the hero in man, may be initiated. (The piercing of the heart is a symbol also of love.)

"We witness the dissection of a heart so that the divine seed enclosed in it may germinate. . . . The heart is the place of union where the luminous consciousness is made. This organ represents the kernel of religious thought, not only because it occupies a central position in the body, and . . . because of the feelings of love . . . it evokes . . . but chiefly because of its dynamic function in the body. What more perfect symbol [Plate 9] could be found for the creative, liberating movement, than this vibrating piece of flesh whose pulsation at every moment rescues corporeal matter from the inertia and decomposition that [lurk] in ambush?" [13]

And then the friction of the wheels that has brought creative energy into being causes still further transformation. So that we are now confronted by day and night — time from the perspective of man.

---

10. PHILOSOPHIES OF INDIA, Heinrich Zimmer, edited by Joseph Campbell, Bollingen Series XXVI, New York: Pantheon Books, 1951, p. 424.

11. In various early cultures the gods and demons periodically altered their roles. In Greek myth the titans or giants who deposed Uranus (sky god, first ruler of the universe), were themselves subsequently overthrown by the Olympians. In Hindu mythology, the Asuras were the gods of the ancient order. Lucifer first represented light, only to descend into darkness. Other analogous reversals abound in myth.

12. THE ART OF INDIAN ASIA, Heinrich Zimmer, edited by Joseph Campbell; Bollingen Series XXXIX; copyright 1955 by Bollingen Foundation, New York; distributed by Pantheon Books; Vol. I, p. 208.

13. BURNING WATER: THOUGHT AND RELIGION IN ANCIENT MEXICO, Laurette Séjourné, New York: Grove Press, 1960, pp. 122, 119.

8. THE CHURNING OF THE MILKY OCEAN
Section of stone relief. Cambodian. Early 12th century. Angkor Wat. Photograph by Beylié.

*9. IMAGES OF PIERCED HEARTS
From representation in the Codex Borgia (14th–15th centuries). Mexican. Pre-Columbian. Biblioteca Vaticana, Vatican City.

10. THE LORD HOLDING THE WHEEL OF CREATION
Manuscript illumination from the Missal of Henry de Midel, Hildesheim. German.[14] c. 1159.

Christ-Logos is depicted flanked by two Cherubim above the wheel of creation in Plate 10. Within the wheel are six medallions — the six days of creation — which lead into the center scene, representing the forming of Eve by the Hand of God (just as Eve herself emerges from the rib of Adam). Below the wheel on the left, the Expulsion from Paradise is portrayed; on the right Cain is shown killing Abel. The half-figure of David holds a scroll with an inscription from Psalm 135:6: "Whatsoever the Lord pleased, that hath he done." Each medallion of the days of creation is encircled by an inscription from the Book of Genesis.

---

6 ADAM AND EVE: THE TREE OF KNOWLEDGE OF GOOD AND EVIL

11. GOD CALLS ADAM AND EVE TO
ACCOUNT. ADAM AND THE TREE
POINT TO EVE, EVE TO THE
SERPENT
Detail of bronze door panel. German. 1015.
Hildesheim Cathedral.

"The struggle between [the] human and [the] divine in the person of the god-descended hero during the process of reaching full humanity."

G. R. LEVY

Although cosmic creation myths speak to us of bringing the world out of chaos or nothingness into form and manifestation, at the very moment when we are born, we enter a mysterious universe apparently lacking in any readily definable order.

In the split second of being plunged into life, we experience myriad bewilderments and ambiguities. We are confronted by conflicting or antithetical, as well as complementary and interdependent forces. We find that even our own impulses are as often destructive as creative.

We are encountered relentlessly by the polarities and interplay of life and death, sky and earth, night and day, male and female, past and future; by what is within us and that which is not. We are confounded not only by the irreducible *two,* but by still further complexities in seemingly infinite variation. Thus we have no alternative save to come to terms with the world's wide range of tensions, as with its conjunctions of opposites; to learn to choose and discriminate.

Adam and Eve are forbidden to eat of the tree of knowledge of good and evil. (Plate 11.) Yet eat they must, or there would be no life on the human plane. And eat they do. Which is not to imagine that man is subsequently able to make an absolute distinction between good and evil. Nor that he dare falsely presume himself to be like unto God. Yet, at least the initial opening of the eyes has been achieved; the path into life has been entered, however difficult the way.

Despite the fact that the fall from Paradise is not to be avoided, there is the merciful counterpoint to Genesis, contained in Deuteronomy 1:39, when the Lord declares: "Moreover your little ones, which ye said should be a prey, and your children, which in that day had no knowledge between good and evil . . . shall go in thither [into the Promised Land], and unto them will I give [the Land], and they shall possess it."

Although Paradise Lost, and the Promised Land that is never gained, may well be but two faces of a single, overriding tragic concept, each motif nonetheless provides crucial clues to the nature of our initiation into life, and into maturity. In one case, as in the other, we must affirm beyond all suffering, in order to attain our most profound and compassionate humanity.

> *"Behold mee then, mee for him, life for life*
> *I offer, on mee let thine anger fall;*
> *Account mee man."*
>
> JOHN MILTON

> *"Man knows of chaos and creation in the cosmogonic myth and he learns that chaos and creation take place in himself, but he does not see the former and the latter together; he listens to the myth of Lucifer and hushes it up in his own life. He needs the bridge."*
>
> MARTIN BUBER

> *"Why hast thou enticed thyself*
> *Into the old serpent's Paradise?*
> *Why hast thou stolen*
> *Into thyself, thyself? . . .*
> *Encaved within thyself,*
> *Burrowing into thyself. . . .*
> *Piled with a hundred burdens. . . .*
> *A knower!*
> *Self-knower! . . .*
> *You sought the heaviest burden*
> *And found yourself."*
>
> FRIEDRICH NIETZSCHE

> *"A lie was possible only after a creature, man, was capable of conceiving the being of truth. It was possible only as directed against the conceived truth. In a lie the spirit practices treason against itself."*
>
> MARTIN BUBER

> *"Without contraries is no progression. Attraction and Repulsion, Reason and Energy, Love and Hate, are necessary to Human existence."*
>
> WILLIAM BLAKE

"The radiance of Paradise alternates with deep, dreadful night."

JOHANN WOLFGANG VON GOETHE

In various ancient myths, in disparate cultures, the birth of consciousness is symbolized by the breaking of the laws of the gods. Adam and Eve eat the prohibited fruit of the tree of knowledge of good and evil, in much the same manner as Prometheus[1] and Coyote (Plate 3) steal the forbidden fire. Whereupon man begins to be liberated from the tyranny of darkness, despite there being an inevitable price to be paid for the breaking — even as for the not breaking — of what have been termed the sacred laws. (Yet there must ever be a reverence, also, for the gods who utter their warnings and commands.)

---

1. "The Greeks . . . developed the myth of the hero overtaken by the divine wrath for having communicated to mankind the use of fire and the possession of knowledge. Prometheus was considered not only to have stolen . . . fire from Zeus by lighting his torch either at the wheel of the sun or at Vulcan's forge, but also to have modelled the first man from clay and then infused into him the spark of life. Without adding comments which no text would justify, we may yet draw attention . . . to a small monument [in which] Prometheus is . . . represented [Plate 12] as engaged in moulding the first man, with the help of Minerva, behind whom stands a tree [and] serpent." (THE MIGRATION OF SYMBOLS, Count Goblet d'Alviella, New York: University Books, 1956, pp. 165–66.)

12. PROMETHEUS MODELING BODY OF MAN, WITH AID OF ATHENA Engraving. MYTHOLOGIE DE LA GRÈCE ANTIQUE, Paul Decharme, Paris: Garnier Frères, 1886, p. 265, fig. 82.

In the alchemical portrayal (Plate 13) the Philosopher's Tree ("the giver of new birth") emerges as a result of the piercing or penetrating of Adam's breast by the arrow of Mercurius.[2]

It was believed that the animation of Adam was caused by the power of Mercurius which, upon being projected into other substances, was capable of transforming them from an imperfect or sleeping, into a perfect or conscious state. Before Adam was so awakened, he was looked upon as representing the "paradise of earth," or as not yet having attained consciousness. It was thought that the arrow of Mercurius ignited the divine flame from which he sprang.[3]

---

2. "In alchemical writings the word 'Mercurius' is used with a . . . wide range of meanings, to denote not only the chemical element mercury or quicksilver . . . Mercury the god (Hermes), and Mercury the planet, but also — and primarily — the secret 'transforming substance' which is at the same time the 'spirit' indwelling in all living creatures." (PSYCHOLOGY AND ALCHEMY, Carl G. Jung, translated by R. F. C. Hull, Bollingen Series XX, New York: Pantheon Books, 1953, p. 26n.)

3. Ibid., pp. 285, 356, 414.

*13.   ADAM AS *PRIMA MATERIA*,
PIERCED BY THE ARROW
OF MERCURIUS
From manuscript illustration, "Miscellanea d'alchimia." Italian. 14th century. Biblioteca Medicea-Laurenziana, Florence.

Just as the hand of day — of the sun — reaches down as though to offer the potential gift of creativity, so, too, does the procreative power of night — of the moon. The figure of Adam is surrounded by freshly emerging vegetation, a further sign of the promise of new life.[4]

In this instance — Plate 14 — it is not a destructive, serpent-like form from without that tempts. It even may be that what is depicted is a higher, positive aspect of new life or fresh growth. Or perhaps the rivers and trees of Paradise portrayed indicate primarily that what is entwined around the form is inextricably a part of it, as are the waters from which it emerges; waters, partially at least — and prophetically — baptismal and initiatory. (The trees of Paradise are nonetheless related to the garden of Eden that must be lost, if man is to achieve a conscious state of being, to enter life with the hard-won gift of awareness.)

---

4. A companion picture to Plate 13 depicts a woman with a tree emerging from her head. (Ibid., p. 257.)

14.

PERSONIFICATION OF THE RIVERS AND TREES OF PARADISE
Stone relief on capital of former Abbey Church of Ss. Peter and Paul, Cluny (Saône-et-Loire). French. 1113–1118.

7 HEAVEN AND EARTH... FINITUDE AND INFINITY... PERFECTION AND IMPERFECTION ...GOOD AND EVIL

Can any understand the spreadings of the Clouds the noise of his Tabernacle

15

Also by watering he wearieth the thick cloud by his counsels
He scattereth the bright cloud also it is turned about

Of Behemoth he saith, He is the chief of the ways of God
Of Leviathan he saith, He is King over all the Children of Pride

Behold now Behemoth which I made with thee

W Blake invenit & sculpt

London Published as the Act directs March 8. 1825 by Will Blake N.° Fountain Court Strand

Proof

"And the original Archangel, or possessor of the command of the heavenly host, is call'd the Devil or Satan."

WILLIAM BLAKE

"**B**ehold now Behemoth, which I made with thee. . . . He is the chief of the ways of God." Job 40:15, 19.

Of Leviathan (below), the Lord saith: "He is a king over all the children of pride." Job 41:34. (The text surrounding the image in Plate 15 was written by Blake, after the Bible.)

There are the inevitable warnings that we are of earth and not merely of heaven.

There is a curious parallel between Blake's attitude toward his *Ancient of Days* (Plate 16), and what occurred in India long ages ago. In order to bring the universe into manifestation, it was necessary for the god Indra to slay the great serpent Vritra, who was attempting to thwart creation. In the first instance, the serpent's opposition to Indra's act was looked upon as destructive. Due, however, to Vritra's having existed before what was considered to be the imperfection of creation, and having attempted originally to prevent it, there were also those who viewed the serpent in quite different, even favorable fashion.

Similarly, in the eyes of Blake, the creator of the world — Jehovah-Urizen — represented "the principle of evil, compelling man to live the bounded and restrained life of reason as opposed to the free life of the imagination."

15. **BEHEMOTH AND LEVIATHAN**
Engraving by William Blake. English. 1825.
The Pierpont Morgan Library, New York.

Hence the compasses in Plate 16, "which the colossal figure holds down onto the black emptiness below him, [symbolized] for Blake not the imposition of order on chaos, but the reduction of the infinite to the finite." [1]

Although the evil angel in Blake's portrayal (Plate 17) is chained, and gropes blindly in darkness, it nevertheless threatens the child held protectively by the good angel.

Whether we adhere to a philosophy preoccupied with making a sharp differentiation between good and evil, or one creating a far less clear distinction, there is an inevitable choice to be exercised in life: The heroic vision forever stresses light and clarity over chaos, annihilation, and ignorance, even while refusing to deny the necessary and challenging role of the "shadow," in whatever its form.

---

1. THE ART OF WILLIAM BLAKE, Anthony Blunt, New York: Columbia University Press, 1959, p. 57.

17. GOOD AND EVIL ANGELS
STRUGGLING FOR POSSESSION
OF A CHILD
Color printed monotype by William Blake.
English. 1795. The Tate Gallery, London.

16. THE ANCIENT OF DAYS
Relief etching by William Blake. English. 1794.
The Library of Congress, Washington, D.C.,
Rosenwald Collection.

8 THE YIN AND THE YANG...
THE DANCE OF SHIVA

*18. THE YIN AND THE YANG
Chinese.

In metaphysical terms, there are philosophies that seem, and do not seem, sharply to distinguish between good and evil; that do and do not look upon creation as having taken place once and for all, in a remote past. There are cultures that appear to view creation as occurring potentially anew, at each moment anew; that consider creation, destruction, and preservation as eternally interactive. Yet although, under certain conditions, we adopt one particular position, in others we find ourselves affirming precisely an opposite one. Thus, whatever our discoveries about, or attitudes toward, such apparently paradoxical situations, it is of primary importance that we expose ourselves to, and comprehend something of each of them; that we cease having preconceptions about any of them.

In contrast to other traditions demanding that a rigid dichotomy be made between Heaven and Earth, light and darkness, good and evil, there is the ancient Chinese *yin* and *yang*. (Plate 18.)

(This concept, representing the two primal forces, was expressed in texts as early as the eleventh century B.C. The period during which the first pictorial representations were made is not, thus far, known.)

"The Great One," it is said, "separated and became Heaven and Earth. It revolved and became the dual forces."

LI CHI

"The dark begets the light and the light begets the dark in ceaseless alternation."

I CHING

"The movement of the Tao *(the universal course or* Way*) is that of reversal."*

LAO TZU

"The alternation of the yin *and* yang *is . . . called* Tao."

I CHING

"Tao's standard is the spontaneous."

LAO TZU

"In unending cycles the good and evil alternate."

HEINRICH ZIMMER

"Tao *is divided into a* principal pair of opposites, Yang *and* Yin.
. . . *This image is* [a] . . . *primordial idea, which we find elsewhere in similar forms; as for* [example] *in the West African myth
where Obatala and Odudua, the first parents* (*heaven and earth*)
*lie together . . . until a son, man, arises between them. Hence as
a microcosm, uniting in himself the world-opposites, man corresponds with the irrational* symbol *which reconciles psychological
antitheses.*"

CARL G. JUNG

"*The primal powers never come to a standstill; the cycle of becoming continues uninterruptedly. . . . Between the two primal powers there arises again and again a state of tension, a potential that
keeps the powers in motion and causes them to unite, whereby they
are constantly regenerated.*"

I CHING

"*God is day and night, winter and summer, war and peace, surfeit
and hunger.*"

"*The unlike is joined together, and from differences results the
most beautiful harmony.*"

HERACLITUS

As Ananda K. Coomaraswamy has written, The Dance of Shiva is "a
representation of . . . Cosmic Activity . . . creation or evolution;
. . . preservation or continued maintenance; . . . destruction or involution; . . . illusion or incarnation; and . . . release or salvation . . .
of the Supreme and Immanent Power.

"It should be noted that from a Hindu point of view creation and destruction are never original nor final, but merely . . . the repeated cycle
of evolution and involution of form in the substance of an eternal energy.
Creation is 'projection,' destruction 'withdrawal;' the process is without a
beginning or end.

"Thus the figure of [Shiva as] Nataraja may be said to represent the
Absolute in manifestation." [1]

---

1. "Saiva Sculptures," Ananda K. Coomaraswamy, MUSEUM OF FINE ARTS BULLETIN, Vol. XX, No. 118, Boston,
April, 1922, p. 20. (Saiva is a variant spelling of Shiva.)

19. NATARAJA (SHIVA AS LORD
OF THE DANCE)
Bronze statue. Indian. Early Chola dynasty. c. 1000.
The Metropolitan Museum of Art, New York.
Harris Brisbane Dick Fund, 1964.

*"This is [the] dance [of Shiva]. Its deepest significance is felt
when it is realised that it takes place within the heart and the self.
Everywhere is God: that Everywhere is the heart."*

ANANDA K. COOMARASWAMY

Shiva, as Nataraja, "in his *Dance of Creation,* stamps down evil in the
shape of Ignorance, which has the body of an infant . . . 'embodiment
of forgetfulness.' This negative aspect of childlike innocence is the
'Demon Ignorance,' forgetful of the primal source and perpetual spring of
the dance of the creative intellect." [2]

2. Stella Kramrisch, as quoted in THE HEROIC ENCOUNTER, Dorothy Norman, New York: distributed by Grove
Press, 1958, p. 14.

Heinrich Zimmer has further noted: "The creation of the world is not an accomplished work, completed within a certain span of time . . . but a process continuing . . . refashioning the universe without cease, and pressing it on, every moment afresh. Like the human body, the cosmos is in part built up anew, every night, every day; by a process of unending regeneration. . . . But the manner of its growth is by abrupt occurrences, crises, surprising events and even mortifying accidents . . . yet, that is precisely the circumstance by which the miraculous development comes to pass." [3]

Even though it is often claimed that the tradition of ancient India differs greatly from that of other cultures, the Babylonian Genesis speaks of the Lord Marduk in terms that conform closely to Hindu thought: "At [Marduk's] command," it is declared, "let there be creation, destruction, alleviation, mercy." [4]

Similarly, an Hasidic Rabbi is quoted as speaking in a manner that appears more closely related to the vision of the Hindus than to that of the Old Testament (as generally understood): "Even now," taught the Rabbi, "the world is still in a state of creation. . . . Day after day, instant after instant, [it] requires the renewal of the powers of the primordial word through which it was created." [5]

Although initially we may imagine it is the East we hear, it is in truth the Testaments, both Old and New, that emphasize: "I form the light, and create darkness: I make peace, and create evil: I the Lord do all these things." [6] "I find then a law, that, when I would do good, evil is present with me." [7] "For that which I do I allow not: for what I would, that do I not; but what I hate, that do I." [8] "What?" it is asked. "Shall we receive good at the hand of God, and shall we not receive evil?" [9] Or again: "The

---

3. THE KING AND THE CORPSE, Heinrich Zimmer, edited by Joseph Campbell, Bollingen Series XI, New York: Pantheon Books, 1948, p. 251.

4. THE BABYLONIAN GENESIS, Alexander Heidel, Chicago and London: Phoenix Books, The University of Chicago Press, 1963, p. 51.

5. TALES OF THE HASIDIM: THE LATER MASTERS, Martin Buber, translated by Olga Marx, New York: Schocken Books, 1948, p. 259.

6. ISAIAH 45:7.

7. ROMANS 7:21.

8. ROMANS 7:15.

9. JOB 2:10.

Lord killeth, and maketh alive: he bringeth down to the grave, and bringeth up. The Lord maketh poor, and maketh rich: he bringeth low, and lifteth up." [10] "I kill, and I make alive; I wound, and I heal: neither is there any that can deliver out of my hand." [11] And then finally there are the, at first glance, paradoxical words of Christ: "But I say unto you, That ye resist not evil," and "Deliver us from evil." [12]

"How translate into terms of 'yes' and 'no' revelations that shatter into meaninglessness every attempt to define the pairs of opposites?"

JOSEPH CAMPBELL

10. I SAMUEL 2:6–7.
11. DEUTERONOMY 32:39.
12. ST. MATTHEW 5:39; 6:13.

9 VARIATIONS ON THE THEME OF HORUS AND SETH... HARI-HARA...THE GUNAS

"You are your own creator; you appear
In the splendor of your own.
Heaven and earth are made light by you."

PYRAMID TEXT

"Hail, O my Creator, I am he who hath no power to walk, the great
Knot who is within yesterday. The might of my strength is within
my hand. I myself am not known, but I am he who knoweth thee.
. . . I am Horus, he who liveth for millions of years. . . . I have
opened a path."

BOOK OF THE DEAD

When reading the following pages about Horus and Seth, it may be helpful to recall the names and certain primary attributes of the nine gods or Ennead of ancient Heliopolis in Egypt. As described by Henri Frankfort, at the head of the Ennead "stood the creator-sun, Atum. Then followed the divine pair whom Atum created out of himself — Shu and Tefnut, air and moisture. The children of this couple followed. They were Geb and Nut, earth and sky; and their children, Osiris and Isis, Seth and Nephthys, were the last four gods of the Ennead. . . .

"Atum, Shu and Tefnut, Geb and Nut represent a cosmology. Their names describe primordial elements; their interrelations imply a story of creation. The four children of Geb and Nut are not involved in this description of the universe. They establish a bridge between nature and man, and that in the only manner in which the Egyptians could conceive such a bond — through kingship. Osiris was the mythological form of the dead ruler forever succeeded by his son Horus. . . .

"Thus the Ennead was formed out of the five cosmic gods and Osiris with the three gods of his circle.[1] Here we [find] the clue to its meaning; it was a theological concept which comprised the order of creation as well as [that] of society. It is peculiar to the Egyptian concept of kingship that it envisaged the incumbent of that office as part of the world of the gods as well as"[2] that of men.

Among other gods to be mentioned are Thoth, who was looked upon, in part, as a god of wisdom (or Lord of Divine Words, Scribe of Truth); and the goddess Maat (personified truth, established order, and the right order).[3]

Although any attempt to define what the deities represent in too narrow or literal a fashion, must be scrupulously avoided, it is nonetheless clear, as Frankfort confirms, that because motifs recur in early Egyptian religious texts with such great frequency, it is possible to "determine certain broad spheres . . . the Egyptians recognized as manifestations of the divine."[4] It is equally feasible to do so as a result of one's own observation of key works of art and artifacts.

---

1. Horus "is sometimes called 'the tenth god.' " (KINGSHIP AND THE GODS, Henri Frankfort, Chicago: The University of Chicago Press, 1948, p. 389n[13].)
2. Ibid., pp. 182–83.
3. Ibid., p. 157.
4. Ibid., p. 145.

In accordance with ancient Egyptian tradition, Horus and Seth, together, represent symbolically the opposing yet complementary forces within ourselves and in the world. Whether viewed as two gods or two principles, their relationship sheds revealing light upon our own nature; upon the entire human condition and struggle. Their battle and interplay are eternally typical of all that is in conflict, yet interdependent within the life-process. It is no more possible to conceive of Horus without Seth than of day without night.

Although it would not be proper to term Horus a hero in literal fashion, he may nevertheless be described as typifying the *heroic principle in man:* the great creative life-force. A formulation to be understood in relationship to the fact that, centuries ago, the king or Pharaoh in Egypt was looked upon as the *embodiment of the two gods, Horus and Seth, in a single person.* Or, as Henri Frankfort has written, the Egyptian king was identified with the Two Lords, "the perennial antagonists, Horus and Seth." This was so "not in the sense that he was considered the incarnation of the one and also . . . of the other," but rather that he embodied both as a pair, as opposites in equilibrium. Hence the ancient title of the king: "The Two Lords." [5]

A traditional Pyramid Text alludes to an Egyptian king as appealing "to the Creator Atum" — the Supreme Sun God, the Complete One[6] — "with the following reference to himself: 'Look upon the two-dwellers-in-the-palace, that is Horus-and-Seth.' " [7]

II.

Seth is, as it were, the shadow of Horus; a god of bondage who sets the problems that the hero in man must solve. It is the very inert quality of Seth that stimulates Horus to develop: to become the ascending one: to follow the path of the hero.

That which resists necessary revitalization is the negative aspect of Seth. Although Horus sees the Seth within himself, it is the deadening force of this obstacle that he must transmute into new life. (The key to what en-

---

5. Ibid., p. 21.

6. Atum was the Heliopolitan form of the Supreme God, Ptah the Memphite. (See ibid., p. 21.)

7. As quoted, ibid., p. 21.

hances development is contained precisely in what obstructs it.) Thus, without the impetus and challenge of Seth there would be no living process of growth in man. This is so despite the fact that liberation can no more be hastened than it is possible to avoid the crises and struggles from which it may alone emerge. Hence, whether in clash or equilibrium, where Horus is, Seth is. Neither can function without the existence of the other.

Seth suggests earth, matter, preservation, prosperity, longevity. He is a basis of life, yet that which opposes change. He is the red, wild bull. From one point of view he is the lower aspect of procreative power. He is both resistance and the instrument of becoming. Horus, on the other hand, represents order. He is the objective of the release of creative energy in man: namely the heroic process and goal.

When it is claimed that Horus follows the path of the hero, this signifies that the qualities he embodies help to reintegrate mankind. He lifts the universe from the netherworld, from chaos, so that all within it may be made whole, or re-formed.

III.

Even when Horus and Seth come into the periodic balance that brings about equilibrium, and thereby unites the "Two Kingdoms" of Egypt,[8] there are invariably other planes on which their conflict resumes. At no point, however, can the antagonism between them be looked upon as involving such oversimplified, or mutually exclusive attributes as good and evil, light and dark, spirit and matter. Inevitably, within each resides the

---

8. In ancient Egypt it was considered that, from a certain perspective, a static balance was attainable or possible only when the forces of the "two lands," or two segments of the country, were equalized. When they were in disequilibrium, a dynamic renewal of their equipoise was required. At the level of the state, when balance was achieved or restored between the "two kingdoms," Egypt was united and peace prevailed. With respect to other aspects, conflict could not therefore be said automatically to have ceased. The fact that Horus was an ascending power, Seth a descending one, over the East and West respectively, did not exclude their being also perennial contenders who represented the North and South of Egypt, as well as the divine order. In other words, they were, in microcosm, the antithetical cosmic principles that must be placed in the right relationship, and thereby united; or, by analogy, a view of the world in what may be termed static equilibrium between conflicting forces. (References to other Egyptian attitudes toward equilibrium are to be found in the pages that follow. Moreover, symbolically, it is of little moment whether "East" and "West" refer to the two banks of the Nile, or the two horizons. For, in any event, the Sun God Re makes his daily journey on a boat, moving westward from the Eastern Horizon at dawn. This concept serves both as an act of faith in the ever-recurrent renewal of life-energy, and a reminder that we ourselves must pass through the darkness of night, in which we are tested, before the rising of the sun.)

seed of the other. It is explicitly warned that Horus must not kill Seth, even though he must periodically oppose him.

Nonetheless, irrespective of historical considerations involving the relationship of Upper and Lower Egypt, "Horus and Seth were," as Frankfort notes, "the antagonists per se . . . mythological symbols for all conflict. Strife is an element in the universe which cannot be ignored; Seth is perennially subdued by Horus but never destroyed. Both Horus and Seth are wounded in the struggle, but in the end there is a reconciliation." [9]

IV.

Seth's followers were known as the *Sons of Rebellion,* who perpetually threaten the "equilibrium" and renewal that Horus brings into being. Thus it was the constant task of the latter to oppose Seth and his rebellious ones, so that a living order might be re-established and/or maintained. An order that could no more be final than Seth and Horus can themselves be viewed as static.

Since, cyclically, Horus governs ascent into the new day, and Seth the reverse, it is the negative aspect of the latter's thrust toward darkness with which Horus — the life-generating force toward day — does battle.

V.

If we consider Horus and Seth in relationship to Osiris, a god of death, light may be shed upon still other aspects of the myth of the hero. Osiris represents the "battleground," in which the drama involving Horus and Seth takes place — the dynamic quality of existence expressed through the conflict leading toward the necessary renewal of the world each morning at sunrise.

---

9. In spite of Frankfort's observation that Horus and Seth also cooperate, he nevertheless calls attention to the pair's antithetical gestures, which "signify that the land [of Egypt] in its totality honors or serves the king. Horus and Seth are therefore called . . . 'the partners,' " even though such solidarity may seem to contrast "strangely with their mythological relationship."

In early Egyptian religious texts Horus and Seth form a pair, yet the bond between them consists also "of an imperishable hostility. It is usual to translate the antagonism between the two gods from the sphere of cosmology, where it belongs, to that of politics, by postulating an ancient conflict between Upper Egypt (Seth) and Lower Egypt (Horus)." (Ibid., pp. 21–22.) See also H. Te Velde's *Seth, God of Confusion,* Leiden: E. J. Brill, 1967, received after this volume had gone to press.

From a certain perspective, Osiris typifies the life already lived that holds within itself the seeds of the future. Osiris enters the Western Horizon, the earth, the netherworld, to reemerge as new life at dawn.[10]

It is Osiris whom Horus must resurrect: namely, that for which we live: the embodiment of fulfilled life. Osiris is the goal achieved, by way of struggle — the primary goal possessed of the power to lead toward meaningful rebirth.

Osiris may be termed the unfinished work of art ever in process of becoming; the work that Horus-in-man perennially labors to perfect. The art Horus attempts to complete is, at one level, an equivalent of the seeing that unmasks what requires change and rebirth; at another, the crystallization of what brings about necessary transformation and revivification.

VI.

In opposing Seth's resistance, Horus is the heroic principle that brings about the necessary resurrection of the dead Osiris, the bound god: imprisoned life awaiting liberation. Horus conquers Apopis, the Serpent of Darkness — created by Seth and called Blind — in the crucial hours before dawn. Thereby Horus transforms the outlived past. For, whether Horus is referred to as the Sun God, the Great God of Heaven, or is identified with the king, his power to release creative energy — to bring about the equilibrium of the divine order or, by analogy, the Two Kingdoms — involves the cyclical overcoming of the collective evil of Apopis, and the rebellious followers of Seth.[11] (The evil or blindness of Apopis is, in reality, a lack of conscience or consciousness.)

The cycle of time into which the Sun God enters is variously spoken of in terms of the Heh, or eternity gods — the cycle of day and night, and also of the year (the latter characterizing, through its periodic religious festivals, the Great Cycle of Creation). The year embodies all of the festivals of the gods, thus graphically alluding, by implication, to the totality of the creative process in life.

---

10. See image in Chapter 24, relating to Osiris, grain, and revivification.

11. According to the predominant tradition in ancient Egypt, Apopis was represented as being overcome by Horus; at certain times, however, by Seth. (An alternate spelling of Apopis is Apophis.)

VII.

When the right eye of Horus is described as the sun or day, the left eye as the moon or night, the struggle between Horus and Seth — as well as their interdependence — is suggested in still other terms. A Pyramid Text states: "Horus is purified with the Eye of his brother Set;[12] Set is purified with the Eye of his brother Horus." [13]

VIII.

At the midpoint in the night — in the netherworld — when the crucial contest between Horus and Seth takes place, the image of their flanking of the ladder comes into being.[14] Just as the ladder, itself, may be viewed as the emergence of Osiris so, from another perspective, the interaction of Horus and Seth is the cause of Osiris' resurrection.

Horus overcomes Seth when Osiris rises like the sun. It is then that the ascending process commences that leads toward the appearance of Osiris — "he of the horizon from which Re goes forth" [15] — in the east: namely the new day. And, as Osiris, the dead king, emerges, he meets the living Sun God, Re, whose complementary force he thus becomes, and returns to life.

From still another point of view: at each moment in which we become aware of the struggle between the potentially divine and the merely mundane within ourselves — in those split seconds during which we decide whether we shall or shall not participate in the heroic battle that may lead toward self-realization — Horus and Seth flank the great ladder.

As the two gods oppose one another in the darkness of our own night, Horus is born as the heroic principle in life. This occurs also at the juncture at which he and Seth hold the ladder that Osiris ascends.

The ladder of conflict unites at the apex: at the androgynous height — the level beyond the oppositions — where there is unification and non-

---

12. A variant spelling of Seth.

13. THE PYRAMID TEXTS, Samuel A. B. Mercer, New York: Longmans, Green and Co., 1952, Vol. I, p. 290, Utterance 667A, lines 1944a + 3 and 1944a + 4.

14. At times it is said that the children of Horus form the ladder.

15. Frankfort, op. cit., p. 195.

differentiation. (Even though, in movement both upward and downward, antagonism and interplay continue without pause. Or, by way of variant, Osiris climbs upon the rungs of discord between Horus and Seth.)

The ascent of Osiris, which takes place by virtue of the power of Horus, exemplifies the effort of the hero in man. It elucidates why Horus is looked upon as treading the path of the hero, or as siding with the gods. (When we awaken to the clash within us and listen; when we are torn between the various directions we might follow, it is at this moment, too, that the essential struggle between Horus and Seth — like our own — takes place.)

Horus and Seth each hold one side of the ladder. Each offers a finger — a rung. Osiris ascends on the rungs, by means of the strength of his integrity, which has been tested in the fire of the netherworld.

Descent down the ladder has as much to do with the potential ability to create, as arising does with the power to destroy. In all areas of life, there are endless cycles through which we must go, every aspect of each cycle being of equally decisive importance. (The ladder, in accordance with Egyptian tradition, has to do primarily with resurrection. Numerous texts mention it as the "Stairway to Heaven." By means of the dual powers that flank it,[16] the ascent to heaven is achieved.)

If we possess any illusion that we can simply climb at top speed, we shall most assuredly find ourselves slipping back in disastrous manner. And, no matter what heights we may achieve, we must be prepared to face the depths. There is a price to be paid for every victory; the next battle to be waged in the wake of every struggle.

IX.

The task of the hero in man is to function in constantly dynamic, positive, creative accord with past, present, future; to live in terms of, and

---

16. In certain PYRAMID TEXTS, as rendered by Budge, the ladder is "set up and held in possession by . . . Horus and Set." It is, however, finally Osiris himself who *becomes* the ladder. (FROM FETISH TO GOD IN ANCIENT EGYPT, Sir E. A. Wallis Budge, London: Oxford University Press, 1934, p. 272.)

Although rarely represented pictorially in Egyptian art, the ladder is depicted in many other traditions even to our own day. There is not only the ladder of Jacob, but we find also such counterparts as the steps of the Sumerian Ziggurat, and the stairs on Meso-American Pyramid Temples, shrines representing seats of the gods. Similarly, in Egypt, Pharaohs' thrones — traditionally elevated — were reached by way of a few steps.

preserve what is life-enhancing; to discard and dismantle what is not.

Osiris is the past transformed into the future, by way of the resurrection effected by Horus, the latter being in filial relationship to Osiris as the new development. Seth shares in the future, but again as the necessary opposition to Horus.

Osiris, in this context, may be termed the "man god," the divine in the human; the capacity to love, to endure. Osiris, like Job, alludes to the suffering self in its own netherworld; what must be faced, gone through, experienced, affirmed, transmuted.

The purpose of the struggle between Horus and Seth involves the unfolding of life. The law and order — the equilibrium, truth, rectitude, justice — that Horus seeks to bring into being are among man's supreme goals.

X.

Ancient Egyptian Pharaohs, writes Frankfort, were under an "obligation to maintain *maat* . . . usually translated 'truth,' but which really means the 'right order' — the inherent structure of creation, of which justice is an integral part." [17] According to this tenet, the Egyptian king — Horus and Seth in one person — must emulate the Creator of the World.

In other words, the hero in man establishes *maat* at the human level, but in pulsating, ever-evolving fashion. He brings about change *toward* the life-giving release of productive energy.

XI.

One of the major elements involved in the struggle between Seth and Horus has to do with the question of the latter's rulership. When Horus is to assume the throne, Seth opposes him. Osiris favors the legitimacy of Horus' succession, which is awarded to the heroic principle in man by Geb, the earth god. The altercation between the opposing forces is cyclically completed when the claim to the inheritance is acknowledged as

---

17. Frankfort, op. cit., p. 51. Maat is personified as "a goddess, the daughter of the sun-god Re whose regular circuit is the most striking manifestation of the established cosmic order. Thus it is said of the king: 'Authoritative Utterance . . . is in thy mouth. Understanding . . . is in thy heart. Thy speech is the shrine of truth (*maat*).' " (Ibid., p. 51.) Maat is often shown as a feather. (See representation of weighing of the heart in Chapter 23.)

rightfully that of Horus. When this takes place, it is Thoth — god of Wisdom — who brings Horus and Seth into equilibrium. (Seth is the eternal adversary of the power of Osiris in the past, that of Horus in the present.)[18]

Whereas Osiris is the justified past, Horus is the legitimate heir to the throne of Egypt. The new king brings about the resurrection of his predecessor. Which is to say that, whenever Seth is vanquished, and Osiris is resurrected by Horus, the latter is the assurance of the future. Balance, law, order are freshly asserted among men.

The ritual referred to as the Opening of the Mouth[19] of dead Pharaohs is the first step to be taken toward revivification. Although in one sense the living struggle is over, still it renews itself; begins again, in eternal succession.

XII.

According to early Egyptian tradition, the equilibrium that is to be established when the two lands of the kingdom are united is often spoken of as static, when viewed from the perspective of the timeless. What transpires at the human level, however, or in time, is by no means static. And

---

18. An incident is recorded in which Seth is said to have challenged Osiris, purporting to be the legitimate heir to the throne. Seth, however, was found to have told a lie.

19. This ceremony, performed for centuries in ancient Egypt at the burial rites of commoner, as of king, was also enacted as part of the daily temple liturgy. There is added evidence that, at the annual new year consecration of the Temple of Horus at Edfu, it was performed in behalf of the temple itself.

The Opening of the Mouth clearly was concerned not merely with death at a literal level but, in each of its forms, it had to do, above all, with purification and revivification.

In the rites enacted at the Temple of Horus (see A. M. Blackman and H. W. Fairman, "The Consecration of an Egyptian Temple According to the Use of Edfu," JOURNAL OF EGYPTIAN ARCHAEOLOGY, Vol. 32, 1946, pp. 75–91), once the Opening of the Mouth had taken place in behalf of the cult statues, the "mouth" of the temple itself then would be opened so that the edifice and everything it contained would have been purified; would become alive and active. All were thus called upon to arouse themselves from slumber after the hours of darkness; to awaken when the sun appeared on the horizon, and shed its light.

Scenes sculptured in relief on temple walls were considered alive, in that the divine spirit entered into them, as it did into the inscribed texts. Actual performance of the Opening the Mouth ceremony, as well as recitation of accompanying texts were, however, regarded as even more efficacious than sculptured representations, and mere written words.

Hence it may be deduced from the above that identification with, and participation in the temple liturgy, as experienced by its celebrants, must have resulted in a sense of personal renewal — possibly a major goal of the Egyptian ritual. (Just as similar revivification is associated with the New Year, Easter, and related ceremonies in still other cultures.)

what is implied, even at the so-called timeless level, is far more closely related to the dynamic concept of the yin and yang (described in Chapter 8), than would, at first glance, seem evident. As expressed in the words of the *Li Chi:* "The Great One separated and became Heaven and Earth. It revolved and became the dual forces." Or, similarly, as stated in Richard Wilhelm's introduction to the *I Ching:* "The circle divided into the light and the dark. . . . An above and a below, a right and left . . . the world of the opposites. These opposites became known under the names yin and yang and created a great stir." Dr. Carl Jung's paraphrase of a passage in the *I Ching* casts still further light upon what is involved: "When *yang* has reached its greatest strength, the dark power of *yin* is born within its depths; night begins at midday when *yang* breaks up . . . to change into *yin*."

It is averred that the two lands of the kingdom of Egypt are set in order by Thoth, god of wisdom — by the grace of knowledge; that, only in equilibrium can either the North or the South — or the two united — survive.

The great or divine pair Shu and Tefnut, in harmony, like Horus and Seth, in conflict, are associated with the unceasing mutability of life; its perpetual ebb and flow, to be seen from various perspectives, and as pertaining to all of the different cycles through which man and nature must go. Whereas Shu and Tefnut, the Prime Pair, represent the great dual powers in the world, Horus and Seth are an aspect of their cosmic duality or interpenetrating unity.

When Horus is told not to kill Seth, the knowledge that he must not do so represents the dawning of mature cognition within himself. (But even awareness can play its tricks. Pride of consciousness can be quite as devastating as the reverse.) And then there is the forever unexpected, never clearly prophesied, nor readily definable next step to be taken: The very deed that was not foreseen as the one we would be called upon to enact is doubtless the one we must perform. Just as what results from our undertakings is so often precisely the reverse of what we had anticipated would occur. Which is merely one additional way of alluding to the many-faceted, yet ever necessary renewal of the battle between the opposing yet interdependent pair: Horus and Seth.

The following illustrations suggest something of the background against which the theme of Horus and Seth may be viewed. In Plate 20, which serves as a prelude, "the horizon at sunrise is represented . . . by the sun god stepping out from the lower region over the Eastern Mountain. On either side the portals, surmounted by the two solar lions, are held by guardian deities. It is probable that the lions on the portals held the same symbolic significance as in Egypt, where as emblems of the horizon they were identified with Shu and Tefnut." [20]

In ancient Egypt, "Shu and Tefnut as a lion pair together represented the horizon of the two mountains of the West and East" or, according to a passage in Chapter 17 of the Egyptian *Book of the Dead,* "yesterday" — or the West — personified descent into the netherworld, "tomorrow" — or the East — ascent into the new day.[21]

---

20. MYTHOLOGICAL PAPYRI, translated by Alexandre Piankoff, edited by N. Rambova, Bollingen Series XL, Vol. 3, New York: Pantheon Books, 1957, pp. 32–33.

21. Ibid., p. 42n[25].

*20.　THE SUN GOD STEPPING OVER THE EASTERN MOUNTAIN
From detail. Cylinder seal. Akkadian. 2334–2154 B.C. The British Museum, London.

*21.　THE EMERGENCE OF THE EGYPTIAN BIRTH GOD SOKARIS IN HIS "EGG"
From detail of diagram based on Thutmosis III version of "Book of What Is in the Netherworld." Egyptian. 18th dynasty, c. 1567–1320 B.C.

The hawk-headed Sokaris — the birth god in his "egg" — typifies emergence of new life or "revivification at the mysterious midpoint of the underworld passage where death first gives way to reawakening life." [22] The egg, in which creation occurs, resembles a coffin. Thus the mystery of the eternal process of life in death, death in life is portrayed (Plate 21), as well as the cyclical manner in which death is transformed into rebirth. (Renewal is achieved by way of inner conquest; of having made the night journey through deepest darkness, agonizing struggle, and conflict.)

The deceased or that which must be revivified, faces a barge on which sails a ram-headed god — Auf-Re, or the Flesh of Re, the form taken by the creator, the sun god Re in his netherworld journey, "with a disk over his head, holding a scepter and the sign of life. He stands in the coils of the serpent," Mehen the Enveloper. On the prow a hawk-headed god, Horus, spears a huge serpent under the barge. On the stern another hawk-headed god, a further aspect or form of Horus, stands by the rudder.[23] The serpent, Apopis — the perennial antagonist representing collective evil — is slain each day at dawn.

The three figures represent variant aspects of the sun god. (Plate 22.) The need to assure the recurrent renewal of the god's power — or, from another perspective, that of Horus — is of primary importance: namely to establish the heroic principle in life.

---

22. Ibid., p. 46.
23. Based on ibid., p. 157.

*22. LORD OF THE WEST
From detail. Papyrus of Djed-Khonsu-iuf-ankh I.
Egyptian. 21st dynasty, c. 1085–935 B.C.
Cairo Museum.

*23. HIS TWO FACES IN THE
MYSTERIES
From detail. Tomb of Ramesses VI, Thebes.
Egyptian. 20th dynasty, c. 1200–1085 B.C.

Horus and Seth are here (Plate 23) joined in one double-headed body. The serpents portray qualities of each of the two gods. The bows on which the double-headed figure and serpents stand are the two nations, or Upper and Lower Egypt, combined in one individual. The serpents and bows allude also to power in the form of a mysterious, enigmatic unity.

Horus — the falcon-headed — holds the Papyrus, heraldic plant of Lower (Northern) Egypt. (According to ancient Egyptian tradition the Falcon was a solar symbol — bird of the sun and sky.) Seth holds the Lily, at times called the Lotus — heraldic plant of Upper or Southern Egypt. In conformity with the foregoing text relating to Horus and Seth, the two lands of Egypt, or the two gods, are shown as symbolically in process of becoming conjoint. (Plate 24.)

(All of the dates utilized in conjunction with ancient Egyptian art throughout this volume conform to the chronology in A GENERAL INTRODUCTORY GUIDE TO THE EGYPTIAN COLLECTIONS IN THE BRITISH MUSEUM, London: The Trustees of the British Museum, 1964. It should be noted that these dates are approximate, and are not always identical with those given by other authorities. Dating for Plates 20, 40, 41, 42, 68 is based on ANCIENT MESOPOTAMIA, PORTRAIT OF A DEAD CIVILIZATION, A. Leo Oppenheim, Chicago: The University of Chicago Press, 1964.)

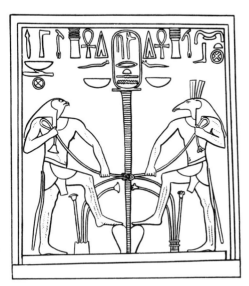

*24. HORUS AND SETH UNITING
THE TWO LANDS
From bas-relief, tablet of Sesostris I. Egyptian.
12th dynasty, c. 1991–1786 B.C. Cairo Museum.

*25. A FORM OF HORUS, "WHO
RISETH UP WITH TWO HEADS,
THE ONE BEARING TRUTH,
AND THE OTHER FALSEHOOD"
From detail. Funerary papyrus of Princess
Nesitanebtashru. Greenfield Papyrus. Egyptian.
21st dynasty, c. 1085–935 B.C. The British
Museum, London.

This version of Horus (Plate 25) as double-headed, from the *Book of the Dead,* is reminiscent of *His Two Faces in the Mysteries* (Plate 23). The depiction exemplifies the duality of the two gods, Horus and Seth, as a fundamental, paradoxical unity.

Horus, as hero, pierces the crocodile — the latter representing Seth — the opposing force. (Plate 26.) Among the Copts in Egypt this theme intermingled with that of St. Sisinnos, St. Mercurius (see Plate 27), St. George and the Dragon, and St. Theodore. The latter two saints were traditionally shown as triumphant "in the strife against the embodiment of Evil." [24] The concept of St. George and the Dragon, in particular, is closely related to the accompanying relief of Horus.

Inevitably, representations of the archangel Michael battling the dragon also come to mind: "And there was war in heaven: Michael and his angels fought against the dragon; and the dragon fought and his angels, And prevailed not; neither was their place found any more in heaven. And the great dragon was cast out, that old serpent, called the Devil, and Satan, which deceiveth the whole world: he was cast out into the earth, and his angels were cast out with him." [25]

Since St. Michael has been shown bearing a shield with the device of the Holy Trinity, this image has been viewed as indicating that the dragon typified heresy overcome by the forces of orthodoxy.[26]

In the Middle Ages, St. Michael [27] also held "the lance and the globe over the portal of churches consecrated to him, or [he was at] the head of the angelic hosts in the great battle that was part of painted or sculptured cycles depicting the Last Day of Judgment." [28]

---

24. THE ICONS OF YUHANNA AND IBRAHIM THE SCRIBE, Cawthra Mulock and Martin Telles Langdon, London: Nicholson and Watson, 1946, p. 9n.

25. REVELATION 12:7–9.

26. THE ANIMAL KINGDOM, The Pierpont Morgan Library, New York, 1940, p. 56.

27. It is also of interest that St. Michael, in his role as weigher of souls, recalls Egyptian Osirian judgment scenes. (See Chapter 23.)

28. "Andrea della Robbia's Saint Michael Lunette," Olga Raggio, THE METROPOLITAN MUSEUM OF ART BULLETIN, Vol. XX, No. 4, December 1961, p. 142.

*26. H O R U S   S P E A R I N G   T H E
      C R O C O D I L E
      From stone relief. Coptic. c. 300–400.
      Musée du Louvre, Paris.

*27. S A I N T   M E R C U R I U S
      From icon by Ibrahim the Scribe. 1765.
      Church of the Virgin Mary al Damshiriya. Cairo.

St. Mercurius, originally named Philopator, became a great soldier.
His "prowess in battle and swiftness in . . . attack won him the name of
Mercurius. In the course of a campaign against the Persians, it became
evident to the emperor Decius that his army was in danger of being overwhelmed. Mercurius reassured him with the words: 'Fear not. We shall
conquer.' An angel thereupon presented Mercurius with a sword, bade
him remember the Almighty, and sent him forth into battle. The Persians
were routed and the Emperor wished to celebrate with a sacrifice to the
gods, and invited Mercurius to participate. The latter refused, confessed
his Faith and threw his belt before the Emperor as an insult. He was
flogged, sent to Caesarea and there beheaded. One hundred years later [it
is alleged], the saint returned to earth in answer to a prayer of Basil, the
Bishop of Caesarea, and slew the apostate emperor Julian during his campaign against the Persians.

"Tradition ascribes to Basil of Caesarea a vision in which he saw St.
Mercurius before the Throne of God, commanded to descend to earth to
slay Julian the Apostate; at the time of Julian's death the divine sword of
St. Mercurius which hung upon the wall of Basil's cell mysteriously disap-
peared, and was restored a day later to its former place upon the wall."
Which implies that, in the vision, St. Mercurius fulfilled "the office of
Mercury, as Messenger of the Gods." [29] (Plate 27.)

---

29. Mulock and Langdon, op. cit., p. 16.

(In the Arabic-Jacobite *Lives of the Saints*[30] there "is no mention . . . of St. Mercurius, who is so great a favorite of the Copts, having had any connection with Egypt during his lifetime. It may be supposed [however] that his triumph in overthrowing the wicked and oppressive apostate Julian so endeared him to the people that on that account he was honoured by the Christians of Egypt." [31])

The myth is eternally ourselves.

When we view a representation of St. George slaying the dragon, or any similar image, what we see is neither an abstraction, nor even, in truth, an historical figure who existed long ago, and killed a particular demon. We are confronted, instead, by a ritualistic depiction of what is occurring all of the time. Hence the important factor is not, essentially, who St. George and various related figures *were,* but what *man is:* what *I am.* Not who *can* vanquish a dragon, but who *has* done so. We do not, after all, slay dragons in order to conquer them, but rather to bring about our own regeneration.

"The highest divine essence . . . in later Hinduism tended to be viewed . . . as a duad; and this could be represented either as a polarity of the male and female forces, Shiva-Shakti, the holy couple in their perennial embrace, or as Vishnu and Shiva — with Shiva standing for the destructive and Vishnu for the creative-and-maintaining aspect of the world process. . . . When . . . the polarity is that of the two males, the functions of bringing into being and carrying on the processes of the cosmos are assigned to Vishnu, who in his character as the creator and maintainer of the universe now enacts the role of the goddess of the male-female duad and absorbs the activity that was formerly assigned (in the symbolism of the Hindu trinity) to Brahma. For the idea has come to prevail that fundamentally the creation and maintenance of the phenomenal world are one, since the life-process, whether in the separate individual or in the giant organism of the universe, is an ever-renewed creation. Living beings are not first created, then simply maintained; they are continu-

---

30. "A collection founded upon an original Greek pattern of homilies or Lives of the Saints, from which extracts are read in the church on the appropriate occasions. Jacobite is a general term used to denote" a certain group of Eastern Christians, so called after Jacobus Baradaeus (Yaqob Burdeana). (Ibid., p. 15.)

31. Ibid., p. 15.

28. H A R I - H A R A
Stone sculpture. Prasat Andet. Cambodian.
2nd half 7th–early 8th centuries. Musée Albert
Sarraut, Pnompenh. Photograph by Eliot Elisofon.

ously becoming. The force that in the beginning shaped their frames carries them on till they are dissolved by the process of decay. Maintenance and creation only *seem* to be different: actually they are identical, as two phases of the one dynamic reality of life. But creation and destruction also are one: for a single divine force brings forms into being and dissolves them. Vishnu and Shiva, therefore, can be thought of as identical. This union is expressed in the term *Hari-Hara*.

"*Hari,* a popular name of Vishnu, means, literally, 'green, greenish yellow, tawny, bay, and reddish brown.' These are the colors of spring and growth, the hues of twigs and young leaves. *Hari* connotes the growth of nature, its eternal capacity to put forth new life, and the unending dynamism that moves through the generations. *Hara,* in contrast, means 'he who takes away,' and is a common epithet of Shiva. *Hara,* 'seizing, grasping, removing, taking, depriving of,' is the gesture by which nature takes back into itself the creatures whom it has produced and supported. *Hara,* this destructive grip, is therefore Shiva in his office of dissolving the individual and the universe when the life-system has reached its term. . . .

"In this image of Hari-Hara [Plate 28], the distinguishing traits of the two conjoined deities are not stressed, yet are clearly given. The tall tiara is vertically divided. On the left side [of the figure] it is plain, but on the other it exhibits, in a flat, subdued ornament, the intertwining tresses of the matted hair of the great ascetic, Shiva. . . .

"The sole immediate and adequate representation of a synthesis of thesis and antithesis, making visible the paradoxical aspect of reality, is an image in which the contrary features are fused in the visible unity of one organism, and Hari-Hara is such a symbol. The meaning of the legend is that you cannot play safe: an unforeseen combination of opposites that seemingly exclude each other can overpower even your strongest defenses. Furthermore, such combinations are bound to come to pass in the course of world history, to restore the cosmic equilibrium, whenever the normal balance of compensating principles has been upset by some self-centered, one-sided, demonic urge.

"Hari-Hara, this coincidence of opposites mutually supporting each other and forming the two vital halves of one living being, is life; is every one of us. Yet who is capable of facing its manifestation with unflinching gaze? An inscrutable mask, flashing forth an ambivalent meaning, it supports an extreme inner tension of antagonistic forces — destruction and growth at the same time. . . . Only perfect equanimity . . . the ability to encompass the two aspects of life, which are delight *and* suffering, growth *and* destruction, the expanding *and* the shrinking, the bright *and* the dark, in the knowledge that they are intrinsically one and the same, complementing each other like day and night . . . can command that divine superiority and aloofness which is necessary if one is to face what at first view seems to be a divine monster. The frightening being is life and truth itself. Hari-Hara is a living duad, symbolic of the reality that is manifest through and contained within all living beings." [32]

The Gunas: The three *gunas* of Hindu tradition cast light upon the Egyptian concept of Horus and Seth, as well as upon Hari-Hara. According to the Hindu view, the universe is said to be composed of three basic qualities, strands, or *gunas: sattva, rajas,* and *tamas.* The *gunas* both support one another and intermingle. It is no more possible to conceive of them as separate entities, than to refer to a certain type of lamp, without considering it in terms of the interplay of oil, wick, and flame. Thus all differentiations in the world are to be traced to the predominance of one or another of the *gunas.*

The three great Hindu gods also may be understood in relation to the *gunas:* Shiva, the embodiment of *tamas,* the destructive tendency; Vishnu, representative of the *sattva guna,* embodiment of the power of preservation; Brahma, the creator, alluding to *rajas,* the principle of activity.[33]

---

32. Zimmer, THE ART OF INDIAN ASIA, Vol. I, pp. 145–49.
33. The last paragraph is based on a Stella Kramrisch letter to the author.

10 SYMBOLICAL CONTESTS OF THE HEROES: THE PROCESS OF SELF-MASTERY

"Truth exists only as the individual himself produces it in action."

SØREN KIERKEGAARD

Since similar attitudes concerning symbolical victories over beasts difficult to tame were so often expressed in diverse early cultures, the illustrations that follow frequently reveal surprisingly analogous imagery.

At one level the heroes portrayed courageously oppose chaos in the outer world: forces capable of destroying crops, the social order, civilization, humanity itself. From another perspective, an inner process is revealed, as a result of which animal qualities deemed positive become identified with the heroes themselves.

In traditional terms, when mythological figures of importance are shown holding aloft, or standing upon, certain beasts, it is because the latter represent creative attributes or vehicles of the former. In addition to which, once a hero has transcended various lower aspects of himself, he has earned the right to carry or bear such beasts, for example, as those illustrated; to wear their skins, as well as to be seated upon them.

The role and quest of the potential hero in man perpetually involve both confrontation with and transformation of the negative elements of such symbolical animals, among others, as lion, bull, dragon; the comprehension of how self-limiting are both material and spiritual pride, how vital it is to liberate our most creative energies.

In various ancient cultures it was believed that stars in an imaginary zone in the sky, arranged in twelve constellations, comprised the zodiac. (Plate 29.) Each of the constellations is equated with a corresponding sign. Their order, eastward from the vernal equinox, is: Aries (Ram), Taurus (Bull), Gemini (Twins), Cancer (Crab), Leo (Lion), Virgo (Virgin), Libra (the Scales or Balance), Scorpio (Scorpion), Sagittarius (Archer), Capricornus (Goat), Aquarius (Water-Bearer), Pisces (Fish).

29. **THE ZODIAC**
   Folios 4 verso, 5 recto, from an illuminated
   Portolan Atlas. Manuscript 507. Battista Agnese.
   Venetian. 1542. The Pierpont Morgan Library,
   New York.

Preoccupation with the significance of ancient initiation and related rites, with the possible meaning of signs of the zodiac, alchemical concepts, animals, and human body parts — as well as such other categories as colors, trees, flowers, minerals — tends more often than not to strike the modern mind either as meaningless or, even worse, dangerously based on superstition. Yet, even when we do not literally believe in or adhere to certain tenets long held sacred in numerous civilizations, there is much to be learned from insights achieved by way of most subtle intuition and profound experience; from perceptions stemming quite as clearly from imaginative and sustained study of natural phenomena, as from wisdom gained in any other manner. Indeed, the combination of all forms of knowledge, like the totality of vision embodied in the major myths of virtually all cultures, represents a most generous gift, irrespective of whether or not we choose to utilize it. Or, as Dr. Carl Jung has phrased it, what long have been termed magical practices are "nothing but the projections of psychic events, which . . . act like a kind of enchantment of one's own personality." [1] A statement further implemented by Esther Harding's: "It did not dawn on man's consciousness until many centuries had passed that while his magic had no actual effect on the order of the external world, it did exert an influence on the . . . force emanating from the depths of his own psyche." [2]

The lion is primarily associated with the sun, its affirmative tendencies being equated with royal courage, will, strength, nobility, power, invincibility — with victory of spirit over matter. In various early cultures this regal animal was regarded as the king of beasts, associated with the hunter — with sky, day, fire, light — with the illumination of the conscious.

The following delineations of heroes combatting lions typify man opposing his own will to power. They allude to the attempt to transcend self-deluding obsessions that stem from a false sense of ego and pride.

In early Near Eastern iconography, "The hero strangling the lion is one of the most ancient and persistent motives." [3] When young Horus is

1. From Carl G. Jung, Commentary to THE SECRET OF THE GOLDEN FLOWER, translated by Richard Wilhelm and Cary Baynes, New York: Harcourt, Brace and Company, 1932, p. 100.

2. PSYCHIC ENERGY, ITS SOURCE AND GOAL, M. Esther Harding, Bollingen Series X, New York: Pantheon Books, 1947, p. 78.

3. "An Achaemenid Sculpture in Cleveland," Dorothy G. Shepherd, ARCHAEOLOGY, Vol. 14, No. 2, Summer 1961, p. 102.

shown standing next to a lion in Egyptian art, he personifies the heroic principle in man. The lion, which so often appears as a royal emblem even today, has long been a feature of thrones, including those, for example, of Pharaohs and the Buddha. Leonine figures also flank or guard sacred gates or portals of antiquity.[4]

The sun — with which the lion is often associated — gives life, yet its too-burning rays can wither; can bring death and destruction. Thus, in turn, there must be the moon and the cooling night — the dews and the rains — to replenish the earth. And then, in endless succession, the waters must themselves recede, else there will be flood and devastation.

The bull long has been considered complementary to the solar lion, although — like the latter — it too has exemplified the sun and kingship in certain early civilizations.

Powerful, wise, majestic, the bull has been widely viewed as the herdsman, the great progenitor, emblem of fertility.[5]

In ancient Greece the bull was deemed to be the animal form of Zeus. As A. B. Cook has noted, "The ultimate reason why both ram and bull were associated with sky-gods in general and with Zeus in particular lay in the fact that these animals possessed [fertilizing force] to an exceptional degree." Hence "bulls and rams were sacrificed to Zeus because, according to the belief of early days, the gift of so much virility increased" the god's power to fertilize and bless.[6]

Cook further observes that, around the shores of the Mediterranean in early times, the Thunder God was envisaged as a bellowing bull. Kings — or priests, as their representatives — donned bull masks, or at least bull horns.

When ritual contests with bulls were fought on the island of Crete, not only did acrobats jump over these majestic, awe-inspiring animals, in

---

4. It is a most curious fact that, in certain parts of the world — such as, for example, China — where the lion itself is not native, it has had profound symbolical significance for many centuries.

5. Whereas the bull — like the lion, dragon, and many other age-old representations of similar importance — has numerous connotations, only those characteristics are emphasized that have special relevance in the present context. Thus it is not possible to treat of such subjects as the bull in relationship to the moon, or to the Great Mother; the fact that, in many representations, the power of the lion is shown as greater than that of the bull; the astrological significance, in any detail, of Leo, Taurus, and still further signs of the zodiac.

6. Cook, op. cit., Vol. I, p. 717.

order to indicate that death was being surmounted and life renewed,[7] but it was essential for the horns of the bull to be grasped — the latter act supposedly possessing power to convey the attribute of fertility to those who came into such contact with the horns.

In the words of G. R. Levy, with the introduction of the dragon, "which causes . . . strife with its promise of perpetual renewal," there "arises the power of the hero." [8]

"The dragon-slaying motif is a high favorite with the mythographers of almost all peoples and ages. In Greece especially, where tales involving gods and heroes were legion, there was hardly a hero who did not slay his dragon. Perhaps Heracles and Perseus are the best-known of the Greek killers of monsters. With the rise of Christianity, the heroic feat was transferred to the saints; witness the story of St. George and the Dragon, and its ubiquitous parallels. The names and the details vary from place to place and story to story. But what is the original source of the incidents? Since the dragon-slaying theme was an important motif in the Sumerian mythology of the third millennium B.C., it is reasonable to assume that many a thread in the texture of the Greek and early Christian dragon tales winds back to Sumerian sources." [9]

At times the dragon, or great serpent, typifies fertility; at others it is representative of vast underwaters in danger of welling up and overflowing, of flooding the earth. Now the dragon is benign, again it is an equivalent of what may overwhelm, thwart, extinguish. It can be fearsome and terrifying — as in a nightmare — its eyes fixed upon us, causing nameless anxiety and dread.

---

7. This practice was similarly regarded elsewhere in the ancient world, and even present-day bull-fights have their origins in age-old rituals possessed of profound religious meaning.

8. THE SWORD FROM THE ROCK, G. R. Levy, London: Faber and Faber, 1953, p. 47.

9. FROM THE TABLETS OF SUMER, Samuel Noah Kramer, Indian Hills, Colorado: The Falcon's Wing Press, 1956, p. 196.

*30. HERAKLES WITH TWO LIONS
From bronze relief, Perugia carriage. Etruscan.
c. 500 B.C. Alte Pinakothek, Munich.

The dragon or serpent has typified such extremes as the temptation of Eve, and a reaching for wisdom — for the potentiality of new life or re-generation.

> *"Appear, appear, whatso thy shape or name,*
> *O Mountain Bull, Snake of the Hundred Heads,*
> *Lion of the Burning Flame!*
> *O God, Beast, Mystery, come!"*

EURIPIDES

From: *The Man with the Blue Guitar*

> "That I may reduce the monster to
> Myself, and then may be myself
>
> In face of the monster, be more than part
> Of it, more than the monstrous player of
>
> One of its monstrous lutes, not be
> Alone, but reduce the monster and be
>
> Two things, the two together as one,
> And play of the monster and of myself,
>
> Or better not of myself at all,
> But of that as its intelligence,
>
> Being the lion in the lute
> Before the lion locked in stone." [10]

WALLACE STEVENS

"The custom of holding public contests between bulls [Plate 31] or between bulls and men is an ancient and widespread one. Its origin is apparently to be sought in some form of nature worship, and it almost always forms part of a ritual observance."

---

10. COLLECTED POEMS OF WALLACE STEVENS, New York: Alfred A. Knopf, 1954, p. 165.

31. TWO BULL-LIKE ANIMALS
LOCKED IN COMBAT
From stone relief. Chinese. Latter period Han
dynasty, 1st–2nd centuries. Nanyang, China.

Early Nanyang reliefs showing men grappling with bulls reveal, as Richard C. Rudolph has indicated, "an excellent attempt to portray man's courage. . . .

"The word bull is used here in a general sense to indicate a fierce male animal with general bovine characteristics ranging from naturalistic to imaginary. . . .

"The non-Chinese Miao tribes of southwest China still kill bulls ritually after a fight and keep their horns as cult objects[11] — a project which reminds . . . of the importance of the bull throughout the ancient world."[12]

Such motifs as those in Plates 32 and 33 appeared in ancient China on various materials. The second image closely resembles later depictions of the hero flanked by mythological animals, as represented in other cultures.[13]

---

11. See also Chapter 22.

12. This entire passage is based on "Bull Grappling in Early Chinese Reliefs," Richard C. Rudolph, ARCHAEOLOGY, Vol. 13, No. 4, Winter 1960, pp. 241 ff.

13. THE BEGINNINGS OF CHINESE CIVILIZATION, Li Chi, Seattle: University of Washington Press, 1957, pp. 27–29.

*32. HERO SUBDUING BEASTS
From bronze inscription. Chinese. Shang dynasty, middle to latter part, 2nd millennium B.C.(?). Anyang, China.

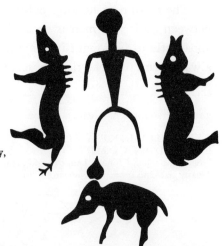

*33. HERO AND BEASTS
From bronze inscription. Chinese. Shang dynasty, middle to latter part, 2nd millennium B.C.(?). Anyang, China.

34. MAN PLUNGING SPEAR INTO
ANIMAL
Detail of rock carving. Swedish. c. 1000–500 B.C.
Fossum, Tanum, Bohuslän, Sweden.

*35. GILGAMESH (?), BULL, BIRD
From decorated stone ritual vase. Sumerian.
Early 3rd millennium B.C. The British
Museum, London.

The dramatic detail of an early carving (Plate 34) shows hunter, hunted, and weapon as unified. The illustration forms part of a scene relating to a seasonal ritual — the transmutation of winter into spring; to sacrifice; to the rites of passage of a fertility god — his marriage, death and resurrection.

The figure in Plate 35, at times described as the epic hero Gilgamesh, is here portrayed with an arm resting on a bull. In other related delineations we find "lions who would otherwise wreak havoc on the livestock." [14]

14. SUMER, THE DAWN OF ART, André Parrot, translated by Stuart Gilbert and James Emmons, New York: Golden Press, 1961, p. 78.

זה שמשון הרוכב על הארי ווזרע פיהו

*36. SAMSON RENDING THE JAW
OF THE LION
From illustration, Hebrew Pentateuch with
Prayers and Commentaries. German. Late 13th
century. The British Museum, London.

*37. HERAKLES AND THE NEMEAN
LION
From vase painting by the Kleophrades
Painter.15
Greek. c. 490 B.C. The University Museum,
University of Pennsylvania, Philadelphia.

The Hebrew (Plate 36) reads "This Samson who rides on the lion and rends its mouth." In the Middle Ages, Samson was envisaged as a prototype of Christ — a symbol of Christ's victory over Satan. Samson's exploits also have been regarded as comparable to those of the Sumerian epic hero Gilgamesh and of Herakles.

Herakles confronts the Nemean lion in its cavern. (Plate 37.) Like Samson, he combats the beast without weapons or assistance. His club, bow, and quiver are placed to one side. Herakles "strangles" the lion by embracing it in his arms, since only his own strength can conquer, and so transmute the destructive "lion forces" within himself.

Having overcome the ruinous lion power within himself, Herakles earns the right to wear the animal's skin — the latter being a traditional garb of the hero-king-priest. (Plate 38.) The release of creative energy that takes place as a result of each of his successful battles enables Herakles, as hero, to perform the ensuing labors assigned to him.

According to certain early versions of the tale, Minos claimed the throne of Crete and, "in proof of his right to reign, boasted that the gods would answer whatever prayer he offered them. First dedicating an altar to

---

15. "Though few actual names of Attic vase painters are known, many different styles can be recognized. Through the intensive work of the last fifty years . . . the chief personalities [who painted] . . . Attic black-figure and red-figure [vases] have become known. To those not known from signatures, invented names have been assigned, derived from the subject or location of the artist's chief work (Nekyia Painter, Berlin Painter) . . . or from the name of the potter with whom he collaborated (Brygos Painter), etc." (A HANDBOOK OF GREEK ART, Gisela M. A. Richter, London: The Phaidon Press, 1965, pp. 315–16.)

38. HERAKLES WEARING THE LION
SKIN
From vase painting by the Berlin Painter. Greek.
490–480 B.C. Martin von Wagner-Museum der
Universität, Würzburg.

*39. THESEUS AND THE
MINOTAUR
From vase painting. Greek. Last quarter
6th century B.C.

Poseidon, and making all preparations for a sacrifice, he . . . prayed that
a bull might emerge from the sea. At once, a dazzlingly-white bull swam
ashore, but Minos was so struck by its beauty that he sent it to join his own
herds, and slaughtered another instead." [16]

Some accounts of the myth claim that it was because Minos had habitu-
ally offered an annual sacrifice of the best bull in his possession to Poseidon — whereas now he withheld his gift for a year, yielding only his sec-
ond-best — that he incurred the god's wrath.

Poseidon, in order to avenge Minos' affront, caused the King's wife,
Pasiphaë, to fall in love with the white bull. Once the Queen had confided
her unnatural passion for the animal to Daedalus, the famed Athenian
craftsman constructed an image of a cow in which Pasiphaë hid herself.[17]

The bull, being deceived, begat by Pasiphaë "the Minotauros, the 'bull
of Minos'. . . . This latter was a child with a bull's head, and it had to be
hidden away." [18] The Minotaur grew up in the Labyrinth that Daedalus
built for the purpose.[19]

It became the task of Theseus to combat the Minotaur. Although it is
most often claimed that he was aided by Ariadne, who provided him with

---

16. THE GREEK MYTHS, Robert Graves, Baltimore: Penguin Books, 1955, Vol. I, p. 293.

17. See ibid., p. 293.

18. Kerényi, THE GODS OF THE GREEKS, p. 111.

19. "The legendary figure of Theseus," notes Mircea Eliade, "and the rites connected with his name, can be more
easily explained if we regard them as dependent upon an initiatory scenario. Many episodes in the saga of Theseus
are in fact initiatory ordeals — for example . . . his entering the labyrinth and fighting the monster, a typical
theme of heroic initiations." (BIRTH AND REBIRTH, Mircea Eliade, translated by Willard R. Trask, New York:
Harper & Brothers, 1958, pp. 108–9.)

*40. KING GRASPING TWO WINGED
BULL-DRAGONS WITH LION
HEADS AND BIRD CLAWS
From limestone cylinder seal. Achaemenian.
c. 6th century B.C. The Pierpont Morgan
Library, New York.

*41. CONTESTANT PAIR: BULL-
MAN AND LION
From detail of steatite cylinder seal.
Akkadian. 2334–2154 B.C. The Pierpont
Morgan Library, New York.

a thread that would permit him "to find his way out of the Labyrinth," [20]
Kerényi calls attention to a variant account according to which Ariadne
used a bejewelled wreath, given her by Dionysos, "to light up Theseus's
passage through the Labyrinth. . . . Originally [moreover] the Labyrinth was not a maze, but a spiral through which one could return after
reaching its centre. [Thus] Ariadne's shining wreath enabled Theseus" [21]
to find his way. He was also successful in killing the Minotaur.

It was doubtless a prime necessity for Theseus to enter the labyrinth or
spiral,[22] as Herakles the cavern: to penetrate his own netherworld; to out-
grow the will to both spiritual and material pride. Only so could he find
his true center; could he serve to liberate the generative, positive forces
both within himself and in the external world. (Plate 39.)

André Gide has written of Theseus (it is Daedalus who speaks): "Believing that no prison can withstand a really obstinate intention to escape,
and that there is no barrier, no ditch, that daring and resolution will not
overcome, I thought that the best way of containing a prisoner in the
labyrinth was to make it of such a kind, not that he couldn't get out (try to
grasp my meaning here), but that he wouldn't want to get out. I therefore
assembled in this one place the means to satisfy every kind of appetite.
The Minotaur's tastes were neither many nor various; but we had to plan
for everybody, whomsoever it might be, who would enter the labyrinth.

---

20. Kerényi, THE GODS OF THE GREEKS, p. 270.

21. Ibid., p. 270.

22. See Chapter 13.

Another and indeed the prime necessity was to fine down the visitor's will-power to the point of extinction. . . .

"Outside of [the labyrinth] reality seems charmless and one no longer has any wish to return to it. And that — that above all — is what keeps one inside the labyrinth. . . . I have thought of this plan: to link you [Theseus] and Ariadne by a thread, the tangible symbol of duty. This thread will allow, indeed will compel you to rejoin her after you have been some time away. Be always determined not to break it, no matter what may be the charms of the labyrinth, the seduction of the unknown, or the headlong urging of your own courage. Go back to her, or all the rest, and the best with it, will be lost. This thread will be your link with the past. Go back to it. Go back to yourself. For nothing can begin from nothing, and it is from your past, and from what you are at this moment, that what you are going to be must spring." [23]

The ancient Near Eastern cylinder seals reproduced (Plates 40–42) are, at times, interpreted as alluding to the Mesopotamian Gilgamesh, or to Marduk — the latter celebrated in the Babylonian Genesis — or again to the Assyrian god Adad. They may also represent still other heroic or epic figures, either within the same or related traditions. The three pictures shown portray conquest — in one manner or another — over the negative powers of the animals depicted or over equally destructive human quali-ties. Yet, whatever the triumph achieved at any given moment, there is the need for eternal struggle. (Plate 43.)

---

23. TWO LEGENDS: OEDIPUS AND THESEUS, André Gide, translated by John Russell, New York: Alfred A. Knopf, 1950, pp. 85–87.

42. HEROIC FIGURE OR CEN-
TAUR ATTACKING LION-
GRIFFIN
From agate cylinder seal.
Neo-Babylonian. Mid-1st millennium
B.C. The Pierpont Morgan Library,
New York.

*43. LION AND BULL
ATTACKING ONE
ANOTHER
From silver coin. Chalcidician. c. 424
B.C. Collection du Cabinet des Médailles
de la Bibliothèque Nationale, Paris.

*44.   FIGURE AND HORSE
From gold coin. Eastern Gallic. Collection
du Cabinet des Médailles de la
Bibliothèque Nationale, Paris.

At first glance the Celtic concept expressed in the accompanying image (Plate 44) may appear to be quite at variance with depictions typical of other traditions. The heroic figure shown on the coin seems not to be riding upon the horse portrayed, in order the more readily to combat some other adversary. He is poised, instead, above the horse, itself, which he is about to spear. The latter fact suggests that what we are witnessing has to do essentially with a symbolical death, brought about as a prerequisite of rebirth and renewal. (Note the phallic form of the weapon, and how both male and female reproductive organs of the horse are emphasized, as is the concept of seven,[24] both on the animal's mane, and above the hero's head.)

In traditional terms, Mithra is a sun god. The voluntary "sacrifice" of his own dark inner powers is suggested by his slaying of the bull in the grotto, at night (the sacrifice of a bull under such circumstances being associated with the forces of light overcoming those of darkness).

Since it is in the night that the seeds of procreation are sown, Mithra personifies birth into the new day. Plate 45 alludes to fertility (note the serpent and other phallic forms); also to the transmutation of what is imprisoned in the realm of the unconscious into the conscious: the emerging sunrise.

From one perspective, overcoming the bull represents both a subjugation and a transcendence of man's lower animal nature. It involves the sacrifice of not yet transformed instinctual drives that control us as in the dark.

---

24. One might readily refer, here, to seven as a number of completion. Yet, although number symbolism recurs in the myth and art of numerous civilizations, and meanings are often identical, they are not invariably so. Hence, despite the fact that various numerals appear in often related context throughout this volume, no effort has been made to prove they possess absolutely uniform significance. Any too literal or generalized explanations concerning this, and analogous matters must, in the end, prove more harmful than helpful.

When, however, there seems to be firm ground for interpretation it is, at times given, in order to clarify how certain numbers are utilized in specific situations and traditions. (A similar approach is used with respect to other categories.)

Jung has written, from another point of view: "Who does not think
. . . of Mithras . . . [taking] his bull . . . namely his love for his
Mater Natura, on his back, and with this heaviest burden [setting] forth
on the *via dolorosa?* . . . The way of this passion leads to the cave in
which the bull is sacrificed. So, too, Christ had to bear the Cross to the
place of sacrifice, where, according to the Christian version, the Lamb was
slain in the form of the god, and was then laid to earth in the sepulchre.
The cross, or whatever other heavy burden the hero carries, is *himself.*" [25]
(Plate 46.)

---

25. SYMBOLS OF TRANSFORMATION, Carl G. Jung, translated by R. F. C. Hull, Bollingen Series XX, New York:
Pantheon Books, 1956, pp. 302–03.

45.   SACRIFICE OF A BULL IN
HONOR OF THE GOD MITHRA
Bas-relief. Roman. c. 3rd century. Musée
du Louvre, Paris. Alinari photograph.

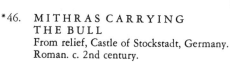

*46.   MITHRAS CARRYING
THE BULL
From relief, Castle of Stockstadt, Germany.
Roman. c. 2nd century.

*47. GUSHTASP KILLING A KARG
From a *Shah-namah* manuscript. Ms.
Supplément persan 1280. Persian. 2nd half
15th century. Biblothèque Nationale,
Paris.

"Scenes in which a legendary hero kills the 'unicorn' are . . . represented in the *Shah-namah* illustrations. . . . The first hero [therein described as performing] this deed of prowess is Gushtasp while exiled in
the land of Rum. When Mirin, a Ruman noble, asks for the hand of the
second daughter of Caesar, he is told that he would be accepted only after
having killed the monster. Being unequal to performing the task, Mirin
enlists the help of Gushtasp who, on foot, vanquishes the beast on his
behalf without revealing the secret" nature of what has transpired.[26]

As is generally the case in myths of the hero, acts considered impossible
of accomplishment by ordinary human beings are performed. Such deeds
also must be carried out without resort to customary external aids.[27]

"Ireland was [being] ravaged by a fierce dragon and the king had
promised the Princess Iseult to the man who should kill it." Tristan, having been sent to Ireland to bring Iseult back to King Mark in Cornwall —
as the latter's bride — "made his plans accordingly. The sight of [an]
Irish court seneschal and several other knights fleeing guided him to the
dragon's lair, and he attacked the monster. After a hard fight he killed the
dragon and cut out its tongue, which he placed in his bosom. Then he
staggered toward a stream and fell unconscious.

"Meanwhile the seneschal returned, found the dragon . . . cut off its
head . . . [and] went to the court to claim the princess." When an at-

26. "The Unicorn," Richard Ettinghausen, FREER GALLERY OF ART OCCASIONAL PAPERS, Washington, 1950,
Vol. I, No. 3, p. 36.

27. Although the beast under attack long has been known simply as the unicorn, in accordance with Ettinghausen's
researches the designations karg, karkadann (rhinoceros), and other Near Eastern descriptions are more specifically
applicable. However, rather than being viewed in literal manner, the above animal forms must be considered in
terms of overtones and aspects that are by no means merely zoological.

*48. **TRISTAN CUTTING OUT
THE DRAGON'S TONGUE**
From detail of wall painting. Austrian.
c. 1400. Summer House, Castle Runkelstein,
Austria.

tempt was made to ascertain whether the knight had, in fact, killed the
beast, it so happened that Tristan was found, unconscious. Once he was
disarmed, the dragon's tongue came to light. After it was clear that Tristan
had slain the monster, he was secretly carried to the palace.

"When the seneschal returned for the princess, bringing the head" of
the beast as proof of his own prowess, "Tristan bade the court look for the
dragon's tongue." When none was found, "Tristan produced it, and all
agreed that he was the slayer. So Tristan won Iseult's hand for Mark." [28]

The cult of Jupiter Dolichenus, named after the little town of Doliche
in Comagene, Syria, where it originated, is an "example of a Hittite god
surviving into the Graeco-Roman age. He seems to have been originally
akin to, or even one with, the Hittite father-god, though . . . he bears
some resemblance to the Hittite son-god also." Extant inscriptions found
near the sites of two Roman sanctuaries of the cult (on the Esquiline and
the Aventine) suggest that Jupiter Dolichenus was "essentially a thunder-
god with solar powers." He is further called "Preserver of the Whole Sky"
and "Provider Invincible" which would indicate he is a fertility god. Like
Mithra, he represents victory of the solar god over the bull, or the winter
rains. He is often related to Apollo in inscriptions, one relief surviving in
which he doubtless personifies the sun itself.

Jupiter Dolichenus, who sometimes holds a thunderbolt in one hand,
and a double axe in the other, is generally represented as a Roman warrior
with a Phrygian cap. Often he wears a breast plate decorated with an

---

28. ABOUT THE ROUND TABLE, Margaret R. Scherer, New York: The Metropolitan Museum of Art, 1945, p. 41.

49. JUPITER DOLICHENUS
Statue. Found at Rome. 2nd–3rd centuries.
Capitoline Museums, Rome.

eagle, a second eagle being perched between the horns of a bull.[29] In Plate 49 the eagle is below the bull upon which the god stands.

"At Sarissa and Karakhna, and probably elsewhere, there was a cult of the god who appears in the texts under a title which seems to mean 'Protective Genius' or 'Providence'. . . . His sacred animal was the stag, and he is represented standing on this animal." [30] (Plate 50.)

The meaning of the stag is often "linked with that of the Tree of Life, because of the resemblance of its antlers to branches. It is also a symbol of the cycles of regeneration and growth. . . . The stag, in several cultures of Asia and pre-Columbian America, came to be thought of as a symbol of regeneration because of the way its antlers are renewed. Like the eagle and the lion, it is the secular enemy of the serpent, which shows that, symbolically, it was viewed favorably; it is closely related to heaven and light. . . . Hence, in the Milky Way, on both sides of the Bridge of Death and Resurrection are figures of eagles, stags and horses acting as mediators between heaven and earth. In the West, during the Middle Ages, the way of solitude and purity was often symbolized by the stag, which actually appears in some emblems with a crucifix between its horns [as in the legend of Saint Eustace. This provides] the last link in the chain of relationships: tree/cross/horns." [31] (See Plate 51.)

29. See Cook, op. cit., Vol. I, pp. 604 ff.

30. THE HITTITES, O. R. Gurney, Baltimore: Penguin Books, 1961, pp. 137–38.

31. A DICTIONARY OF SYMBOLS, J. E. Cirlot, translated by Jack Sage, New York: Philosophical Library, 1962, p. 294.

0. THE GOD ON THE STAG
From steatite relief. Hittite. c. 2nd
millennium B.C. From Yenikoy, Asia
Minor.

1. SAINT EUSTACE
Hand-colored woodcut from *Leben der
Heiligen,* Jacobus de Voragine, J. Bämler,
Augsburg. 1480. Collection Dorothy
Norman, New York.

One day, *The Golden Legend* tells us, when Placidus (later called
Saint Eustace), who was master of soldiers under the Roman Emperor
Trajan, "was riding to the hunt, he came upon a herd of deer, in the midst
of which he saw a stag larger and fairer to the eye than the rest; and this
stag left the herd, and bounded off into a deep forest. While the soldiers
went after the other deer, Placidus pursued the stag at full speed, and bent
all his efforts to capture it. . . . As he chased it with all his might, the
stag mounted at last upon a height of rock, and Placidus, drawing near,
pondered means of taking it. Then, looking closely at the stag, he saw
between its horns the form of the holy cross, gleaming more brightly than
the sun, and upon it the image of Jesus Christ; Who then spoke to him
through the stag's mouth . . . and said: 'O Placidus, why dost thou pursue Me? For thy sake I have appeared in this beast, for I am Christ,
Whom thou unwitting adorest; thine alms-deeds have ascended before
Me, and therefore am I come, that in this stag which thou didst hunt, I
Myself might hunt thee!' Others say, however, that these words were
spoken by the image itself, that appeared between the stag's horns." [32]

32. THE GOLDEN LEGEND, Jacobus de Voragine, translated by Granger Ryan and Helmut Ripperger, New York:
Longmans, Green and Co., 1941, Part II, p. 555.

The accompanying figure, which throws a certain light on the portrayals that follow, represents a deity in the form of "Lord of the Animals."
The manner in which the god is seated on a throne suggests the goal
toward which various of the heroes depicted aspire.

The majestic Lord of the Animals sits cross-legged, in yogic position.
As Coomaraswamy has written, "The deity . . . has been identified,
probably rightly, with [Shiva]." [33] Both his contemplative sitting position
and his ithyphallic powers typify ascetic control. (Plate 52 suggests also
the manner in which the Buddha and other equivalent *yogis* are often
portrayed.)

Just as numerous other figures have had manifold meanings throughout
the ages, so has the widely known sphinx, in which a human head is combined with a leonine body. (Plate 53.) In one of its aspects, the sphinx
was long an emblem of the achievement of wisdom in Egypt: ideal of
mature, evolved kingship. The solar mane of the sphinx further linked
Pharaoh with the sun.

---

33. ELEMENTS OF BUDDHIST ICONOGRAPHY, Ananda K. Coomaraswamy, Cambridge: Harvard University Press,
1935, page facing Plate VI, fig. 22.

52. SEATED FIGURE (LORD
OF THE ANIMALS—
POSSIBLY SHIVA?)
Indus Valley seal. Mohenjo-daro. Indian.
3000–1500 B.C. The National
Museum, New Delhi.

The king-hero, or Pharaoh, having conquered the destructive elements of the "lion" within himself: namely material and spiritual ego — pride and the will to power — became identified with the positive attributes of the king of beasts. Thus we see Pharaoh seated upon the lion throne, image of self-mastery. The throne supports the king. (Plate 54.)

53. SPHINX OF TANIS
Statue. Egyptian. 12th dynasty,
c. 1991–1786 B.C. Cairo Museum.

*54. KING KHAF-RE ON
LION THRONE
From diorite statue. Egyptian. 4th
dynasty, c. 2613–2494 B.C. Cairo
Museum.

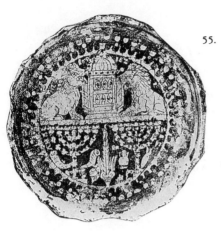

55. TORAH SHRINE
FLANKED BY LIONS
Depiction on gold glass. Found at Rome.
c. 4th century. Biblioteca Vaticana,
Vatican City.

*56. MAN BEARING SEVEN-
BRANCHED CANDLESTICK
(MENORAH) ON HIS HEAD
c. 2nd century. From catacomb at
Beth-Shearim, Palestine.

In ancient Hebraic art, when lions are shown on both sides of the Torah Shrine, such usage is said to derive from the Biblical Cherubim. The lion which, in Plate 55, alludes to the tribe of Judah guarding the Holy Law, was the heraldic beast of Judah.[34] It is not unusual to find two seven-branched candlestands — the Menorah as Tree of Life — under two lions flanking the Torah Shrine. The candlestands and lions depicted signify divine light: the Torah, the law. The combined images relate to the solar principle: the life- and light-giving, life- and light-sustaining power of the sun.

How to say Torah: "I shall teach you the best way to say Torah. You must cease to be aware of yourselves. You must be nothing but an ear that hears what the universe of the word is constantly saying within you. The moment you start hearing what you yourself are saying, you must stop." [35]

"God commanded Moses to make a golden candelabrum having seven branches to be placed in the Ark of the Covenant. [Plate 56.] The mystic number seven is traditionally the number of perfection and is used in both the Old and the New Testament innumerable times in that sense. In the Talmud it is stated that over the throne of king Solomon hung a chandelier of gold with seven branches and on these the names of the seven patriarchs (Adam, Noah, Shem, Abraham, Isaac, Jacob, and Job) were engraved. On the second row of the branches were the names of the 'seven pious ones of the world.' " [36]

34. See ANCIENT HEBREW ARTS, A. Reifenberg, New York: Schocken Books, 1950, p. 117.

35. Reprinted by permission of Schocken Books Inc. from TEN RUNGS, Martin Buber, translated by Olga Marx. Copyright © 1947 by Schocken Books Inc. Pp. 65–66.

36. SIXTEEN ILLUSTRATIONS FROM AN EXHIBITION OF RELIGIOUS SYMBOLISM IN ILLUMINATED MANU-SCRIPTS, The Pierpont Morgan Library, New York, 1944, unnumbered page.

Just as many of the other figures portrayed surmount inner obstacles, so here the attribute of light itself alludes to what, having been assimilated, may now be positively projected.

> *"Neither was there any beast with me, save the beast that I rode upon."*
>
> NEHEMIAH 2:12

> *"A righteous man regardeth the life of his beast."*
>
> PROVERBS 12:10

"A distinction is made between the epithets Bodhisattva and Buddha. The Bodhisattva is an awakening being, or one of wakeful nature; the Buddha is awake." [37]

Of the Buddha's lion throne: It "is the common seat and symbol of regal dignity in the secular realm, where the king is the lion among men. Comparably, the Enlightened One [the Buddha] is the lion among spiritual teachers, philosophers, and divines, and when he lifts his voice to announce the doctrine every other voice is silenced, unable to refute him. His sermon is therefore the 'lion's roar' . . . for when the lion's voice is heard in the wilderness all the other animals fall silent, fearing his approach." [38] (Plate 57.)

---

37. HINDUISM AND BUDDHISM, Ananda K. Coomaraswamy, New York: Philosophical Library, 1948, p. 50.
38. Zimmer, THE ART OF INDIAN ASIA, Vol. I, p. 169.

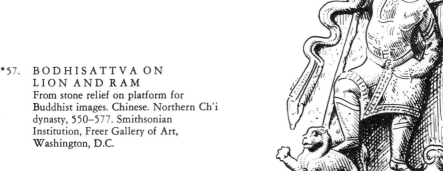

*57. BODHISATTVA ON LION AND RAM
From stone relief on platform for Buddhist images. Chinese. Northern Ch'i dynasty, 550–577. Smithsonian Institution, Freer Gallery of Art, Washington, D.C.

58. NINE-DRAGON SCROLL
(Detail)
Ink on paper by Ch'en-Jung. Chinese.
1244. Museum of Fine Arts, Boston.
Francis Gardner Curtis Fund.

In China the dragon, which ascends and descends, is considered a benevolent beast not connected with the powers of darkness. It suggests "fertilizing rain, the genius of waters, especially petitioned in times of drought
or flood." It is looked upon as a paragon of strength and goodness. Its
benevolent life-giving services have been compared with the good admin-
istration of officials, and the dragon has become an image of imperial dignity.

"The fact that the dragon is manifest as a purely emblematic figment
of the imagination makes him none the less real and natural. . . . For
many centuries, there have been reports and records which tell us that the
dragon is a mythological animal, a symbolic figure and a metaphysical
concept. In Chinese art, the dragon is one of the most significant motifs; a
mystic, fantastic, and awe-inspiring being, swift as lightning and strong as
a storm wind; a being which appears among clouds and mist, visible only
to those whose enlightened minds are open to the great spiritual forces of
nature." [39]

Okakura Kakuzo has written: In the Far East the dragon has been associated "with the supreme power or that sovereign cause which pervades
everything, taking new forms according to its surroundings, yet never seen
in final shape. The dragon is the great mystery itself. Hidden in the cav-
erns of inaccessible mountains, or coiled in the unfathomed depths of the
sea, he awaits the time when he slowly rouses himself to activity. He unfolds himself in the storm clouds; he washes his mane in the blackness of
the seething whirlpools. His claws are in the forks of the lightning, his
scales begin to glisten in the bark of rain-swept pine trees. His voice is
heard in the hurricane which, scattering the withered leaves of the forest,
quickens the new spring. The dragon reveals himself only to vanish." [40]

39. "A Study of the Nine-Dragon Scroll," Hsien-chi Tseng, ARCHIVES OF THE CHINESE ART SOCIETY OF
AMERICA, Vol. XI, 1957, p. 22.

40. THE ART AND ARCHITECTURE OF CHINA, Laurence Sickman and Alexander Soper, Baltimore: Penguin
Books, 1956, p. 143.

59. CHRIST AS THE GOOD
SHEPHERD: ECCE HOMO
Etching by Cornelis Galle the Younger.
Flemish. Mid-17th century. Collection
Dorothy Norman, New York.

*"I am the good shepherd: the good shepherd giveth his life for
the sheep. . . . I am the good shepherd, and know my sheep, and
am known of mine. . . . And other sheep I have, which are not of
this fold: them also I must bring, and they shall hear my voice; and
there shall be one fold, and one shepherd. . . . My sheep hear my
voice, and I know them, and they follow me: And I give unto them
eternal life; and they shall never perish, neither shall any man pluck
them out of my hand."* (Plate 59.)

St. John 10:11, 14, 16, 27-28

60. CRUCIFIXION WITH
SERPENT
Engraving by Francïscus Wauters. Dutch.
1791. Collection Dorothy Norman,
New York.

11 THE FOUNDING OF CIVILIZATIONS...DANGERS INHERENT IN EXCESSIVE LAW, ORDER, REASON... NEGATIVE ASPECTS OF THE UNCONSCIOUS AND CONSCIOUS...NOAH... JONAH...DURGA

"In the beginning was the Word, and the Word was with God, and the Word was God."

ST. JOHN 1:1

"The very naming of a subject by a man of genius is the beginning of insight."

RALPH WALDO EMERSON

"The soul stands fast that gave them shape and speech."

ALGERNON SWINBURNE

"To determine the import of names is the same as to determine the fundamental character of concepts."

THEODORE STCHERBATSKY

"A new World has just been born, a fresh, pure, rich world with all its potentialities intact and unworn by time . . . the World as it was on the first day of Creation. This idea, which is . . . very widespread, reveals the religious man's desire to deliver himself from the weight of his past, to escape the work of Time, and to begin his life again ab ovo.*"*

MIRCEA ELIADE

*61. KADMOS KILLING THE DRAGON
From detail of vase painting by Asteas.
Paestan. 3rd quarter 4th century B.C.
Museo Nazionale, Naples.

"Hold fast the form of sound words."

2 TIMOTHY 1:13

"Whatever is Name (nama), is indeed Form."

STELLA KRAMRISCH

" 'He thinks things, and behold they are'; to know the true 'name' of a thing is to evoke it."

ANANDA K. COOMARASWAMY

"We must do what the Gods did erst."

SATAPATHA BRAHMANAS

"The depths of the human soul are also 'Primordial Times,' that deep 'Well of Time' in which Myth has its home and from which the original norms and forms of life are derived. For Myth is the foundation of life; it is the timeless pattern, the religious formula to which life shapes itself, inasmuch as its characteristics are a reproduction of the Unconscious. There is no doubt about it, the moment when the story-teller acquires the mythical way of looking at things . . . that moment marks a beginning in his life. It means a peculiar intensification of his artistic mood, a new serenity in his powers of perception and creation. This is usually reserved for the later years of life; for whereas in the life of mankind the mythical represents an early and primitive stage, in the life of the individual it represents a late and mature one."

THOMAS MANN

"Work as though no one existed, no one lived, no one had ever come upon the earth."

MEISTER ECKHART

Among various peoples throughout the world, certain mythical heroes long have been regarded as the first to bring into being law, order, form, knowledge, civilization, the word. They have acted, purportedly, much in the manner of Kadmos[1] who, in Kerényi's words, behaved as "at the beginning of the world . . . in primaeval loneliness."[2]

Indeed, each hero who founds a particular city or civilization is considered the sole individual who possibly could have done so *just then, in that place, as at the very center of the universe.*

> *"In the ancient rites of fire, the ritual offering made to the flames was as much a sacrifice to the universal order as to the personal order, the sacrificial act being intended to re-create primordial unity and to bind again into the total being the man torn to pieces by history."*
>
> St.-John Perse

That each citadel should be looked upon as sacred, the first, and at the center is no more contradictory than that every sacrifice we make, every creative act we perform, is necessarily achieved with utter spontaneity, virginally. For do we not inevitably feel each of our most wondrous experiences to be unique and primordial? Is not the bliss of dawning love; our sense of ecstasy in the presence of a new-born child; the making or beholding of a work of art — or any other overwhelming vision — equally pristine?

As Mircea Eliade[3] has noted: "Every human being tends, even unconsciously, towards the Centre, and towards his own centre, where he can find integral reality — sacredness. This desire, so deeply rooted in man, to find himself at the very heart of the real — at the Centre of the World . . . explains the ubiquitous use of [the phrase] 'Centres of the World.' "[4]

---

1. Often referred to, in accord with the Latin spelling, as Cadmus.

2. THE HEROES OF THE GREEKS, C. Kerényi, translated by H. J. Rose, New York: Grove Press, 1960, pp. 29–30.

3. IMAGES AND SYMBOLS, Mircea Eliade, translated by Philip Mairet, New York: Sheed and Ward, 1961, p. 54.

4. As for example, in the case of the Buddha's First Meditation, "it is evidently just because he is for the time being . . . situated at the 'navel of the earth,' the nether pole of the Axis, that the Sun above him casts an unmoving shadow, while the shadows of other trees than the one under which he is seated change their place. We need hardly say that the position of the Axis of the Universe is a universal and not a local position: the 'navel of the earth' is 'within you'. . . . In the same way the centre of every habitation is analogically *the* centre, an hypostasized centre, of the world, and immediately underlies the similarly hypostasized centre of the sky at what

It has been narrated that Kadmos — shown in conflict with a dragon, with which he alone must do battle, and which he attacks without weapons other than a stone — was the mythological founder of Thebes in Boeotia; that he civilized the Boeotians and was instrumental in bringing to them the Pelasgian alphabet.[5] (Is it not possible, also, that Athena, Goddess of Wisdom, advised Kadmos to sow the ground with the teeth of the dragon, much as mankind was admonished not to ignore the significance of Behemoth and Leviathan? See Chapter 7.)

But then, just as each city or civilization must be founded sacredly, must bring order out of chaos, so must what has been created retain its liberating power. Let it become too rigid or, in reverse, again disordered, and there is the recurrent danger that a replica of the very situation from which a Kadmos, a Romulus and a Remus, and still other related figures, have rescued man will come into being once more; that the dragon that has been overcome must again be vanquished, in repeated imitation of what certain of the gods themselves did at the very beginning. Or, if it is not, it may in turn devour.

As Jessie Weston has written, "The detail that the ruling sovereign is sometimes regarded as the re-incarnation of the original founder" of a race strengthens the point that "the king never dies — *Le Roi est mort, Vive le Roi* is very emphatically the motto of this Faith. It is the insistence on Life, Life continuous, and ever-renewing." [6] That not all kings or gods[7] die to be symbolically reborn, does not significantly alter the fact that the basic preoccupation of virtually all great myths is with creation and renewal.

---

is the other pole of the Axis at once of the edifice and of the universe it represents." ("Symbolism of the Dome," Ananda K. Coomaraswamy, THE INDIAN HISTORICAL QUARTERLY, Vol. XIV, No. 1, March, 1938, pp. 9–10.)

In Hindu thought "the Centre" is even "greater than the Circumference, whatever be the extension of the latter," since no one can possibly "conceive the full glory or greatness of the divine reality." (SHIVA MAHADEVA, THE GREAT GOD, Vasudeva Agrawala, Varanasi (India): Veda Academy, 1966, p. 3.)

5. Graves, op. cit., Vol. I, p. 182.

6. FROM RITUAL TO ROMANCE, Jessie L. Weston, New York: Doubleday and Company, 1957, p. 9.

7. Samuel Noah Kramer has called attention to the fact that, in conjunction with "Ishtar's Descent to the Nether World," ever since the early Semitic version of the myth, it had been assumed that Inanna (or Ishtar) "descended to the lower regions in order to free her husband Dumuzi and bring him back to earth." But this is not so: "Inanna did not save her husband Dumuzi from the nether world. Rather, it was she who, angered by his contemptuous attitude, actually handed him over to the demons to be carried off to the land of no return." (Kramer, FROM THE TABLETS OF SUMER, pp. 194–95.)

Although the founders of civilization create,[8] release and renew, any excessive reliance upon the law and order they bring into being — like irrationality, itself — can become a potential danger. (See Plates 62–63.)

"The greater the consciousness, the greater the artist."

LEONARDO DA VINCI

"Where there is no conscience, there can be no art."

ALFRED STIEGLITZ

"By understanding the unconscious we free ourselves from its domination."

CARL G. JUNG

The Goya picture (Plate 62), which reveals a state of nightmare, emphasizes the relationship between varying levels of the artist's vision. A commentary, attributed to Goya, reads: "Imagination deserted by reason begets impossible monsters. United with reason, she is the mother of all art, and the source of its wonders." [9]

On the Blake that follows (Plate 63), we read: "When I say, My bed shall comfort me, my couch shall ease my complaint; Then thou scarest me with dreams, and terrifiest me through visions: So that my soul chooseth strangling, and death rather than my life." [10]

"My bones are pierced in me in the night season & my sinews take no rest. My skin is black upon me & my bones are burned with heat. The triumphing of the wicked is short, the joy of the hypocrite is but for a moment. Satan himself is transformed into an Angel of Light & his Ministers into Ministers of Righteousness." [11]

---

8. In various traditions the manifest world is said to have been fashioned out of chaos; from on high or from below; also from primeval unity before duality existed. The ancient Indian Rig Veda speaks of there having been neither the existent nor the nonexistent prior to creation in time.

9. As quoted in ARS MEDICA, compiled by Carl Zigrosser, Philadelphia Museum of Art, 1955 and 1959, p. 40.

10. JOB 7:13-15.

11. From Blake text around image, after the Bible.

62. "THE SLEEP OF REASON PRODUCES MONSTERS" Etching and aquatint by Francisco José de Goya y Lucientes. Spanish. From first issue of *Los Caprichos,* Madrid, 1797. The Philadelphia Museum of Art: Ars Medica Collection. Photograph by A. J. Wyatt, Staff Photographer.

63. "WITH DREAMS UPON MY
BED THOU SCAREST ME
AND AFFRIGHTEST ME
WITH VISIONS"
Engraving by William Blake. English. 1825.
The Pierpont Morgan Library, New York.

The waters are often associated in myth with both the male and female creative principles, as with the unconscious. Yet, since they may have still other connotations, there is no single, undifferentiated meaning that can be applied to all of their aspects. Thus, although Noah and Jonah have terrifying experiences — which tell us much about ourselves — the terms in which the Bible speaks of the waters in relationship to these two figures are by no means identical. (Plates 64 and 65.)

In the time of Noah, "God saw that the wickedness of man was great in the earth, and that every imagination of the thoughts of his heart was only evil continually. . . . And the Lord said, I will destroy man whom I have created from the face of the earth; both man, and beast, and the creeping thing, and the fowls of the air; for it repenteth me that I have made them. But Noah found grace in the eyes of the Lord. . . . Noah was a just man and perfect in his generations, and Noah walked with God. . . . And God looked upon the earth, and, behold, it was corrupt; for all flesh had corrupted his way upon the earth. And God said unto Noah, The end of all flesh is come before me; for the earth is filled with violence through them; and, behold, I will destroy them with the earth. Make thee an ark. . . . And, behold, I, even I, do bring a flood of waters upon the earth, to destroy all flesh, wherein is the breath of life, from under heaven; and every thing that is in the earth shall die. But with thee will I establish my covenant; and thou shalt come into the ark, thou, and thy sons, and thy wife, and thy sons' wives with thee. And of every living thing of all flesh, two of every sort shalt thou bring into the ark, to keep them alive with thee; they shall be male and female. Of fowls after their kind, and of cattle after their kind, of every creeping thing of the earth after his kind, two of every sort shall come unto thee, to keep them alive. And take thou unto thee of all food that is eaten, and thou shalt gather it to thee; and it shall be for food for thee, and for them. Thus did Noah; according to all that God commanded him, so did he. . . . And the flood was forty days upon the earth; and the waters increased, and bare up the ark, and it was lift up above the earth. And the waters prevailed, and were increased greatly upon the earth; and the ark went upon the face of the waters. And the waters prevailed exceedingly upon the earth; and all the high hills, that were under the whole heaven, were covered. . . . And every living substance was destroyed which was upon the face of the

64. NOAH'S ARK
Woodcut from a Bible in Low German.
Heinrich Quentell. 1478. The Pierpont
Morgan Library, New York.

ground, both man, and cattle, and the creeping things, and the fowl of the heaven; and they were destroyed from the earth: and Noah only remained alive, and they that were with him in the ark. And the waters prevailed upon the earth an hundred and fifty days. . . . And it came to pass at the end of forty days, that Noah opened the window of the ark which he had made: And he sent forth a raven, which went forth to and fro, until the waters were dried up from off the earth. Also he sent forth a dove from him, to see if the waters were abated from off the face of the ground; But the dove found no rest for the sole of her foot, and she returned unto him into the ark, for the waters were on the face of the whole earth: then he put forth his hand, and took her, and pulled her in unto him into the ark. And he stayed yet other seven days; and again he sent forth the dove out of the ark; And the dove came in to him in the evening; and, lo, in her mouth was an olive leaf pluckt off: so Noah knew that the waters were abated from off the earth. And he stayed yet other seven days; and sent forth the dove; which returned not again unto him any more. And it came to pass in the six hundredth and first year, in the first month, the first day of the month, the waters were dried up from off the earth: and Noah removed the covering of the ark, and looked, and, behold, the face of the ground was dry. . . . And God spake unto Noah, saying, Go forth of the ark, thou, and thy wife, and thy sons, and thy sons' wives with thee. Bring forth with thee every living thing that is with thee, of all flesh, both of fowl, and of cattle, and of every creeping thing that creepeth upon the earth; that they may breed abundantly in the earth, and be fruitful, and multiply upon the earth. And Noah went forth, and his sons, and his wife, and his sons' wives with him: Every beast, every creeping thing, and every fowl, and whatsoever creepeth upon the earth, after their kinds, went forth out of the ark. And Noah builded an altar unto the Lord; and took of every clean beast, and of every clean fowl, and offered burnt offerings on the altar. And the Lord smelled a sweet savour; and the Lord said . . . While the earth remaineth, seedtime and harvest, and cold and heat, and summer and winter, and day and night shall not cease." [12]

The story of Noah has been interpreted in ways other than those identified with Genesis — ways that cast additional light upon the Biblical version, as upon the dormant and awakening — the dissolute and regenerative — forces within ourselves.

One version involves a mythological explanation that "illicit and unnatural" sins were committed by the generation of the deluge.[13] Such sins involved men looking "at strange women . . . inviting them to immorality." As a result, an "unnatural union between . . . two kinds of waters" occurred.[14]

---

12. GENESIS 6:5–8:22.

13. Water has had "a dual role in mythology . . . sometimes [being] . . . the fountain of life . . . at [others] . . . 'the depths' into which one should dread to fall. Thus to fall into the 'nether waters' is to regress to a pre-human state, to be swamped by unconscious contents and to lose all rational control. For there are two ways of becoming ego-less or un-self-ish: to descend into the lower waters so that one is not *even* an ego, and to ascend into the upper waters by the increase of consciousness, thus outgrowing the illusion of individual isolation." (MYTH AND RITUAL IN CHRISTIANITY, Alan W. Watts, New York: Vanguard Press, 1954, p. 48n^2.)

14. MAN AND TEMPLE, Raphael Patai, London: Thomas Nelson and Sons, 1947, p. 142.

Thus, when "all the creatures entered [Noah's] Ark . . . there descended onto the earth the waters of the deluge which are male waters, and [those that] came up from the Deeps (Tehomoth) which are female waters, and they united and grew mighty to destroy the world." [15]

The belief "that floods and inundations are the result of a union between male and female waters goes back to age-old traditions in the ancient East. . . . The annual life-giving floods, caused by the rising of the waters of the Tigris and Euphrates, in consequence of which the dry fields were irrigated, were mythically represented as being the result of a union between male and female deities." [16]

The concept of Noah, himself, had an early counterpart in the "god-fearing king" — the Sumerian Ziusudra — who stationed himself by a wall where he heard "the voice of a deity informing him of the decision taken by the assembly of the gods to send a flood and 'to destroy the seed of mankind.' " [17] As described in Chapter 22, the epic hero Gilgamesh journeyed to Utnapishtim — also a prototype of Noah — to seek the "secret of eternal life." [18]

On Palm Sunday, "the priest . . . blesses the branches with incense and holy water, recalling in his prayer not only the palms with which Christ was greeted at Jerusalem, but also the olive-branch . . . the dove brought to Noah as a sign of the ending of the Flood and of peace between God and man. For the Flood," writes Alan Watts, ever typifies that "unconsciousness of the Spirit, the true Self, into which the Divine — as the Sun — descends at night, and from which it arises at dawn, since these are the same waters from which the world was made in the beginning." [19]

In the ancient midnight mass between Holy Saturday and Easter Sunday the priest consecrates the baptismal waters: "O God, who by water didst wash away the crimes of an evil world, and in the overflowing of the Flood didst give a figure of regeneration." [20]

---

15. Rabbi Zadoq, as quoted, ibid., p. 65.
16. Ibid., pp. 65–66.
17. Kramer, op. cit., p. 179.
18. Ibid., p. 218.
19. Watts, op. cit., pp. 143–44.
20. Quoted, ibid., p. 178.

65. JONAS AND THE WHALE
Details from manuscript illumination. *Biblia Pauperum,* Folio 1362. German. 14th century. Staatsbibliothek der Stiftung Preussischer Kulturbesitz, Berlin.

"The conscious processes [depend] so much upon the functioning of the unconscious that if the unconscious should fail to function on a certain day, we would be unable to say a single word."

CARL G. JUNG

"This thing of darkness I acknowledge mine."

WILLIAM SHAKESPEARE

"What does your conscience say? — You shall become who you are."

FRIEDRICH NIETZSCHE

Was it from his own voice that Jonah fled — from both self-knowledge and self-challenge? Was Jonah not yet quite ready to heed the word of the Lord; to arise and go forth, as he was bidden, "to Nineveh, that great city, and cry against it," because of the wickedness there? Was it because of a need to escape from himself that Jonah rose up and fled, instead, "unto Tarshish from the presence of the Lord?"

When Jonah ignored "the word of the Lord," and found a ship going to Tarshish, "the Lord sent out a great wind into the sea, and there was a mighty tempest . . . so that the ship was like to be broken." Whereupon the mariners whom Jonah had joined became afraid, "and cried every man unto his god, and cast forth the wares that were in the ship into the sea, to lighten it of them.

"But Jonah was gone down into the sides of the ship; and he lay, and was fast asleep. So the shipmaster came to him, and said unto him, What meanest thou, O sleeper? arise, call upon thy God, if so be that God will think upon us, that we perish not. And they said every one to his fellow, Come, and let us cast lots, that we may know for whose cause this evil is upon us. So they cast lots, and the lot fell upon Jonah. Then said [the mariners] unto him, Tell us, we pray thee, for whose cause this evil is upon us. . . ."

When Jonah answered that he feared the Lord, the God of heaven, the men again became "exceedingly afraid, and said unto him, Why hast thou done this? For the men knew that he fled from the presence of the Lord, because he had told them. Then said they unto him, What shall we do unto thee, that the sea may be calm unto us? for the sea wrought, and was tempestuous. And he said unto them, Take me up, and cast me forth into the sea; so shall the sea be calm unto you: for I know that for my sake this great tempest is upon you. Nevertheless the men rowed hard to bring it to the land; but they could not: for the sea wrought, and was tempestuous against them. Wherefore they cried unto the Lord, and said, We beseech thee, O Lord, we beseech thee, let us not perish for this man's life, and lay not upon us innocent blood: for thou, O Lord, hast done as it pleased thee.

"So they took up Jonah, and cast him forth into the sea: and the sea ceased from her raging. Then the men feared the Lord exceedingly, and offered a sacrifice unto the Lord, and made vows. Now the Lord had prepared a great fish to swallow up Jonah. And Jonah was in the belly of the fish three days and three nights. Then Jonah prayed unto the Lord his God out of the fish's belly, And said, I cried by reason of mine affliction unto the Lord, and he heard me; out of the belly of hell cried I, and thou heardest my voice. For thou hadst cast me into the deep, in the midst of the seas; and the floods compassed me about: all thy billows and thy waves passed over me. Then I said, I am cast out of thy sight; yet I will look again toward thy holy temple. The waters compassed me about, even to the soul: the depth closed me round about, the weeds were wrapped about my head. I went down to the bottoms of the mountains; the earth with her bars was about me for ever: yet hast thou brought up my life from corruption, O Lord my God. When my soul fainted within me I remembered

the Lord: and my prayer came in unto thee, into thine holy temple. They
that observe lying vanities forsake their own mercy. But I will sacrifice
unto thee with the voice of thanksgiving; I will pay that that I have
vowed. Salvation is of the Lord. And the Lord spake unto the fish, and it
vomited out Jonah upon the dry land. And the word of the Lord came
unto Jonah the second time, saying, Arise, go unto Nineveh, that great
city, and preach unto it the preaching that I bid thee. So Jonah arose, and
went unto Nineveh, according to the word of the Lord. Now Nineveh
was an exceeding great city of three days' journey. And Jonah began to
enter into the city a day's journey, and he cried, and said, Yet forty days,
and Nineveh shall be overthrown. So the people of Nineveh believed
God, and proclaimed a fast, and put on sackcloth, from the greatest of
them even to the least of them. For word came unto the king of Nineveh,
and he arose from his throne, and he laid his robe from him, and covered
him with sackcloth, and sat in ashes. And he caused it to be proclaimed
and published through Nineveh by the decree of the king and his nobles,
saying, Let neither man nor beast, herd nor flock, taste any thing: let them
not feed, nor drink water: But let man and beast be covered with sackcloth, and cry mightily unto God: yea, let them turn every one from his
evil way, and from the violence that is in their hands. Who can tell if God
will turn and repent, and turn away from his fierce anger, that we perish
not? And God saw their works, that they turned from their evil way; and
God repented of the evil, that he had said that he would do unto them;
and he did it not. But it displeased Jonah exceedingly, and he was very
angry. And he prayed unto the Lord, and said, I pray thee, O Lord, was not
this my saying, when I was yet in my country? Therefore I fled before
unto Tarshish: for I knew that thou art a gracious God, and merciful, slow
to anger, and of great kindness, and repentest thee of the evil. Therefore
now, O Lord, take, I beseech thee, my life from me; for it is better for me
to die than to live. Then said the Lord, Doest thou well to be angry? So
Jonah went out of the city, and sat on the east side of the city, and there
made him a booth, and sat under it in the shadow, till he might see what
would become of the city. And the Lord God prepared a gourd, and made
it to come up over Jonah, that it might be a shadow over his head, to
deliver him from his grief. So Jonah was exceeding glad of the gourd. But
God prepared a worm when the morning rose the next day, and it smote

the gourd that it withered. And it came to pass, when the sun did arise, that God prepared a vehement east wind; and the sun beat upon the head of Jonah, that he fainted, and wished in himself to die, and said, It is better for me to die than to live. And God said to Jonah, Doest thou well to be angry for the gourd? And he said, I do well to be angry, even unto death. Then said the Lord, Thou hast had pity on the gourd, for the which thou hast not labored, neither madest it grow; which came up in a night, and perished in a night: And should not I spare Nineveh, that great city, wherein are more than sixscore thousand persons that cannot discern between their right hand and their left hand; and also much cattle?" [21]

Noah, on the one hand, in obeying sacred law, functioned as a righteous man, a seer who averted disaster. Due to his covenant with the Lord, and in spite of the flood he was made to endure, he both escaped total destruction, and was able to preserve for the future what was worth saving from the past and present. In sharp contrast, there is the experience of Jonah, who, having failed to follow the dictates of his most profound inner voice, was first cast into the waters, and then into the body of the whale: into the flood or waters of the unconscious — into his own inchoate conflict, darkness, or netherworld. He remained there until he could gain the courage to listen to the voice of God, although, even then — despite having erred himself — he was far less compassionate than was the Lord.

An illuminating variant of the story of Jonah: In the great Indian epic, *The Mahabharata,* the inability to notice and pay homage to a saint, described below, is closely related to Jonah's not heeding the word of the Lord; the being burnt to ashes also closely resembling the whale's swallowing Jonah.

The Mahabharata recounts that "Sixty thousand sons of a certain Cakravartin named 'Ocean' . . . were riding as the armed guard of their father's sacrificial horse while it wandered over the kingdoms of the land, during its symbolical solar year of victorious freedom." Suddenly, to the profound distress of the sons, "the animal vanished from before their very eyes. They set to work digging where it had disappeared and came upon it, finally, deep in the earth, down in the underworld, with a saint sitting

---

21. JONAH 1:1–4:11.

66. DURGA—
MAHISHASURAMARDINI
(SHE WHO KILLS THE
BUFFALO DEMON)
Stone relief. Indian. 13th century. Shiva
Temple, Chidambaram. Photograph by
Allen Atwell.

beside it in meditation. Over-eager to recapture their sacred charge, the young warriors disregarded the saint," omitting to pay the homage to him "traditionally due to a holy man. Whereupon, with a flash of his eye, he burnt them all to ashes." [22] Like Jonah, they must, through ultimate understanding, be symbolically redeemed or revivified.

Durga, the Great Goddess — "unattainable," even by force — being supreme, and thus eternally victorious, effortlessly severs the head of the monstrous Buffalo Demon in a periodically repeated ritual.

In his demonic form, the Buffalo-Titan is an example of the brutality of ignorance that must be transformed. Through cutting off his head, Durga succeeds in releasing the dark forces of the unconscious within him — powers that impede the gaining of consciousness. Subdued by the Divine Calm of the Goddess, the Buffalo, in certain sculptures, is shown as her support, even while she is in the act of doing battle with him. (Plate 66.)

---

22. Zimmer, PHILOSOPHIES OF INDIA, p. 282.

12 GUARDIANS OF THE TREASURE...CLINGING TO THE TREASURE... CONSANGUINITY

"Who is this god, who is invoked 'O Liberator . . . help us find the treasure . . . by our inner vision?' "

STELLA KRAMRISCH

"For where your treasure is, there will your heart be also."

ST. LUKE 12:34

"The aim of the extraverted type of hero is action: he is the founder, leader, and liberator whose deeds change the face of the world. The introverted type is the culture-bringer, the redeemer and savior who discovers the inner values, exalting them as knowledge and wisdom, as a law and a faith, a work to be accomplished and an example to be followed. The creative act of raising the buried treasure is common to both types of hero, and the prerequisite for this is union with the liberated captive."

ERICH NEUMANN

"When Indra made the sun shine . . . so that there was light . . . he hung up a treasure which he had found hidden in darkness."

STELLA KRAMRISCH

The hero's search for the treasure of difficult access is by no means a simple one. He is neither invariably prepared nor even permitted to attain what he seeks merely because he wishes to do so.

At times it is the gods themselves who interfere with the hero's quest. In a manner that seems often contradictory, they decree that dragons, serpents, and equivalents thereof should guard the very treasure the hero most passionately desires. Yet we find these same monstrous figures also tempting the hero with what the gods have forbidden him to acquire.

In still other situations the hero dare not obtain treasure at all, but must rather relinquish it. This is so because it is often necessary to sacrifice the most precious of objects in order that there shall not be demeaning dependence upon it.

In the case of Adam and Eve, for example, the apple they preempt is prohibited to them, yet it is necessary that they eat of it as part of their initiation into a more highly developed state of being — at whatever the cost. There is, however, a point beyond which no mortal dare pass, despite the most profound longing to grasp the ungraspable. So it is that, after having eaten of the tree of knowledge of good and evil, Adam is sent "forth from the garden of Eden" by the Lord God, lest now "he put forth his hand, and take also of the tree of life, and eat, and live for ever." [1]

In certain instances the treasure is the very moment of revelation that spells our release. Just as, in reverse, what obstructs us from completing our quest is, more often than not, an inner chaos or conflict we have not yet resolved. When we are most relentlessly challenged, the dragon may be said to personify our lack of illumination about the next step we must take. For what both *is* the treasure and guards it, resides primarily within ourselves. (Thus it is that those who jealously desire treasure they are not yet prepared to attain, can become so cruelly menacing to others who rightfully find what is sought.)

Portrayals of the serpent or dragon coiled about a tree may be interpreted in varying manner, in diverse circumstances. Movement upward toward a higher state may be involved, or downward toward a lower one. Rather than being either totally beneficent or maleficent, serpentine forms

---

1. GENESIS 3:22–23.

*67. THE DRAGON AND THE
HESPERIDES
From detail of vase painting by Asteas.
Paestan. 3rd quarter 4th century B.C.
Museo Nazionale, Naples.

may, at times, be viewed simultaneously in terms of "good" and "evil";
also as eluding or transcending both states of being.

The serpent (or dragon), shown in Plate 67, is dreaded in its role as
guardian "of certain symbols of immortality, the approach to which it
forbids. Thus we find it coiled round the tree with the golden apples in the
garden of the Hesperides, or the beech tree in the wood at Colchis on
which the Golden Fleece hangs; these trees [being] clearly further forms
of the 'Tree of Life,' and accordingly . . . also [representative of] the
'World Axis.'" [2]

"In Greece . . . [we find] mythical tales which refer us . . . directly to the Hindu tradition of the Sacred Tree; this is the expedition of
Hercules to the garden of the Hesperides, whence he carries off the
Golden Apples guarded by dragons.[3] Whether these Apples represent the
luminous rays or the healing waters, another reading of the myth records
that Hercules handed them over to Minerva, who put them back in the
place where they must always remain, 'for they are immortal.' It is note-
worthy that, on a Greek vase . . . the Tree round which the dragon is
coiled is depicted between two Hesperides, one of whom gathers the fruit
for Hercules whilst the other diverts the attention of the dragon." [4]

---

2. SYMBOLISM OF THE CROSS, René Guénon, translated by Angus Macnab, London: Luzac and Company, 1958,
pp. 110–12.

3. A further variant concerning the interplay of the forces of good and evil: "Herakles' slaughter of the Serpent
and theft of the Golden Apples are from the point of view of Jason's companions heroic feats, but from the point
of view of the Hesperides themselves acts of wanton violence." (SYMPLEGADES, Ananda K. Coomaraswamy, reprinted from STUDIES AND ESSAYS IN THE HISTORY OF SCIENCE AND LEARNING IN HONOR OF GEORGE
SARTON, 1946, p. 55n[8].)

4. d'Alviella, op. cit., p. 166.

68. GRIMACING MASK OF THE
GIANT HUMBABA[5]
Terracotta. Babylonian. Early 2nd millennium
B.C. The British Museum, London.

"The deepest significance of each of [the] archetypal masterpieces lies in the reduction of [the] pride [of the hero] by means of a bereavement which imposes the recognition of a common humanity."

G. R. LEVY

"The Gorgons . . . are not to be likened to old women, but to masks. . . . Anyone who wanted to go to [them] needed the help of their sisters, the Graiai. For the Gorgons lived . . . in the direction of Night, beyond Okeanos, with the clear-singing Hesperides. They were three in number." One of them, Medousa, was mortal. "Poseidon, the dark-haired god, lay with [her] . . . in soft grass, under spring blossom. This tale brings Medousa quite close to Persephone. She, too, the goddess of the Underworld, was ravished by a dark god and went, as if she were a mortal, down among the dead. She sends the Gorgon's head, 'the gigantic shape of fear,' to meet those who seek to invade her Underworld. This head is, in a sort, the other aspect of the beautiful Persephone. And this is the most remarkable thing about Medousa: although she, too, was 'beautiful-cheeked,' like her mother the sea-monster Keto, she and her sisters also resembled the Erinyes [spirits of anger and revenge]. The Gorgons had golden wings, but their hands were of brass. They had mighty tusks like a boar's, and their heads and bodies were girdled with serpents. If anyone looked at [their] terrible [faces] . . . his breath left him, and on the spot he was turned to stone.

"As for the question of how the Gorgon's head could appear by itself — which it did, according to one version, in the Underworld as a self-protection by Persephone; and, according to another . . . on the breast

---

5. See Gilgamesh, in Chapter 22.

*69. GORGON
From detail of vase painting. Greek. 580–570
B.C. Musée du Louvre, Paris.

of Pallas Athene — this was explained in the story of Perseus. This hero
was named [Eurymedon] by his mother . . . as if he were a 'ruler of the
sea' and Medousa's husband, not merely her slayer. It was chiefly Athene
who protected and guided Perseus in his task of winning the Gorgon's
head. She had instructed him not to look at the Gorgon when he advanced
upon her, but to see only her reflection in his bright shield. (The same
procedure was followed by . . . youths in certain initiation rites, in
which they were required to look at a mask mirrored in a silver vessel.) In
this manner Perseus succeeded. . . . He struck the [Gorgon's] head off
with the sickle . . . he had received from Athene. . . .

"From the . . . head sprang the winged horse named Pegasos. . . .
With it was also born Chrysaor, the hero whose name means 'he of the
golden sword.' The mask-like Gorgon's head . . . was thenceforth worn
by Athene, either as a sign on her shield or attached to her breastplate." [6]

It is just because Perseus could view the Gorgon-head (Plate 69) reflected in his shield (the shining mirror of truth, or his own evolving
clarity) — rather than having to sink into the darkness of Medousa's am-
bience in order to confront her — that he was liberated from fear; from
the slumbering, destructive aspect of the netherworld. Whereupon the
winged horse, Pegasus, associated with the sun, became his vehicle.

6. Kerényi, THE GODS OF THE GREEKS, pp. 48–50.

In various ancient traditions the Great Mother is shown both in her mild or benign, and malevolent aspects. As the creative principle, the Great Goddess gives birth, protects, and nurtures. She also challenges, leading us into the darkest reaches of ourselves, initiating us into what may be termed the "mysteries" — the latter representing the necessity to descend into the netherworld of ourselves. As a result of which process we may gain the strength to overcome, assimilate, and transmute our less exemplary traits; to achieve a measure of self-mastery.

When the terrifying powers of the Mother Goddess are operative, we are in danger of being engulfed, blinded, or emasculated by her. Yet, although she sets the problems the hero in man must resolve, she also holds the key to the very treasure in which reside the answers to our dilemmas.

With respect to the Good Mother, there is the ever-present possibility that we shall simply fall in love with her; that we shall permanently depend upon her, fearing ever to leave her, to forge our own way.[7]

In order to win his own freedom and, thereby, that of others, the heroic Marduk of the Babylonian Genesis split asunder the Great Mother Goddess Tiamat in her destructive aspect. "When on high the heavens had not been named," the Genesis tells us, "Apsu the Begetter and Mother Tiamat mingled chaotically and produced a brood of dragon-like monsters. Several ages passed before a younger generation of gods arose. One of these, Ea god of Wisdom, challenged and killed Apsu. Tiamat thereupon married her own son Kingu, bred monsters from him, and prepared to take vengeance on Ea.

"The only god who now dared oppose Tiamat was Ea's son Marduk. Tiamat's allies were her eleven monsters. Marduk relied upon the seven winds, his bow and arrow and storm-chariot, and a terrible coat of mail. . . . Flames crowned his head. Before their combat, Tiamat and Marduk exchanged taunts, curses and incantations. When they came to grips, Marduk soon caught Tiamat in his net, sent one of his winds into her belly," struck her upon the head, "and shot her full of arrows. He bound the corpse with chains and stood victoriously upon it. Having chained the eleven monsters and cast them into prison — where they became gods of

---

7. The Great Mother of Christianity — the Virgin — is viewed solely as beneficent. In spite of this fact, Jesus becomes and remains free of all sense of dependence.

70. SPHINX
Bronze statuette from Perachora. Greek.
c. 550 B.C. National Museum, Athens.

the underworld — he snatched the 'Tablets of Fate' from Kingu's breast and, fastening them upon his own, split Tiamat into halves like a shell-fish. One of these [halves] he used as firmament, to impede the upper waters from flooding the earth . . . the other as a rocky foundation for earth and sea. He also created the sun, the moon, the five lesser planets and the constellations, giving his kinsmen charge over them; and finally created man from the blood of Kingu, whom he had condemned to death as the instigator of Tiamat's rebellion." [8] (The fact that man should have been formed from Kingu's blood again calls to mind the warnings in Job about Behemoth. Chapter 7.)

Oedipus was greatly punished because of his incestuous relationship with his mother, Jocasta, despite being described as unconscious of his regressive act.

"Oedipus," in the words of Jung, "thinking he had overcome the Sphinx sent by the mother-goddess [Hera] merely because he had solved her childishly simple riddle, fell a victim to matriarchal incest and had to marry Jocasta, his mother, for the throne and the hand of the widowed queen belonged to him who freed the land from the plague of the Sphinx. This had all [the] tragic consequences [that] could easily have been avoided if only Oedipus had been sufficiently intimidated by the frightening appearance of the 'terrible' or 'devouring' Mother whom the Sphinx personified. . . . The genealogy of the Sphinx (Plate 70) has manifold connections with the problem touched upon here: she was a daughter of

8. HEBREW MYTHS, THE BOOK OF GENESIS, Robert Graves and Raphael Patai, Garden City, New York: Double-day and Company, 1964, p. 23.

Echidna, a monster with the top half of a beautiful maiden, and a hideous serpent below. This double being corresponds to the [mother-image]: above, the lovely and attractive human half; below, the horrible animal half, changed into a fear-animal by the incest prohibition. . . . With . . . her own son, Echidna incestuously begat the Sphinx. This should be sufficient to characterize the complex whose symbol is the Sphinx. . . . The riddle was . . . the trap which the Sphinx laid for the unwary wanderer. . . . The riddle of the Sphinx was *herself* — the terrible [mother-image], which Oedipus would not take as a warning." [9]

Despite the fact that the answer to the riddle[10] Oedipus solved was indeed man, it is, after all, by no means possible to know the reply's meaning in significant fashion without having lived fully, oneself. Merely to perceive at an intellectual level is clearly insufficient.

"In medieval times, by legal prohibition, consanguinity or relationship as far as the fourth degree of kinship was a bar to marriage. . . . [The] illuminated Table of Consanguinity [shown] . . . is a graphic representation of how this legal provision actually worked and how it affected the family." [11] (Plate 71.)

What is depicted is a table of degrees of blood relationship within one family. In order to determine what amounted to incest, the Church worked out such tables. Each medallion is numbered to establish the degree of relationship.

---

9. Jung, SYMBOLS OF TRANSFORMATION, pp. 181–82.

10. The Sphinx was said to live "on a high rock near Thebes, and asked the following riddle of all who came near: 'What walks on four feet in the morning, on two at noon, and on three in the evening?' She killed all who failed to answer her until Oedipus solved the riddle by saying, 'Man crawls on all fours as a baby, walks upright in the prime of life, and uses a staff in old age.' The Sphinx then leaped from her rock and died, and Oedipus became king of Thebes." (Quoted from THE COLUMBIA ENCYCLOPEDIA.)

The Sphinx is "a hybrid monster, usually described as having the head of a woman and the (winged) body of a lion . . . also, any monster of a similar form and character . . . one who propounds or presents a difficult question or problem . . . a thing or subject of an inscrutable or mysterious nature . . . a sculptured, carved or moulded figure of an imaginary creature having a human head and breast combined with the body of a lion." The word Sphinx is said to derive from a Greek root: "To draw tight." (THE OXFORD UNIVERSAL DICTIONARY.)

"The Sphinx," writes Kerényi, "may well have been proud of her riddle, and also it confused people; for they likewise did not understand that riddle which was carved, as a sage's warning, on the porch of Apollo's temple at Delphi, 'Know thyself.' The answer [being], 'Know that thou art man.'" (Kerényi, THE HEROES OF THE GREEKS, p. 98.)

11. "A Thirteenth-Century Table of Consanguinity," William M. Milliken, THE BULLETIN OF THE CLEVELAND MUSEUM OF ART, Vol. 41, No. 3, March 1954, p. 46.

71. TABLE OF CONSANGUINITY
Manuscript illumination from *Summa Aurea*
by Henry of Segusio. French. Last
third 13th century. The Cleveland Museum of
Art, J. H. Wade Collection.

The above portrayal is taken from "one of the path-making books on
Canon Law . . . so important legally . . . it is understandable that
quite a number of complete manuscripts have been preserved. . . . The
finest often contain three miniatures — Tables of Bigamy, Affinity, and
Consanguinity. . . . The figure of the king [holding the table] . . .
wears a crown of gold and holds in either hand a scepter, while under his
feet . . . are two fantastic cocks with tails of serpents entwined, symbolic
of the evil against which he inveighs and which he treads underfoot." [12]

The reason Tables of Consanguinity evolved becomes more understandable if we consider the manner in which early kinship systems functioned. According to the latter, strict rules were followed so that families
— indeed entire social organisms — were protected. When a harmfully
incestuous pattern of life resulted, however, it became necessary to alter
such systems.

---

12. Ibid., pp. 46–47.

Both the narrowing and the widening of our horizons can cause a sense of unease. It is our task to transcend what we fear in both cases. Moreover, it is as incestuous to depend too long upon those who are young, in order to resolve our problems, as it is to cling to a past that should properly be outgrown and relinquished.

> *"Do not confine your children to your own learning, for they were born in another time."*
>
> PROVERBIAL HEBRAIC SAYING

According to the artist, the ants portrayed have closed in avidly, around one particular circle. They have done so to protect the treasure contained within it. But what they do not seem to realize is that the same treasure exists within the other circles they have not surrounded. (Plate 72.)

72. ANT WAR
Brush and ink drawing by Morris Graves.
American. 1958. Collection Dorothy
Norman, New York.

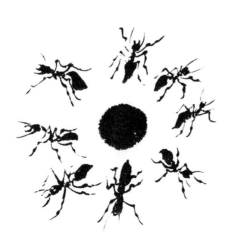

13 LABYRINTH AND CONCATENATION

*73. LABYRINTH WITH OCULI-
FORM FACE AT CENTER
From rock carving. Prehistoric.
Valcamonica, Italy.

"A course
Confusing as the Labyrinth in Crete
Whose path runs through blind walls, where craft has hidden
A thousand wandering ways, mistake and error ·
Threading insoluble mazes, so the children,
The sons of Troy, wove in and out, in conflict."

VIRGIL

A Link: And now we move through still further mazes and labyrinths, coming ever closer to the center. At which point we shall arrive at the Birth of the Hero.

The search for clarity is long, circuitous, labyrinthine. Our conflicts are not readily resolved, once and for all. Our relationships with others are not invariably releasing. The threads to be woven, the paths to be followed, are many and complex.

A number of ancient rock carvings of labyrinths have been found in Italy in the Camonica Valley. "In certain cases a demon is represented in abstract and stylized manner, as a labyrinth whose twistings end at the center of the image in two dots standing for eyes; a third dot sometimes [marking] the mouth or the nose. [Plate 73.] These [demons] are probably monsters comparable to those of ancient Greece: the legend of the Minotaur doubtless draws its origins from this kind of concept. Sometimes the monster is pictured within the labyrinth; sometimes he seems to be one with it, to be himself the labyrinth." [1]

"The battles and the monsters associated with the labyrinth probably have some connection with Cerberus and . . . other strange hybrid creatures" of mythology. "Death and life are associated; one must die to be reborn, whether it be by true death or by symbolic death in the initiation rites and other rituals . . . among primitive peoples." [2]

Or, as John Layard has observed, among many similarities in labyrinth ceremonials and beliefs "certain facts stand out as being of special import." The rites invariably have to do with "death and rebirth." They are "almost always connected with a cave (or more rarely a constructed dwelling). . . . In those cases where the ritual has been preserved, the labyrinth itself, or a drawing of it, is invariably situated at the entrance to the cave or dwelling." [3]

---

1. CAMONICA VALLEY, Emmanuel Anati, translated by Linda Asher, New York: Alfred A. Knopf, 1961, p. 217. (Oculiform: In the form of, or resembling an eye.)
2. Ibid., p. 220.
3. STONE MEN OF MALEKULA, John Layard, London: Chatto and Windus, 1942, p. 652.

74. LABYRINTH
Nave of Chartres Cathedral. French.[4]

Certain "famous medieval examples [of constructed labyrinths] are inlaid on cathedral floors . . . and of those still existing, the most notable
is that of Chartres [Plate 74] with a pathway some six hundred and fifty
feet in length, leading round and about until the center is reached. . . .

---

4. The greater part of the present Chartres Cathedral was built between 1195 and 1220. Its "labyrinth consists of a
geometrical figure in the form of a circle . . . in which the 'labyrinthine ways' are arranged concentrically about a
sixfoil centre-piece. The idea goes back to the legendary labyrinth of Daedalus in the palace of Minos in Crete, and
commemorates him as the ancestor of all the celebrated architects of the Western world. The figure became, so to
speak, his" emblem. The Chartres labyrinth, which was "inlaid in the nave floor, contained the names of the master
builders. . . . Unfortunately no traces [of the names] have survived." (HIGH GOTHIC, Hans Jantzen, translated
by James Palmes, New York: Pantheon Books, 1962, pp. 83–85.)

W. R. Lethaby quotes Didron, who says that 'the whole device was deemed to be indicative of the complicated folds of sin by which man is surrounded, and how impossible it would be to extricate himself from them except through the assisting hand of Providence.' . . . Lethaby says that the French labyrinths 'appear to have been called *la lieue* or *Chemin de Jerusalem;* they were placed at the west end of the nave and people made a pilgrimage[5] on their knees, following the pathway to the center, which is said to have been called *Sancta Ecclesia* or *Ciel.*' Of numerous English examples cut in turf it is of great interest that one is called by the name of 'Troy Town.' The Italian examples of pavement labyrinths at Ravenna, Rome, Pavia, etc., are descendants, through Roman pavements . . . and gems, from . . . representations of the labyrinth of Dedalus which occur on Cretan coins. . . . At Pavia the Minotaur is represented at the vortex in the form of a centaur. As Lethaby remarks, the exact form of the original designs is preserved throughout the Middle Ages, but 'when the root of tradition was broken away from at the Renaissance, all this was altered, and mazes became inventions, every one different from the others — spiders' webs of enticing false paths.' " [6]

The names of Leonardo da Vinci and Albrecht Dürer were inscribed in the centers of their Knot designs (Plate 75), in the same manner as those of various medieval church architects occupied the central points of cathedral labyrinths. The affiliation of such knots to labyrinths is thus clearly established.

"That the lines of the *Knots*," notes Coomaraswamy, "are superposed and intersect involves no difference in principle, but represents a translation of the idea of the maze into three-dimensional . . . terms." [7]

---

5. Although labyrinths long had existed before such a "pilgrimage" as that described above was made, it seems entirely clear how the mazes found in holy places in the West came to be associated with a treading of the path to Jerusalem. For, just as the Western sanctuaries in which such constructions were placed represented the center of the world, so did Jerusalem itself.

A. B. Cook notes that "Towards the close of the Crusades men who had broken vows of pilgrimage to the Holy Land did penance by treading these tortuous *chemins de Jerusalem* until they reached the central space, often termed *le ciel*. Later the same Labyrinths were used as a means of penance for sins of omission and commission in general." (Cook, op. cit., Vol. I, p. 486.)

6. "THE ICONOGRAPHY OF DÜRER'S 'KNOTS' AND LEONARDO'S 'CONCATENATION,' " Ananda K. Coomaraswamy, THE ART QUARTERLY, The Detroit Institute of Arts, Vol. VII, No. 2, Spring 1944, pp. 110, 113.

7. Ibid., p. 113.

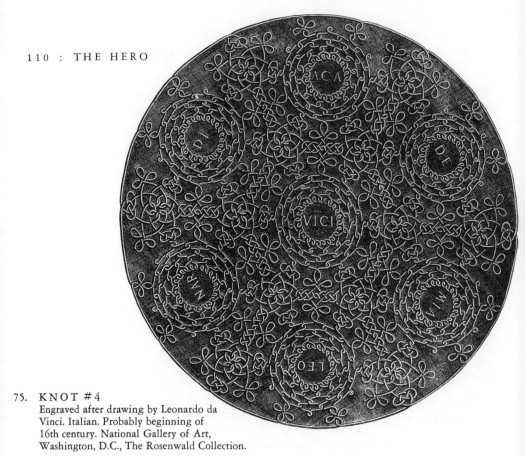

75. KNOT #4
Engraved after drawing by Leonardo da
Vinci. Italian. Probably beginning of
16th century. National Gallery of Art,
Washington, D.C., The Rosenwald Collection.

"Knots and labyrinths approximate to spiral forms. In the case of the
single spiral, which resembles a coiled rope or snake, it is evident that if
we follow round the line from the outside we reach a center, just as in
following round the thread of a spider's web we should reach the spider's
'parlor.' "[8] "The spiral itself is a growth form."[9]

8. "The mention of spider's webs is strictly appropriate, for the Sun is the primordial spinner, moving along the
threads he spins . . . and [is] often explicitly likened to a spider . . . who 'makes his net with a single thread'
. . . and 'wise is he who layeth hold upon it.' . . . There is more in the words, 'Come into my parlor, said the
spider to the fly,' than catches the ear. The remarkable perfection of the 'spider' symbolism extends to the fact that
the radii (warp, threads) of the web are not sticky, while the spiral (woof) is adhesive; the spider himself walks
only on the radii while the flies are caught on the sticky threads." (Ibid., p. 126n^9.) Which further reminds of the
Stickfast motif, in general. (See Coomaraswamy, JOURNAL OF AMERICAN FOLKLORE, Vol. LVII, 1944, pp.
128–31). When, for example, we grasp greedily, we become stuck fast to what then holds us in bondage. The
Stickfast motif appears also when we tread upon forbidden ground, are trapped by it, and are inevitably discovered
where we should not be.
9. Coomaraswamy, "THE ICONOGRAPHY OF DÜRER'S 'KNOTS' AND LEONARDO'S 'CONCATENATION,' " p.
119.

Neither the Shakers depicted (Plate 76), nor those who have walked upon such a labyrinth as the one found in the cathedral at Chartres, could dare merely to depend upon a distant Zion or Jerusalem, to supply authentic religious experience, *in absentia*. Unless identification, concentration, participation — deeds — are profoundly involved, one can no more reach "the center of the world," than, by implication, one's own center.

76. THE SACRED DANCE ON THE
HOLY HILL OF ZION
Wood engraving from *Gleanings from Old
Shaker Journals,* C. E. Sears, Boston, 1916.[10]

10. As reproduced in PHILADELPHIA MUSEUM OF ART BULLETIN, Vol. LVII, No. 273, Spring 1962, p. 79.

14 THE BIRTH OF THE HERO...THE EXPOSURE OF THE HERO

"The hero-deed is a continuous shattering of the crystallizations of the moment. The cycle rolls: mythology focuses on the growing-point. Transformation, fluidity, not stubborn ponderosity. . . . The ogre-tyrant is the champion of the prodigious fact, the hero the champion of creative life."

JOSEPH CAMPBELL

*"For whenever of the right
A languishing appears . . .
A rising up of unright,
Then I send Myself forth.*

*"For protection of the good,
And for destruction of evil-doers,
To make a firm footing for the right,
I come into being in age after age."*

BHAGAVAD GITA

At first glance it may appear somewhat strange that pictorial and literary references to the Birth of the Hero should be introduced only now, rather than having been presented at the outset of this volume. It has seemed scarcely possible, however, to discuss so important a theme before describing the nature of the heroic principle in some detail, and various of the most challenging forces to be both encountered and transmuted. For the birth of the hero heralds the return of fundamental life-giving values in danger of extinction. It foreshadows the overthrow and transformation of tyrannical powers that would thwart the release of creative energy in man.

Thus when it was foretold that Christ was to come to earth to save the people from their sins, this prophecy filled King Herod with foreboding. Being guilty himself of one of man's paramount transgressions — the will to cling to power — the despotic ruler sensed at once how dangerous to his own future the impending birth of the Saviour would be.

In order to insure the continuity of his reign, Herod was determined to destroy the Christ child. When, as recounted in St. Matthew, the three wise men refused to inform the king where the new-born infant lay, the tyrant took it upon himself to have "all the children that were in Bethlehem" [1] slain, in a blindly enraged attempt to avoid his own otherwise certain doom.

In similar manner, King Kansa of Hindu myth dreaded the prediction that the Lord Krishna — who would be "ever free from fear" — was to appear on earth in order to lift its too great burdens. The ruthless monarch's inability even to distinguish between his true adversary and others, led him cruelly to murder brothers and sisters of the not yet born Krishna. Kansa's evil cohorts further advised him to slay additional children in every city, village, pasture, or any other place — much as did Herod — so that his own rulership might be safeguarded.

---

1. ST. MATTHEW 2:16.

The Coming of Christ: "Now the birth of Jesus Christ was on this wise: When as his mother Mary was espoused to Joseph, before they came together, she was found with child of the Holy Ghost." And behold, the angel of the Lord appeared unto Joseph in a dream, saying that Mary his wife would bring forth a son to be named Jesus, "for he shall save his people from their sins." [2]

And the angel said unto Mary, "The power of the Highest shall overshadow thee: therefore also that holy thing which shall be born of thee shall be called the Son of God." [3]

It was then further prophesied of the child Jesus: Thou "shalt be called the prophet of the Highest: for thou shalt go before the face of the Lord to prepare his ways; To give knowledge of salvation unto his people by the remission of their sins, Through the tender mercy of our God; whereby the dayspring from on high hath visited us, To give light to them that sit in darkness and in the shadow of death, to guide our feet into the way of peace." [4]

"Now when Jesus was born in Bethlehem of Judaea in the days of Herod the king, behold, there came wise men from the east to Jerusalem, Saying, Where is he that is born King of the Jews? for we have seen his star in the east, and are come to worship him. When Herod the king had heard these things, he was troubled, and all Jerusalem with him. And when he had gathered all the chief priests and scribes of the people together, he demanded of them where Christ should be born. And they said unto him, In Bethlehem of Judaea: for thus it is written by the prophet, And thou Bethlehem, in the land of Juda, art not the least among the princes of Juda: for out of thee shall come a Governor, that shall rule my people Israel. Then Herod, when he had privily called the wise men, inquired of them diligently what time the star appeared. And he sent them to Bethlehem, and said, Go and search diligently for the young child; and when ye have found him, bring me word again, that I may come and worship him also. When they had heard the king, they departed; and, lo, the star, which they saw in the east, went before them, till it came and stood over where the young child was. When they saw the star, they

---

2. Ibid., 1:18,21.
3. ST. LUKE 1:35.
4. Ibid., 1:76–79.

77. PSALTER
South German. 12th century. Spencer
Collection, Ms. 11, The New York Public
Library. Astor, Lenox and Tilden Foundations.

rejoiced with exceeding great joy. And when they were come into the house, they saw the young child with Mary his mother, and fell down, and worshipped him: and when they had opened their treasures, they presented unto him gifts; gold, and frankincense, and myrrh. And being warned of God in a dream that they should not return to Herod, they departed into their own country another way. And when they were departed, behold, the angel of the Lord appeareth to Joseph in a dream, saying, Arise, and take the young child and his mother, and flee into Egypt, and be thou there until I bring thee word: for Herod will seek the young child to destroy him. When he arose, he took the young child and his mother by night, and departed into Egypt: And was there until the death of Herod: that it might be fulfilled which was spoken of the Lord by the prophet, saying, Out of Egypt have I called my son. Then Herod, when he saw that he was mocked of the wise men, was exceeding wroth, and sent forth, and slew all the children that were in Bethlehem, and in all the coasts thereof, from two years old and under, according to the time which he had diligently inquired of the wise men." [5]

5. ST. MATTHEW 2:1-16.

After his baptism, Reprobus, or the outcast, was named Christopher, or Christ-bearer. It has been said of Christopher, who "was twelve cubits in height and fearful of aspect," that he decided to "go in search of the most powerful king on earth [to] enter his service. Thus he went to a certain very great king, of whom it was commonly said that no other king on earth equalled him in power. . . . When the king saw [Christopher], he gladly received him, and gave him lodgings in his palace. But one day, in the presence of the king, a minstrel sang a song in which the Devil was named several times. . . . The king, who was a Christian, made the sign of the cross each time that the Devil's name was mentioned. Christopher was astonished thereat, and wondered why the king did this, and what the sign meant. But the king refused to tell him, until he said: 'Unless thou tell me, I shall no longer remain with thee!' Then the king said: 'Each time that I hear the Devil's name, I make this sign as a safeguard, lest he gain power over me and do me harm!' Then Christopher replied: 'If thou fearest that the Devil harm thee, he must be more puissant than thou! Therefore am I thwarted in my hope, for I thought to be in the service of the most powerful king on earth. So now farewell, for I shall seek out the Devil, and take him for my lord and give myself into his service!' Then he left the king and hurried off in search of the Devil. . . . In the desert he came face to face with a great host, whose leader, a soldier fierce and terrible of visage, came to him and asked whither he was going. . . . Christopher answered: 'I am in search of my lord the Devil, that I may take service with him.' . . . The soldier answered: 'I am he whom thou seekest!' Christopher rejoiced, and bound himself forever to the Devil. But as they marched along a common road, they came upon a cross, and the Devil, terrified, took flight, and leaving the road, led Christopher through a wild desert, and returned to the road at some distance. He asked the reason thereof, and when the Devil refused to answer, said: 'Then shall I quit thy service, unless thou tell me!' . . . The Devil was forced to reply: 'A certain man named Christ was once nailed to a cross, and since that time, at the sight of the cross, I take fright and flee!' 'This Christ,' answered Christopher, 'must therefore be greater and more puissant than

78. **SAINT CHRISTOPHER CARRYING CHRIST**
Oil painting by the Master of Messkirch (?).
German. 2nd quarter 16th century.
Oeffentliche Kunstsammlung, Kunstmuseum,
Basel.

thou; and once more I have laboured in vain, for I have not yet found the most powerful king on earth! Farewell then, for I go to seek Christ!'

"Long he sought for someone who could give him word of Christ, until at last he found a hermit, who preached Christ to him and diligently instructed him in the faith. . . . The hermit said to him: 'The King whom thou desirest to serve demands of thee that thou fast oftentimes in His honour!' And Christopher answered: 'Let him demand somewhat else, for to fast I am not able!' 'Then He demands,' said the hermit, 'that thou offer Him many prayers!' 'Nor can I do this service,' answered Christopher, 'for I know not how to pray!' Then the hermit said: 'Knowest thou a certain river, into which many who attempt to cross tumble and are drowned?' 'I know it,' replied Christopher. 'Since thou art mighty of stature and strong of arm,' responded the hermit, 'thou couldst dwell beside the river, and carry over all who wished to cross. This would be most pleasing to Christ, the King Whom thou desirest to serve; and I hope that He may show Himself to thee there!' 'This at last is a thing that I can do,' said Christopher, 'and I promise to do it for the service of Christ!' He betook himself therefore to the river, built a hut upon its bank, and using a great pole as a staff to steady himself in the water, he bore across all who sought his aid.

"When many days had passed, he lay asleep one night in his hut, when he heard a child's voice calling him . . . saying: 'Christopher, come out and carry me across the river!' . . . He went out, and found a child standing on the river bank, who earnestly besought him to carry him across. Christopher took the child upon his shoulders, and taking up his staff, set out through the water. But little by little the water rose, and the child became heavier than a leaden weight; and the farther he went, the higher rose the water, and the heavier grew the child, until Christopher was so sorely tried that he thought he would founder in the waves. But at last he made his way to the other bank, and set the child down, saying: 'Child, thou hast put me in dire peril, and hast weighed so heavy upon me that if I had borne the whole world upon my shoulders, it could not have burdened me more heavily!' . . . The child answered: 'Wonder not, Christopher, for not only hast thou borne the whole world upon thy shoulders, but Him Who created the world. For I am Christ thy King, Whom thou servest in this work! And as a sign that I say the truth, when thou shalt have returned to the other side of the river, plant thy staff in the earth near thy hut, and in the morning thou shall see it laden with flowers and fruits!' . . . Straightway He disappeared. . . . Christopher planted his staff in the earth, and rising in the morning he saw that it had borne leaves and fruits, like to a palm tree." [6]

Christopher "bore Christ in four ways: upon his shoulders when he carried Him, in his body by his mortifications, in his mind by his devotion, and in his mouth by professing and preaching Him."

The gigantic size of Christopher corresponds to his ability to endure great battles; the tree he carries, to a firm belief in the word of God. His journey through the water suggests the prophets' tribulations. [7]

Christopher goes as from the far shore of non-knowing to the near shore of awakening. His staff, bearing leaves and fruit in the morning, further typifies the concept of transformation.

———————◆————————

The Birth of Krishna: Despite the fact that the East is so often viewed as making no distinction whatever between good and evil, it is an accepted tenet among Hindu devotees of Vishnu (the latter being the symbolical form the Lord who maintains life assumes), that incarnations of that great God will appear whenever the burdens of the earth — including oppression by tyrants, or the prevalence of ignorance — become too great for mankind to bear. This expression of faith could, to be sure, echo merely a passive doctrine were men simply to wait until avatars (or incarnations) of Vishnu might appear on earth in order to save them. On the other hand, what is implied is that man must himself act in the manner in which both the gods and their mediators on earth — the heroes — ideally behave.

Thus, in accordance with Hindu myth, avatars of Vishnu appear periodically to protect the world from disaster during epochs when it is bent upon its own destruction and evil prevails. That is, the god "descends," as it were, at such times, "from his state of glory" [8] and, taking the form

6. THE GOLDEN LEGEND, Part II, pp. 377–80.

7. Based on unpublished NOTES ON THE SAINT, by Jessie Fraser.

8. INDIAN SCULPTURE IN THE PHILADELPHIA MUSEUM OF ART, Stella Kramrisch, Philadelphia: University of Pennsylvania Press, 1960, pp. 41–42.

*79. THE INFANT KRISHNA
BEING CARRIED ACROSS
THE RIVER JUMNA, WITH
SERPENT AND LION
From segment of painting. Indian. Late 18th
century. Collection Dorothy Norman,
New York.

adequate to meet each particular crisis, rescues creation.[9] He does so whether as the Buddha, as the heroic Krishna and Rama (see Plates 79–80), or in still other incarnations.

When Krishna — son of Vasudeva and Devaki — is born, as described in the Hindu Puranas, he is brought to earth to rid the world of King Kansa, the latter personifying uncontrolled energy and a ruthless clinging to power.

Aware that the infant hero poses a threat to his life, the demonic ruler decides that Krishna must be destroyed. The life of his son being thus endangered, Vasudeva — father of an incarnation of Vishnu — approaches the prison in which Krishna is confined, in order to rescue him from henchmen of the king. Although the doors of the prison have been "secured with iron chains and bolts," they open "of their own accord like

---

9. Of Vishnu, the Puranas further declare that "eternal righteousness abides" with him, among whose manifestations are said to be such qualities as "truth, quietude, self-control, reverence, benevolence, forgiveness and sacrifices." Vishnu, who is himself the sacrifice, is thus "the enemy of the Asuras [or demons]." (The Puranas — purana: ancient, legendary — are sacred books of mythological and epic lore, said to have been compiled by the legendary sage and poet, Vyasa.)

unto darkness flying before the rising sun." [10] Thereupon Vasudeva covertly bears his beloved Krishna across the holy river Jumna — which rises in a torrential flood — to an encampment of cowherds.

The flight itself is protected by the magical power of Vishnu. A "rain-cloud [pours] down showers accompanied by low thunder; and the serpent Sesha," who supports the universe, follows. Sesha protects "Vasudeva from the rains by spreading on him his hood."

Because the god Indra is responsible for producing "continuous showers, a strong current [has been] generated in the river." Although the waters become frightening, they nevertheless permit Vasudeva to proceed. Indeed, they are "like unto the ocean affording passage," or the Red Sea permitting the Israelites to proceed.

"On reaching the kingdom of Nanda, Vasudeva [sees] cowherds . . . profoundly asleep through the influence" of the gods. Leaving his son Krishna on the bed of Jashoda, wife of the cowherd King Nanda, Vasudeva exchanges the new-born hero for Jashoda's infant daughter. He then returns to the prison, in which his wife, Devaki, is still detained, leaving the female child on her bed.

Despite the latter's prayerful plea to her brother, King Kansa, that he spare Jashoda's child — which is now held at Devaki's own breast — the wicked tyrant snatches it away, "and with vehemence [dashes it] against the surface of a stone." Flying out of Kansa's grasp, Jashoda's daughter rises "upwards and assuming the form of a goddess [stations] herself in the heavens." She addresses Kansa: " 'O wicked one! . . . Thy adversary hath been born as thy death somewhere else. Do thou not slay other innocent children in vain.' "

In the kingdom of Nanda, where Krishna is reared, great joy is expressed, a "rare object of love" having created a desire to make all things pure: "Objects are purified in various ways; some in the course of time; some by being washed with water; some by being cleansed . . . by . . . austerities . . . [and] the celebration of sacrifices; some . . . by being given unto others."

When Krishna's parents, Vasudeva and Devaki, finally gaze upon him, they, too, are "struck with reverence, and . . . delight." They extol him:

---

10. The account of Krishna in this chapter is, in the main, paraphrased from THE SRIMAD-BHAGABATAM, translated by J. M. Sanyal, Oriental Publishing Co., Calcutta, 1952, Vol. IV, pp. 13 passim.

"Thy only semblance is feeling and [ecstasy]. Thou art the witness of all intellects. Verily thy semblance is beyond any description. . . . Being ever undiscerned, thou hast neither inside nor outside. Thou art everything . . . the essence and origin of all things and . . . the real entity. . . . O Lord! the creation, preservation and destruction of this universe are said to proceed from thyself."

Krishna is praised further: "Thou art verily the Lord Vishnu, who art described in the Vedas as the primordial cause and hence inscrutable, omnific, omniscient . . . attributeless, immutable, undifferentiated. . . . Thou art the lamp, so to say, of spirituality which illumines the intellect and senses."

Later, when Krishna and his brother, Balarama (the life of each having been miraculously saved), reach manhood, King Kansa realizes that the two boys have been created to cause his "Death by the celestials, whose sole refuge is Vishnu."

After Kansa attempts, but fails to defeat the brothers by various ruses, he finally realizes that all is lost. Whereupon Krishna, the indestructible lord and "refuge of the universe . . . subject only to his own will," throws down the tyrant. "Thereafter like a lion dragging a dead elephant, the almighty Krishna [begins] to drag Kansa on the ground," and thus ultimately slays him. Kansa, who up to that moment has been filled with thoughts of Vishnu, now that he is dead "at [the] Lord's hand [achieves] the self-same appearance with the Lord which is difficult of being attained."

In other words, through slaying Kansa, Krishna symbolically performs the essential task of the hero. He combats and transforms what would otherwise thwart the release of creative energy in man.

The lunar serpent, at left (in Plate 79), closely associated with the Lord Vishnu, protects the infant hero, Krishna — an avatar of the god Vishnu. The solar lion, at right, further suggests the hero. (In one of his incarnations, Vishnu is a man-lion.)

Like so many other mythological heroes, Krishna is a combination of night — of procreative, unconscious forces (exemplified, in part, by the serpent), and day — the creative, conscious forces in man (typified by the lion). "The human avatar is a blending of opposites. Such a blending also, are we ourselves, though unaware of our twofold nature: we are at once the illimited, unconditioned, divine Self, and the shrouding attributes of personality-experience and ego-consciousness." [11]

A variation of the tale of Krishna: In the Hindu epic, *The Ramayana,* the heroic Rama, a partial incarnation of the god Vishnu, is sent to earth to deliver the world from the mighty titan or demon, Ravana, and his rule by black magic. In fulfillment of a vow made to assuage the jealousy of his second queen, King Dasaratha, Rama's father, banishes his son to the forest for fourteen years. Rama's wife, the Princess Sita, is kidnapped by Ravana. After rescuing her from the latter, Rama kills the titan (Plate 80) and returns to his own capital, where he begins what has been termed a long and glorious reign.

---

11. Zimmer, MYTHS AND SYMBOLS IN INDIAN ART AND CIVILIZATION, p. 89.

80. RAMA AND RAVANA
Painting. Nurpur, Punjab. Indian. 1720.
The Cleveland Museum of Art, E. L.
Whittemore Collection.

For many Hindus, "Rama and Sita are the ideal man and woman, the model husband and wife." The story of Rama "may also be taken as an allegory. Symbolically Rama and Ravana represent the forces of light and darkness operating in the human heart, as well as in the world. . . . The real triumph of man means conquest of the forces of darkness. In India a festival is celebrated each year on the day traditionally held to be that on which Ravana fell and the rule of tyranny, injustice, savagery and un-righteousness ended." [12]

The Exposure of the Hero

When it is noted that various infant "heroes" of myth are "exposed" to danger, what is meant is that one or another such figure is forcibly separated from a parent or parents, because the latter wish either to destroy an illustrious son or daughter or to remove them from some external threat.

In general, the expulsion of the hero occurs because, since he possesses extraordinary, creative attributes, unless he is banished or opposed he will displace those desirous of maintaining their own tyrannical power.

Occasionally those who succeed in rescuing the hero from jealously menacing adversaries thrust him into a situation that seems even more threatening than the one from which he has been saved.

At times the hero is secretly transferred to the care of certain kindly animals, or to human foster-parents who are less exalted than his own mother or father, so that he may be reared close to nature, and/or without benefit of special privilege.

Removal from parental shelter often has to do with a necessary cutting away of bonds of dependence — upon either the real parent or still other aspects of the past.

As already described, both the Christ child and the infant Krishna are "exposed" to danger in traditionally symbolical manner, as is Rama.

Dr. Otto Rank has listed a wealth of examples of expulsion in *The Myth of the Birth of the Hero*.[13] Among other well-known "exposures":

---

12. Introduction to THE RAMAYANA OF VALMIKI, translated by Hari Prasad Shastri, London: Shanti Sadan, 1952, Vol. I, pp. xvi–xviii.

13. New York: Vintage Books, 1959, pp. 15 passim.

1.) The child Perseus is enclosed with his mother "in a box, which is cast into the sea." 2.) When his mother has died in childbirth, and his father is killed, Tristan is reared by a retainer. By spreading the rumor that the infant has been born dead, the faithful liege saves Tristan from the enemy. 3.) One of the reasons Alcmene, mother of Herakles, exposes her son in a place long known as the "Field of Hercules" is her fear of the goddess Hera. 4.) The new-born Sargon, traditionally known as founder of Babylonia, is brought forth in a hidden place and then "laid in a vessel of reeds," whose door is closed "with pitch, and dropped . . . into the river." 5.) When a Pharaoh of ancient Egypt commanded that all sons born to Hebrews be cast into the river, Moses was protected by being placed in the bulrushes. 6.) The future King Arthur was brought up by a father not his own, without his being aware of it. 7.) Oedipus was reared by a shepherd. Similar examples abound.

15 SNOW-WHITE

"All the doctrines of the philosophers are hidden within fables."

NATALE CONTI

Our most seemingly simple fairy tales — known widely in the modern world — are casually recounted without thought of their possible derivation from ancient myth, or their often profound, even inevitable, original significance. To take but a single example: "Snow-White and the Seven Dwarfs," [1] despite its obviously popularized form, clearly relates in most meaningful manner to various important themes touched upon throughout these pages — themes that resound with deep echoes in the psyche of each of us.

Since the story begins with a reference to the "middle of winter," and the heroine's name is Snow-White, it is scarcely surprising that we are being told about a process of transformation. Indeed, the relationship between the forces of light and darkness plays a consistently crucial role throughout the entire tale.

We are informed, to begin with, that a Queen works at her embroidery[2] on an *ebony* frame, while *snowflakes* fall. As the Queen sews, she pricks her finger with *three* drops of blood that fall upon *snow*. Here we have the traditional three of creation: The dark wood; snow, the ground of purity; and red, coursing blood — red foreshadowing the life-force of the hero or heroine about to be born.

Wishing for a child "as white as snow, as red as blood, and as black as the wood of" her embroidery frame, the Queen dies while giving birth to Snow-White.

It would seem not only that the Queen's creative, positive qualities are reborn in the form of her beautiful daughter, but that the latter is liberated

---

1. Quotations from "Snow-White and the Seven Dwarfs" have been taken from GRIMM'S FAIRY TALES, translated by Lucas, Crane and Edwardes, New York: Grosset and Dunlap, 1945, pp. 166–77. Details in other translations sometimes vary. (Italics throughout this section are mine.)

2. For a revealing description of the symbolism of weaving and embroidery, see Coomaraswamy, "THE ICONOGRAPHY OF DÜRER'S 'KNOTS' AND LEONARDO'S 'CONCATENATION,' " pp. 109–28.

from depending upon the past, due to her mother's symbolical death. Snow-White, as we shall see, is also cruelly "exposed" thereby — a theme already described in Chapter 14, on the birth of the hero.

As the story progresses, Snow-White is repeatedly at the mercy of a cruel second Queen, her stepmother. Like numerous other heroes or heroines of myth, Snow-White is possessed of two quite different mothers, one serving as a symbol of the Terrible, the other of love.

In wishing ruthlessly to cling to her power as the fairest of all, the demonic stepmother is a typical tyrant who must be overthrown. Yet — as is so in analogous cases in other myths — her very envy of Snow-White's loveliness helps to set the problems that the hero or heroine in life must resolve.

In order to be rid of Snow-White as an emerging rival once and for all, the Queen gives the exquisite child to a huntsman, so that he may murder her.

A young wild boar appears just as the huntsman, through pity, decides to spare Snow-White's life. Catching and killing the beast, he gives its heart to the wicked stepmother to prove he has fulfilled her command.[3] The Queen's immediate conviction that he has done her bidding clearly stems from sinister qualities capable of preventing her from distinguishing between what she receives, and the loving aspect of the heart, typified both by Snow-White and by the huntsman's compassionate gesture toward the child. (It becomes evident that the Queen is blind to love in any form.)

When the huntsman abandons Snow-White, she wanders filled with terror in the forest, until she finds a little house, clean and inviting, within

---

3. In accordance with the ancient Indian Rig Veda, the boar was considered a hostile power insofar as it kept the wealth of the Asuras (the Gods of the ancient order) on the other side of the *seven hills,* and was slain by Indra. In this context the boar may be identified with the great serpent, described at the beginning of this volume: namely Vritra. (From a Stella Kramrisch letter to the author.)

Also significant: Herakles' fourth labor involved the capturing alive of the fierce Erymanthian Boar. Without going into other aspects of what is involved, it may suffice to note that, as phrased by Robert Graves, "The snow drift in which the Erymanthian Boar was overcome indicates that [Herakles'] labour took place at midwinter." (Graves, op. cit., Vol. II, p. 115.)

John Layard has written of Boar sacrifices in various cultures; about the manner in which such rituals have had to do both with placating powers of the evil mother, and initiating the virgin. ("Boar-Sacrifice and Schizophrenia," John Layard, THE JOURNAL OF ANALYTICAL PSYCHOLOGY, Vol. I, No. I, 1955, London: Tavistock Publications, pp. 13–14.) Such references, which can be multiplied, are of special relevance to the tale of Snow-White.

which there is a table covered by a *white* cloth. Laid upon it are *"seven* plates and *seven* knives and forks." By the wall stand *seven* little beds "covered with clean *white* quilts."

When the *seven* dwarfs — dwarfs, if affirmative in nature, being small, represent that which may grow within each of us — return home, they light *seven* candles in the house of which they are masters. The work they perform throughout the day is to dig underground among the mountains for gold.[4] (As so often occurs, the treasure of difficult access lies hidden. In this case gold, signifying — among other attributes — life and light, is buried under towering heights.)

Finally discovering the lovely young creature who lies, asleep, in their abode, the dwarfs are struck by her radiance. In the morning, when Snow-White awakens and confronts them, they offer her a haven, in return for which she agrees to tend their house. The dwarfs warn her, however, to be on guard, since her stepmother is certain to find out where she is.

When the Queen, now that Snow-White is supposedly murdered, consults her mirror (symbol of vanity, as well as truth) to make certain she is the fairest of us all, she learns both about Snow-White's being with the dwarfs, and that her step-daughter's beauty is, in fact, considered superior to her own.

The Queen thereupon adopts a disguise, crossing *seven* mountains (a recurrent image in myth) in order to reach the house of the dwarfs and, again, to attempt to destroy Snow-White.

On the Queen's initial visit, she dupes Snow-White into permitting herself to be so tightly laced that her breathing will cease. (Not only is breath obviously essential to human life, but its control long has been associated with still other disciplines to be undergone by the hero or heroine.) The dwarfs fortunately cut the fabric that binds Snow-White.

Next the Queen offers a poisoned comb to the unsuspecting child who, not yet having transcended the false lure of vanity herself, again permits the Queen to do what she pleases. (Here, as in the case of Samson and other similar figures, the heroic power that resides in the hair is attacked.) Once more the friendly dwarfs come to the rescue.

---

4. For a mythological interpretation of the seven dwarfs, and certain other elements in "Snow-White," see ATMAYAJNA: SELF-SACRIFICE, Ananda K. Coomaraswamy, Harvard Yenching Institute, 1942.

The Queen finally tries to delude Snow-White with the eternally tempting apple. The cunning woman offers the poisoned half that is *red,* keeping the *white* for herself, thus tricking Snow-White by way of the negative aspect of each of the colors involved.

Once the Queen has performed this most monstrous of deeds, and Snow-White appears at long last to be mortally poisoned, her stepmother is told by her mirror that she is the "fairest now of all."

The dwarfs place Snow-White in a clear glass coffin. A Prince who happens to come by, and sees how ravishing she is, beseeches the dwarfs to permit him to take the transparent box with him, since he cannot live "without looking upon Snow-White." The seven good little creatures acquiesce.

In carrying the coffin away, the Prince's servants stumble over a bush, whereupon the bit of poisoned apple lodged in Snow-White's throat flies out. After she awakens, and the Prince takes her to his father's castle, they are joyfully married.

The evil Queen, who ultimately agrees to attend the wedding, finds she must dance there in "red-hot iron shoes" until she falls down dead. Thus, instead of being purified by the fire through which she must go, the destructive force of her own wickedness burns her out of existence. As with Achilles, the vulnerable aspect of the foot is emphasized. The positive power, on the contrary, alludes to the ability to walk forward as a result of one's own developed strength — an attribute not of tyrants, but of the evolved hero or heroine.

Snow-White, having eaten her half of the apple, and gone through the ordeal of being placed in a coffin or "tomb," assimilated the final poison with which it was possible for the evil Queen to delude her. Having thereby transcended her former state of being, the lovely child succeeded in freeing herself from the Terrible Mother. Only then could she be loved, deservedly, by the Prince — personification of insight and completion — who alone comprehended the true nature of what lay behind the glass.

Whereas the second Queen was burned out of existence, Snow-White justified her lineage from the good Queen, and — united with her Prince — became the promise of the future.

16 TYRANNICAL CLINGING TO POWER... ILLUSORY AND DISTORTED ATTRIBUTIONS OF HEROIC DEEDS...PRIDE, SELF-ADULATION, GREED, REPRESSION... INTERROGATION POINT

Not only are our own self-serving fantasies in danger of tricking us into believing that false values are true, but various figures herewith represented are themselves credited with having performed acts they clearly did not.[1] (Plates 81–97.)

Once a meaningful sense of reality has been lost, the specious is bound to be mistaken for the valid, the destructive for the virtuous, the non-existent or non-experienced for that which *is*. Most dangerous of all, perhaps, is our failure to see and acknowledge self-deceptive tendencies within ourselves.

In conjunction with the image of David and Goliath reproduced, although the giant is the explicit enemy to be fought, King Saul's ruthless desire for power, revealed by his fear that David will succeed him, constitutes an equally insidious threat.

---

1. For centuries conflicting views have been held both about deeds supposedly performed by Alexander the Great, and about his character: "On the one hand he was exalted as a model of . . . virtues — courage, liberality, magnanimity and even chastity; on the other, he was charged with cruelty, drunkenness and ambition, while his ascent to the skies, borne up by gryphons, was interpreted as an example of the deadliest of sins, pride. . . . Needless to say, history has been overlaid by a mass of prodigies and marvels, and it gives one quite a start to read that Homer and Ptolemy were among Alexander's tutors, teaching him Latin, falconry and fencing!" (MEDIEVAL ROMANCES, edited by Roger Sherman Loomis and Laura Hibbard Loomis, New York: Modern Library, 1957, pp. 234–35.)

*81. DAVID AND GOLIATH
From stone relief on capital of Basilica of the
Madeleine. Vézelay (Yonne). French. 11th–
12th centuries. Musée lapidaire, Vézelay.

Since Moses is one of the world's great
heroic figures, it is by no means surprising
either that he should be portrayed in a
Persian miniature of the fourteenth century, or be almost universally admired —
and often depicted — even to the present
day.

There is the ever-present danger, nonetheless, that images deriving at
second- or third-hand from distant cultures may become merely formal-
ized, decorative objects. It is equally possible that we shall simply give lip-
service to what they are attempting to make us realize. Only if a work of
art — whether created in the remote past, or in our own time — profoundly moves us, illuminating what has not hitherto been revealed to us;
only if it expresses authentic affirmation and wonder, can it have significance.

In the picture of Rustam, the demon under attack is not intended to be
what it seems, namely a traditional, mythological beast. It is, instead, a
demeaning equivalent of the dreaded "white foreigner."

Whatever the Emperor Jahangir's positive attainments may have been,
the two portrayals that follow must be considered in terms of the self-
deluding behavior they reflect.

Just as Faust trusts that no harm will befall him if he sells his soul to
Mephistopheles, so we find Peter Schlemihl, with similar lack of self-
knowledge, mistakenly relinquishing his shadow to the Devil, believing
that he will, in return, be spared the need to toil for whatever he may receive in life.

In further illustrations included in this section, self-love, greed, illusion,
are relentlessly delineated. (Even St. Anthony's effort merely to repress
the demons by which he is tempted can have no positive significance.
Rather, we must directly face and come to terms with the dark forces
within ourselves.)

Indeed, whatever acts we perform that are based on distorted attitudes
of any variety — be they of a spiritual or physical nature — must cause us
ultimately to answer to the "whirlwind."

According to a legend recounted by Louis Ginzberg,[2] Goliath was intent upon doing away with King Saul. The giant's grievance against the king had to do with the fact "that once, when, in a skirmish between the Philistines and the Israelites, Goliath had succeeded in capturing the holy tables of the law, Saul had wrested them" away. Because of a malady from which the latter suffered, he could not subsequently "venture to cross swords with Goliath," accepting instead, "David's offer to enter into combat in his place." When David donned the powerfully-built king's armor, and it clearly fit him, Saul recognized that the younger man "had been predestined for the serious task he was about to undertake."

Since "David's miraculous transformation" aroused the king's jealousy, "the erstwhile slender youth. . . . declined to array himself as a warrior for his contest with Goliath." He wished, instead, to meet the giant as a simple shepherd. (Plate 81.) Scarcely had he begun to move toward Goliath, than his overwhelming opponent became "conscious of the magic power of the youth."

Goliath stood rooted to the ground, being so confused by his own "impotence that he scarcely knew what he was saying, and he uttered the foolish threat that he would give David's flesh to the cattle of the field, as though cattle ate flesh. One can see, David said to himself, [Goliath is crazed] and there can be no doubt he is doomed. Sure of victory, David retorted . . . he would cast the carcass of the Philistine to the fowls of the air. At the mention of fowls, Goliath raised his eyes skyward, to see whether there were any birds about. The upward motion of his head pushed his visor slightly away from his forehead, and in that instant the pebble aimed by David struck him on the exposed spot. An angel descended and cast him to the ground face downward, so that the mouth that had blasphemed God might be choked with earth. [Goliath thus] fell in such wise that the image of Dagon[3] which he wore on his breast touched the ground, and his head came to lie between the feet of David, who now had no difficulty in dispatching him."

---

2. LEGENDS OF THE BIBLE, Louis Ginzberg, New York: Jewish Publication Society of America, 1956, pp. 536-37.
3. A god or idol of the Philistines.

Goliath's fall personifies the doom of the destructive aspect of the giant — that which must be displaced, so that the newly emergent present may develop in creative manner.

Through slaying Goliath, David transcends outlived, external power, thereby liberating inner growth. The fact that Goliath is choked with earth further suggests that the past dare not be permitted to suffocate the productive energy of the evolving future.

'Uj is Og, king of Bashan. References to this obscure figure, contained in Numbers and Deuteronomy, seem to have fired the imagination of the Rabbis of Talmudic times, who embellished existing tradition with many fanciful tales. One of these relates how Og, beholding the camp of the Israelites — which was three parasangs in length — uprooted a mountain of equal dimensions, in order to hurl it against the Israelites, and thus destroy them. The Lord, however, sent swarms of ants (locusts in another account), which burrowed through the center of the mountain, so that it fell like a huge tight collar encircling Og's throat. With Og thus incapacitated, Moses leaped ten ells into the air, slaying his adversary by striking him in the heel with his staff. This version was taken up by the early Muslims, and expanded still further.

According to one narrative, 'Uj's full name was 'Uj ibn 'Unq, because of the stone necklace that encased his neck. (Plate 82.) The Hebrew term

82. MOSES STRIKES THE
GIANT 'UJ
From page of manuscript: *Majma' al-Tawarikh*
of Hafiz-I Abru. Written and illustrated
in Herat. c. 1425. Cincinnati Art Museum.

*83. ALEXANDER THE GREAT
SLAYING A DRAGON
From detail in the Emir of Bokhara's Album,
Ms. M. 386, folio 6. Persian. Early 17th
century. The Pierpont Morgan Library,
New York.

applied to him means "giant," and this is probably the origin of the Arabic
surname.[4]

It is significant that, just as Goliath, upon being vanquished, was cast
downward and choked with earth, so the enormous 'Uj was weakened by
the Lord, as a result of the constricting band that descended about his
neck. In both cases what had grown oppressively menacing must give way
to the authentically spiritual; to the release — the breath of new life —
that is the hero himself. The negative aspect of what has been overcome is
replaced by its opposing positive force.

Alexander became a legendary figure almost during his lifetime — an
oft-repeated example of an historic individual being transformed by others
into a purportedly allegorical, yet in fact illusory equivalent of already
existing mythological prototypes. (Plate 83.)

---

4. The above is based on information contained in a letter from Norman Golb of the Hebrew Union College —
Jewish Institute of Religion, Cincinnati, Ohio.

*84. RUSTAM KILLING THE DIV-I
SAFID (WHITE DEMON)
IN THE CAVERN
From manuscript illustration to the *Shah-Nama* (*Book of Kings*) by Firdausi. Folio 80a. Persian. 16th century. The Metropolitan Museum of Art, New York. Gift of Mr. Alexander Smith Cochran, 1913.

To Iranian or Persian worshippers of Ahura Mazdah (the force of light), the *daevas* came to represent "false gods, who had not sided with the Good Spirit; to this day they survive as demons under the name of *divs*. Whatever belonged to their world was defined as *daevic* and opposed to the *ahuric* sphere. This religious dualism even affected the language." If a good being ate, Avestan writers used one verb, if a *daevic* being ate, a different verb was used. The same applied to speaking, running, dying.[5]

Although what is *dark* often is regarded as "sinister," "white" (simply the "white foreigner," who was feared) is identified with the mythological demon or *div* in Plate 84.

The two images relating to the Emperor Jahangir (Plates 85 and 86) represent falsifications of reality, or misleading re-creations of it.

In the first painting, although Jahangir appears in the role of conqueror, he was, in fact, defeated. Shown standing on a lion (with which he obviously identified himself), he arranged to have the figure of his enemy, Shah 'Abbas, made smaller than his own, and to have it placed on a lamb.

Whereas Jahangir towers over, and embraces his enemy, it was Shah 'Abbas who was victorious. It was by no means Jahangir who achieved "peace on earth," despite the fact that amity was brought into being. Thus it is entirely unwarranted to have the supposedly conquered one submitting to him. The notion that the Messianic Age had arrived, in which the lion and lamb could lie down together, because of any act performed by Jahangir, remains in the realm of mere dream. Hence, however realistic the details in the two pictures may be, they totally distort truth.

---

5. "Iranian Literature," I. Gershevitch, LITERATURES OF THE EAST, edited by Eric B. Ceadel, London: John Murray, 1953, p. 62.

85. JAHANGIR'S DREAM OF
SHAH 'ABBAS' VISIT
Painting by Abu'l-Hasan. Mughal. Indian.
Early 17th century. Smithsonian Institution,
Freer Gallery of Art, Washington, D.C.

The historical background of this delineation relates to the tension between India and Iran concerning Qandahar, which was finally captured by
the Shah of Iran, Shah 'Abbas, in 1622. The picture "represents a dream
in a well of light . . . experienced by Jahangir. In it the Shah of Iran
appeared to the emperor and thus made him happy."

In this remarkable painting, Jahangir indicates "his psychological effort
to overcome his anxieties about [a] political problem. In his vision the
tension is relieved and the adversary comes submissively to be received and
forgiven in brotherly love. Both are united in the immense halo composed
of sun and moon, an allusion to Jahangir's name Nur ad-din (Light of
Religion). . . . The symbolic animals [lamb and lion] on which the
sovereigns stand indicate Jahangir's wishful thinking about their relative
strength; at the same time the peaceful association of lion and sheep shows
that the Messianic age has arrived in the world, which is shown in the
form of a partially visible globe." [6]

---

6. PAINTINGS OF THE SULTANS AND EMPERORS OF INDIA IN AMERICAN COLLECTIONS, Richard Ettinghausen, New Delhi: Lalit Kala Akademi, 1961, opp. Pl. 12.

86. JAHANGIR VANQUISHING
HIS ENEMY MALIK 'ANBAR
Painting by Abu'l-Hasan. Mughal. Indian.
Early 17th century. Smithsonian Institution,
Freer Gallery of Art, Washington, D.C.

The Emperor Jahangir is astride a globe on which is shown the world, covered with symbolical animal figures. The globe rests upon an ox which in turn stands on a large fish. (According to popular Islamic tradition, the earth was often portrayed supported by a great fish.)

The Emperor is shooting an arrow at the dark head of his enemy, Malik 'Anbar, "an Abyssinian who vigorously opposed the progress of Jahangir's armies . . . and succeeded in recovering much of the territory that had been conquered . . . by the Mughals. Jahangir sent one army after another in vain, to check him." [7] As in other instances, when "baffled or angered by failure of attainment," the Emperor "took to pictorial allegory to counteract . . . evil forces and to assuage his feelings." [8]

---

7. THE LIBRARY OF A. CHESTER BEATTY. A CATALOGUE OF THE INDIAN MINIATURES, Sir Thomas W. Arnold and J. V. S. Wilkinson, London, 1936, Vol. I, p. 32.

8. "The Emperor's Choice," Richard Ettinghausen, reprinted from DE ARTIBUS OPUSCULA XL, ESSAYS IN HONOR OF ERWIN PANOFSKY, New York: New York University Press, 1961, p. 117.

*87.   ALLEGORY OF HUMAN LIFE,
FROM THE LEGEND OF
BARLAAM AND JOSAPHAT
From miniature in *Psalter and Hours of the
Virgin.* Ms. 729. French. 13th century. The
Pierpont Morgan Library, New York.

A further example of illusion: "Those who crave for the delights of the body, and suffer their souls to die of hunger . . . are like to a man who was fleeing from an unicorn,[9] for fear of being devoured. In his flight he fell into a deep abyss; but as he fell, he grasped a little bush in his hands, and set his feet upon a slippery and unstable support. Looking up, he saw two mice, one white and one black, gnawing at the roots of the bush, and perceived that they had almost cut it through. . . . Looking up again, he found a little bit of honey dripping from the branches of the bush; and completely forgetting the dangers which beset him on all sides he gave himself wholly to the enjoyment of a few drops of honey. The unicorn is death, which is ever in pursuit of man, and seeks to lay hold of him. The abyss is the world, which is full of every evil. The little bush is each man's life, which is consumed by the hours of the day and the night as by the white and black mice, and comes nigher and nigher to breaking. . . . The dreadful dragon is the mouth of Hell, which yawns to devour all men. The sweetness of the honey is the false pleasure of the world, which beguiles man, and distracts him from giving thought to his peril." [10]

---

9. The unicorn has not consistently been utilized as an emblem of purity or virginity, but has also typified death, as in the above miniature.

10. de Voragine, op. cit., p. 726.

Plate 88 is reproduced from a Russian work, "Concerning the Passions." The text closes with the following: "The first and primary cause, the mother of all of [the passions] is Self-love." The Genealogy of the Passions appears in the form of an iconographical analogy to the genealogy of the Mother of God, or the Tree of Jesse. The Passions, or Vices, represent demons.[11]

---

11. Based on PARADIES UND HÖLLE: RUSSISCHE BUCHMALEREI, Dmitrij Tschizewskij, Recklinghausen: Verlag Aurel Bongers, 1957, p. 36.

88. THE GENEALOGY OF THE
VICES: SELF-LOVE
ENTHRONED, THE MOTHER
OF ALL VICES
Book illustration. Russian. 18th century.
Slavisches Institut der Universität Heidelberg.

"Since in fact we see that avarice, anger, envy, pride, sloth, lust and stupidity commonly profit far beyond humility, chastity, fortitude, justice and thought, and [we] have to choose, [in order] to be human at all . . . why then perhaps we must stand fast a little — even at the risk of being heroes."

ROBERT BOLT

After Peter Schlemihl had sold his shadow, so that he might avoid facing life's realities, the devil took the ill-gotten treasure "out of his pocket, and with a dexterous fling it was unrolled and spread out on the heath on the sunny side of [the devil's] feet [Plate 89], so that he stood between the two attendant shadows, [Peter's] and his, and walked away." [12]

Peter Schlemihl's relinquishing of his shadow is reminiscent of Faust's selling his soul to Mephistopheles. However seemingly alluring both bargains may appear at first glance we can no more live without our shadows than our souls.

But then, having taken a moral position concerning Peter Schlemihl's blind abandonment of his shadow to the devil, and Faust's similar bargain with Mephistopheles, we must pay heed, at a different level, not only to the wisdom mirrored in Erich Neumann's words, but also to Mircea Eliade's hypothesis: "In myths," wrote Neumann, "the shadow often appears as a twin, for he is not just the 'hostile brother,' but the companion and friend, and it is sometimes difficult to tell whether this twin is the shadow or the self." [13]

Understood in the context of Goethe's entire work, what Eliade has termed the "unexpected 'sympathy' between God and the Spirit of Negation" becomes entirely comprehensible. In *Faust,* notes Eliade, Mephistopheles actually stimulates human action. This is so because, to Goethe, evil, as well as error, are productive: "It is contradiction," he wrote to Eckermann, on March 28, 1827, "that makes us productive."

"In Goethe's conception," Eliade adds, "Mephistopheles is the spirit who denies, protests and, above all, *halts* the flux of life and prevents things from being done. Mephistopheles' activity is not directed against God, but against Life. Mephistopheles is 'the father of all hindrance'. . . . What [he] asks . . . Faust to do is to *stop.*" He "knows that the moment Faust stops [the latter] will have lost his soul. But a stop is not a negation of the Creator; it is a negation of Life. Mephistopheles does not directly oppose God, but his principal creation, Life. In place of movement and Life he tries to impose rest, immobility, death. For whatever ceases to change and transform itself decays and perishes. This 'death in Life' can be translated as spiritual sterility. . . . A man who has let the roots of Life, in the deepest part of himself, perish falls into the power of the negating Spirit. . . .

---

12. PETER SCHLEMIHL, Adelbert von Chamisso, translated by Sir John Bowring, New York: A. Denham and Co., 1874, p. 75.
13. THE ORIGINS AND HISTORY OF CONSCIOUSNESS, Erich Neumann, translated by R. F. C. Hull, Bollingen Series XLII, New York: Pantheon Books, 1954, p. 353.

"However, as has often been observed, though Mephistopheles uses every means to oppose the flux of Life, he stimulates Life. He fights against the Good but ends by doing Good." [14]

"Co-operating with the beneficent forces, though antagonistically," states Heinrich Zimmer, "those of evil . . . assist in the weaving of the tapestry of life; hence the experience of evil, and to some extent this experience alone, produces maturity, real life, real command of the powers and tasks of life. The forbidden fruit — the fruit of guilt through experience, knowledge through experience — had to be swallowed in the Garden of Innocence before human history could begin. Evil had to be accepted and assimilated, not avoided." [15]

A whale rests upon the surface of the sea. (Plate 90.) Unwary seamen, thinking it to be an island, anchor their boat to it. The text accompanying the picture in an early bestiary calls attention to the vast size of the illusory beast, which closely resembles the whale that swallowed Jonah. The whale's "belly was so huge," it is stated, that, as Jonah himself said, "he thought he was in the Infernal regions." [16]

---

14. MEPHISTOPHELES AND THE ANDROGYNE: STUDIES IN RELIGIOUS MYTH AND SYMBOL, Mircea Eliade, translated by J. M. Cohen, New York: Sheed and Ward, 1965, pp. 79–80.

15. Zimmer, THE KING AND THE CORPSE, p. 49.

16. Based on letter to the author from the Department of Western Mss., Bodleian Library, Oxford.

*90. WHALE
From a bestiary. Ms. Ashmole 1511, folio 86 verso. English. Late 12th century. Bodleian Library, Oxford.

91. THE FALL OF THE BEAST
AND THE FALSE PROPHET
Detail of manuscript illumination. *L'Apocalypse
de Saint-Sever,* Ms. 8878, folio 201. Abbey
of Saint-Sever-sur-l'Adour (Landes). French.
11th century. Bibliothèque Nationale, Paris.

"And the beast was taken, and with him the false prophet that wrought miracles before him. . . . These both were cast alive into a lake of fire burning with brimstone." [17] (Plate 91.)

As indicated in Chapter 12, Perseus avoided being turned into stone because he heeded Athena's advice. Instead of looking directly at Medousa's Gorgon-head, he gazed at its reflection in his own shield. When he had succeeded in cutting off the head, there sprang into being from it the winged horse, Pegasus.

Plate 92 reflects one of the major themes emphasized throughout this volume: Not only does every battle of the hero necessarily lead to a further one, but each victory can all too readily be but the prelude to a subsequent disaster.

In the depiction that follows, the monster Chimaera (a child of Echidna, as was the Sphinx whose riddle Oedipus solved) is about to be killed by Bellerophon, who rides Pegasus.

The Chimaera appears "in the traditional form of a lion with a tail terminating in a snake, while the forepart of a goat grows out of its back. Hesiod was the first among the ancient writers to call the monster 'fire-breathing.'" The Chimaera "has felled a stag which lies on its back, the

---

17. REVELATION 19:20.

*92. BELLEROPHON ON PEGASUS
IN THE ACT OF KILLING
THE CHIMAERA
From plaque of engraved bronze sheathing.
Greek. c. 660 B.C. The Metropolitan Museum
of Art, New York.

legs stretched out stiffly. Pegasus is aloft. . . . The winged horse is bri-
dled; Bellerophon holds the reins in one hand and poises a javelin in the
other. As often in Greek art the decisive phase of [such] a combat or
hunt . . . is not that of the actual killing of the enemy or prey, but the
moment immediately before: both combatants are shown at the height of
their strength and power, and as the ending of the story is already known
to the spectator, the outcome of the struggle cannot be in doubt." [18]

But then, in turn, Bellerophon himself falls, due to his exaggerated
pride of spirit. Icarus, also, who flies too near the sun, crashes to earth.
Indeed, writes Erich Neumann, "just because he is begotten by God, the
hero must be 'devout' and fully conscious of what he is doing. If he acts in
the arrogance of egomania, which the Greeks called hybris, and does not
reverence [that] against which he strives, then his deeds will infallibly
come to nought. To fly too high and fall, to go too deep and get stuck,
these are alike symptoms of an overvaluation of the ego that ends in disaster, death, or madness. An overweening contempt for the transpersonal
powers above and below means falling victim to them, whether the hero
crashes to earth . . . or plunges into the sea." [19]

18. "Newly Acquired Bronzes — Greek, Etruscan, and Roman," Dietrich von Bothmer, THE METROPOLITAN
MUSEUM OF ART BULLETIN, January 1961, pp. 136, 138.
19. Neumann, op. cit., p. 188.

With a certain incisive humor, the lines from Revelation that follow puncture self-delusion. They pronounce, in subtle prophecy, how we dare not imagine it is possible to cast out our demons once and for all.

"And I saw an angel come down from heaven, having the key of the bottomless pit and a great chain in his hand. And he laid hold on the dragon, that old serpent, which is the Devil, and Satan, and bound him a thousand years, And cast him into the bottomless pit, and shut him up, and set a seal upon him, that he should deceive the nations no more, till the thousand years should be fulfilled: and after that he must be loosed a little season." [20] (Plate 93.)

---

20. REVELATION 20:1–3.

*93.   THE DRAGON ENCHAINED
From manuscript illumination. *L'Apocalypse de Saint-Sever,* Ms. 8878, folio 202 verso.
Abbey of Saint-Sever-sur-l'Adour (Landes).
French. 11th century. Bibliothèque Nationale, Paris.

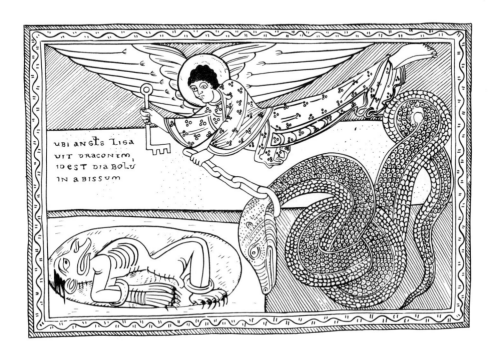

*94. SIGURD SLAYING FAFNIR
From stone carving, the Ramsund Rock.
Swedish. 11th century. Södermanland,
Sweden.

Sigurd, hero of Iceland's *Poetic Edda,* was reared by the cunning dwarf, Regin. Fafnir, a brother of Regin, hoarded the great Andvari treasure, brooding over it in the form of an enormous snake or dragon. Regin, who hoped to possess the treasure himself, urged Sigurd to slay the mighty Fafnir. (Plate 94.) After Sigurd had struck the dragon — symbol of unmitigated greed — with his sword, he took Fafnir's heart and cooked it on a spit. When the blood foamed out of the heart, he tested it with his finger to see whether it was fully cooked. Burning his finger, he put it in his mouth, and when Fafnir's heart's-blood came upon his tongue, he understood the speech of birds.[21]

Thus a bird was able to warn of the dwarf's perfidy, in time for Sigurd to protect himself by killing Regin. (In various other myths the speech of birds is also understood at decisive moments by the hero — the bird, in its positive aspect, signifying higher or spiritual realization. Unless he had finally identified with Fafnir, thereby experiencing his own capacity to be treacherous, Sigurd could not, however, have protected himself, nor comprehended what the birds were saying.)

---

21. Based on THE POETIC EDDA, translated by Henry Adams Bellows, New York: The American-Scandinavian Foundation, 1957, p. 380.

95. SAINT ANTHONY
TORMENTED BY DEMONS
Engraving by Martin Schongauer. German.
Last quarter 15th century. Philadelphia
Museum of Art: Ars Medica Collection.

"The Temptation of St. Anthony [is] one of the famous examples of hallucination. . . . The founder and organizer of ascetic monasticism . . . was often, according to his own belief, sorely tempted during his fasting and solitude by the devil, who appeared in many forms, such as a seductive woman, a deceptive friend, a banquet of delectable food, and as wild beasts, dragons, and demons to torment him. [Plate 95.] In many representations St. Anthony was accompanied by his familiar, the pig. . . . The pig may have been one form of diabolic visitation, or it may have symbolized the saint's animal nature." [22]

Is it not always when we seek merely to control, rather than transmute our demons, that they inevitably erupt in more virulent form to mock, beset, and tempt us anew?

---

22. Zigrosser, op. cit., p. 80.

96. THE LORD ANSWERING JOB
OUT OF THE WHIRLWIND
Engraving by William Blake. English. 1825.
The Pierpont Morgan Library, New York.

"Who is this that darkeneth counsel by words without knowledge?" [23]

Challenge, Paradox, Interrogation Point: A mounted Don Quixote-like figure is poised off-center, front, upon the top of a monumental question mark. (Plate 97.) Will he permit his elegant steed to plunge into the space before him, or will he remain immobilized, tilting head-on into a void; holding aloft, with absurd splendor, his oversize banner, his unsheathed, yet unmenacing sword, his grandiose lance?

And what of the featureless, motionless, dummy-like human beings at the base of the monument? Are they either more or less heroic than the posturing knight above?

Saul Steinberg's picture confronts us with our collective and individual dilemma. To observe the silent drama not being played out is to glimpse a most shrewd portrait of our own all too frequent no-way-out and our excruciating self-delusions. Perhaps the drawing fascinates both because it alludes to a concept widely popular today — the anti- or false-hero — and illustrates what so often has to, and does occur to each of us, despite our failure to admit what is involved.

---

23. JOB 38:2.

97. UNTITLED
Black and white line drawing by Saul
Steinberg. American. 1960. © 1965 by
Saul Steinberg. Originally in The New
Yorker.[24] Drawing in Collection
Dorothy Norman, New York.

Whether we set forth to fight against windmills in the outer world —
in the manner of a Don Quixote — or against equally grotesque interior
dragons, we are interminably confronted by our weaknesses; by a distress-
ing inability to distinguish between spurious heroes *or* dragons, and real
ones. Yet we harbor a curious necessity to tilt, even when not altogether
certain against what, just as we are so often timorous — lance in hand —
when faced by tyranny we had best overthrow.

Among any number of other irritating, albeit persistent contradictions
and quandaries that plague us, is the propensity to be a non-hero, while
masquerading as the reverse. When such a plight is viewed with a certain
sympathy, we may say with a measure of truth: There is a time for this,
and a time for that. When less favorably disposed toward our inadequa-
cies, it is necessary to confess how seldom we are able to choose the right
moment for either suitable action or inaction. Absurd and wrong decisions
are made again and again, just as right ones are avoided. We attempt, with
ludicrously hollow gestures, to impress ourselves, as well as others. Most
disquieting of all is being reminded of battles undertaken by true heroes,

---

24. From THE NEW WORLD, New York: Harper & Row, 1965.

since our uncertainty about being prepared to perform feats requiring equivalent courage painfully haunts us.

Plate 97 also suggests that to adopt the posture of the hero is the most unheroic of all acts. From one point of view, there are only split-seconds, at best, during which it is feasible to descend into any abyss by which we may be confronted. And who can be certain, even during those moments of suspension when we do decide to leap, what will result? Is it not essentially the courage to risk everything, without knowledge of the outcome, that is our most basic solidity?

If we labor under the illusion that we shall automatically arrive safely, or arrive at all, and then be free placidly to play the role of the hero, we are mistaken. If we imagine we can bask in the glory of success in the wake of any achievement whatever, we have already become the dragon.

No situation can serve as a permanent solution or displacement of another. Mutation, suspense, suspension, flux — plunging, as an act of faith — are the sole forms of assurance we are permitted to enjoy.

Even with regard to jumping into the mystery of awesome space, how often in a lifetime can we set forth into the formidable unknown for some noble purpose? Certainly not with total consistency.

Nonetheless, if anyone has ever performed a single deed that may be termed heroic — even if he never does so again — still he remains the hero.

For Steinberg, perhaps the most crucial point in the picture shown is the challenging space between the upper curve of the large question mark and the dot at its base. Yet even the incomplete and overflorid cloud forms, like the dubiously heraldic emblems on the pretentious buildings, represent but further variants of his major interrogation point.

"Be true! Be true! Show freely to the world, if not your worst, yet some trait whereby the worst may be inferred!"

NATHANIEL HAWTHORNE

17 THE JESTER...THE RIGHT QUESTION...THE ACT OF TRUTH...THE TRICKSTER

The jester — the satirist, the clown, the "fool" — are healthy antidotes to pomposity and tyranny. In such context, these figures — depending upon the spirit in which they operate — are in part, at least, heroic, although unable to perform a totally valorous role.

Like everyone else, those who are exceptional must subject themselves to mockery or protest, no matter how irreverent and seemingly irrational their critics may be, else they, too, become the dragon. Yet when the truly great are ridiculed, it is paradoxical that those who identify with thrusts at them, should thereby experience a fraudulent sense of release. This occurs temporarily, at least, when those who are, in fact, inferior, feel they are not.[1]

At times, the "fool" as a symbol of innocence can have great power. At others, in being unaware of, or miscalculating, what is required of him, he can be a negative character, harmful both to himself and the social order.

There are situations in which simply knowing the right questions to ask, and asking them, can be heroic, as can the ability to perform the act of truth.

It is of importance both to question ourselves, and to stand up to the questioning of others. It is necessary, also, to be extraordinarily flexible in such matters, since the queries and criticisms to be made inevitably change.

Jessie Weston has noted,[2] for example, in conjunction with the Grail, whether we consider Gawain, Perceval or Galahad, that we find both "a uniformity which assures us of the essential identity of the tradition underlying the varying forms, and a diversity indicating that" the customary "has undergone a gradual, but radical modification."

In the case of Gawain, we gather "he ought to have enquired concerning the nature of the Grail, and that this enquiry would have resulted in the restoration to fruitfulness of a Waste Land."

---

1. When the jester is free to attack the hero, this may, of course, suggest that a given society is stable, and that those in power feel secure. Just as periodic Saturnalias — during which unusual license is permitted — most certainly would not be countenanced in cultures unsure of their survival.

2. Quotations are from Weston, op. cit., pp. 12 ff.

Indeed, when Gawain does ask a question of consequence, this helps, at least partially, to restore the land. Whereupon the waters flow again through "their channel,[3] and all the woods" are "turned to verdure."

However, the Perceval versions, "which form the bulk of . . . existing Grail texts, differ considerably . . . one from the other, alike in the task to be achieved, and the effects resulting from the hero's success, or failure." The distinctive feature of these texts is, nonetheless, that emphasis is placed upon the sickness and disability of the ruler of the land, the Lord of the Grail Castle — possessor of the Grail — the Fisher King.[4]

"Regarded first as the direct cause of the wasting of the land," the King's languishing condition "gradually assumes overwhelming importance." Thus what is ultimately necessary is to heal the King. "The restoration of the land not only falls into the background but the operating cause of its desolation is changed."

When the *motif* of the Waste Land has disappeared, then the "task of the hero consists in asking concerning the Grail, and by so doing, [he restores] the Fisher King, who is suffering from extreme old age, to health and youth. . . . Here we have the introduction of a new element, the restoration to youth of the sick King. . . .

"The question is [altered in that] the hero no longer asks what the Grail is, but . . . whom it serves? a departure from an essential and primitive simplicity." Even more important a change: "While the malady of the Fisher King is antecedent to the hero's visit, and capable of cure if the question be asked, the failure to fulfil the prescribed conditions . . . itself entails disaster upon the land. Thus the sickness of the King, and the desolation of the land, are not necessarily connected as cause and effect, but . . . the latter is directly attributable to the Quester himself."

The idea "that the misfortunes of the land are not antecedent to, but dependent upon, the hero's abortive visit to the Grail castle, is carried still

---

3. As described in Chapter 5, when the god Indra smites the serpent Vritra, because the latter would thwart the creation of the manifest universe, the waters are similarly released.

4. "Wounded by a spear thrust through his thighs," it is claimed, the King's only solace is "in fishing. He can be healed only through the help of the Grail-seeker and when he is healed the waste land which surrounds his castle will become productive again. . . . The epithet fisher applied to [the King] may derive from Christ's . . . 'I shall make ye fishers of men.' " (STANDARD DICTIONARY OF FOLKLORE, MYTHOLOGY AND LEGEND, edited by Maria Leach, New York: Funk and Wagnalls Company, 1949, Vol. I.)

further by the compiler of the *Perlesvaus,* where the failure of the predestined hero to ask concerning the office of the Grail is alone responsible for
the illness of the King and the misfortunes of the country."

Or, as Dr. Carl Jung has noted, there is the mythological truth that the
"wounded wounder is the agent of healing," the sufferer taking away
suffering.

The questions to be asked alter, because life itself is in constant flux.
They can no more remain static than can we ourselves.

Performing the "act of truth" is quite as important as is asking the right
question. The manner in which both are done affects not merely the fate
of individuals, but that of entire societies.

II.

As noted in the section on Horus and Seth (Chapter 9), ancient Egyptian Pharaohs were under an obligation to maintain *maat,* generally translated as truth, but which meant, rather, the "right order," the inherent
structure of creation, of which justice was said to be an integral part. The
King's speech was itself looked upon as "the shrine of truth," or, again, as
maat.

"In very early times in India," too, "the speaking of truth became in-
vested with magic power." [5] Thus a traditional tale is told concerning an
Indian priest who asks the wife of a "sacrificer with whom she consorts,
other than her husband. It is essential that she . . . confess, since [other-
wise] it will go badly with her kinsfolk, an interesting assertion of the
solidarity of the kin." To confess her sin diminishes it, even though, it
appears, not in any other way "than that it brings exactitude again into the
order of things." This is so because, symbolically, an offense has been committed against Varuna, the Vedic god to whom truth and cosmic order are
subject. Hence, although the wife of the sacrificer has consorted with an-

---

5. Brown, op. cit., p. 6.

other, her "statement of the true fact removes . . . inexactitude, and re-pairs in so far the defect" for which she has been responsible.[6]

Such narratives have far more collective relevance than incidents in which we confess, merely to seek our own absolution, or ask right questions, only to demonstrate our individual brilliance.

III.

The Beginning of Teaching: "*Rabbi Bunam began teaching with these words: 'We thank You, who are blessed and who are the source of blessing, that you are manifest and hidden.' Then he continued: 'A fearless man must feel God as he feels the place on which he stands. And just as he cannot imagine himself without a place to stand on, so he must in all simplicity grow aware of God who is the Place of the world, and comprises it. But at the same time he must know that He is the hidden life which fills the world.'*"

MARTIN BUBER

It is enlightening that an act of truth relating to our own misconduct can be of greater import than exaggerated ecstasy before even the Most High. Thus we find the Talmud warning that "He who multiplies the praise of God to excess shall be torn from the world." It cautions also concerning how perilous it can be to give wrong answers or ask wrong questions. There is, for example, the tale of the four who entered Paradise, in which Rabbi Akiba addresses his companions: "When you come to the place of the pure marble plates, do not say 'Water! Water!' For it is said: He that telleth lies shall not tarry in my sight" — a passage alluding to dangers that confront "the mystic in his ascent through the seven palaces of the seventh heaven."[7]

It has been written of Ben Azai, one of Akiba's colleagues, that he "was deemed worthy and stood at the gate of the sixth palace and saw the ethe-

---

6. As quoted from Keith, RELIGION AND PHILOSOPHY OF THE VEDA AND UPANISHADS, in Brown, op. cit., p. 7.

7. As quoted in JEWISH GNOSTICISM, MERKABAH MYSTICISM, AND TALMUDIC TRADITION, Gershom G. Scholem, New York: The Jewish Theological Seminary of America, 1960, p. 14.

real splendor of the pure marble plates. He opened his mouth and said twice, 'Water! Water!' " In the twinkling of an eye he was decapitated: "This shall be a sign for all generations that no one should err at the gate of the sixth palace." [8]

It has been asked whether Ben Azai may have uttered his fatal question because he was a descendant of those who kissed the Golden Calf, and was therefore unworthy to see "the King in his beauty." [9]

In accordance with still other ancient traditions, water, which may be life-giving at a positive level, can also connote illusion in a negative sense. Or, perhaps Ben Azai was unprepared for the final phase of his journey, since the appearance of God on the "throne of Glory" must, in any event, remain forever secret, a mystery, transcendent, incapable of being visualized, or described. [10]

IV.

The Trickster myth that appears among both the simplest aboriginal tribes, and those that are more complex, [11] surprises by upsetting preconceived notions. Yet it can be a symbol, too, of unexpected growth.

The right order is restored by the Trickster's acts, just as it is in preceding passages, when the correct questions have been asked, and the act of truth has been performed. That so notable an end should be achieved by the seemingly irrational Trickster is no more surprising, however, than that a dream — rising out of the depths of our unconscious — should

---

8. Ibid., p. 15. Those subject to illusion, who mistake what is nameable for that which is not, are clearly unprepared to undergo the highest experiences in life. To decapitate, as above, is not a physical, but rather a symbolical act. Thus, when one is decapitated, or burned to ashes — see also Chapter 11 — it is suggested that purification must be attained by way of suffering and the gaining of further insight.

9. MAJOR TRENDS IN JEWISH MYSTICISM, Gershom G. Scholem, New York: Schocken Books, 1954, p. 53.

10. Ibid., p. 66.

11. THE TRICKSTER, Paul Radin, New York: Philosophical Library, 1956, p. ix. The Trickster is encountered in African and American Indian (Winnebago) mythology, as well as among the ancient Greeks, Chinese, Japanese, "and in the Semitic world. Many of the Trickster's traits," notes Radin, "were perpetuated in the figure of the mediaeval jester, and have survived right up to the present day in the Punch-and-Judy plays and in the clown. Although repeatedly combined with other myths and frequently drastically reorganized and reinterpreted," the basic plot of the Trickster narratives "seems always to have succeeded in reasserting itself." (Ibid., p. ix.)

bring disorder to our attention, thereby helping us to develop at a conscious level.

Joseph Campbell has retold a tale of the African trickster-divinity, Edshu[12]: "One day, this odd god came walking along a path between two fields. 'He beheld in either field a farmer at work and proposed to play the two a turn. He donned a hat that was on the one side red but on the other white, green before and black behind [these being the colors of the four World Directions: i.e., Edshu was a personification of the Center . . . or the World Navel]; so that when the two friendly farmers had gone home to their village and the one had said to the other, "Did you see that old fellow go by today in the white hat?" the other replied, "Why, the hat was red." To which the first retorted, "It was not; it was white." "But it was red," insisted the friend, "I saw it with my own two eyes." "Well, you must be blind," declared the first. "You must be drunk," rejoined the other. And so the argument developed and the two came to blows. When they began to knife each other, they were brought by neighbors before the headman for judgment. Edshu was among the crowd at the trial, and when the headman sat at a loss to know where justice lay, the old trickster revealed himself, made known his prank, and showed the hat.[13] "The two could not help but quarrel," he said. "I wanted it that way. Spreading strife is my greatest joy." ' "

But, it may be asked, why spread strife? Doubtless the Trickster, in his way, behaves much as does the Lord Shiva, when the latter lays waste what is merely static; when the god puts an end to self-centered illusions — to "the fetters that bind each separate soul"— thereby bringing about renewal.

In what must be regarded as the earliest and most archaic form of the Trickster myth — as found among the North American Indians — the central figure further recalls East Indian myth in that the Trickster "is at one and the same time creator and destroyer, giver and negator." [14]

In a Winnebago — North American Indian — narrative about the Trickster, the latter at first behaves in primitive fashion, but gradually

12. A Trickster tale quoted from Leo Frobenius, UND AFRIKA SPRACH . . . (Berlin: Vita, Deutsches Verlagshaus, 1912) in THE HERO WITH A THOUSAND FACES, Joseph Campbell, New York: Meridian Books, 1956, p. 45.
13. To this very day, jesters' caps are multicolored.
14. Radin, op. cit., p. ix.

evolves as an integrated, purposeful, and socially motivated being. In describing the Trickster's development, Paul Radin points out its essentially psychological import, and how it indicates what occurs when "man's instinctual side is given free reign."

"A normal individual," writes Radin, "the chief of the community, takes it upon himself to defy all customs, sacred and profane. As a result, he finds himself deserted and alone and is thrown back, externally, upon the vaguest type of relationship with nature as symbolized by the birds who taunt and mock him. Internally, he is thrown back upon his primitive undisciplined appetites, hunger and sex. Instead of embarking upon . . . a highly socialized, cooperative enterprise, he finds himself proceeding aimlessly from place to place to satisfy his hunger and an undifferentiated sex drive, in the course of which he destroys and kills wantonly and sins against all human values. When he attempts once more to establish a connection with other human beings he has to do it indirectly, through animals . . . and on the basis of hunger, and of sex inversion." [15]

The Trickster "dupes others and . . . is always duped himself. He wills nothing consciously. At all times he is constrained to behave as he does from impulses over which he has no control. He knows neither good nor evil yet he is responsible for both. He possesses no values, moral or social, is at the mercy of his passions and appetites, yet through his actions all values come into being. But not only he, so our myth tells us, possesses these traits. So, likewise, do the other figures of the plot connected with him: the animals, the various supernatural beings and monsters, and man." [16]

Although, basically, the Trickster possesses no well-defined and fixed form, as Radin observes, his myth nonetheless foreshadows "the shape of man. . . . Laughter, humour and irony permeate everything [he] does. The reaction of the audience in aboriginal societies to both him and his exploits is prevailingly one of laughter tempered by awe. There is no reason for believing this is secondary or a late development. Yet it is difficult to say whether the audience is laughing at him, at the tricks he plays on others, or at the implications his behaviour and activities have for them." [17]

---

15. THE WORLD OF PRIMITIVE MAN, Paul Radin, New York: Henry Schuman, 1953, pp. 336–37.
16. Radin, THE TRICKSTER, p. ix.
17. Ibid., p. x.

Nonetheless, as the Winnebago myth unfolds, the Trickster ceases "to laugh at the discomfiture of others" and to walk aimlessly into further adventures. Instead, he flees from the latter, returning "to his family and to socialization."

The first return is, to be sure, of "short duration," since the Trickster's character, like that of each of us, cannot fully evolve with excessive speed. Neither he, nor we, can immediately discern and comprehend what will result from unbridled behavior.

The very projection of the Trickster's irritations, dissatisfactions, and maladjustments "serve as a mechanism for expressing . . . the negativisms and frustrations" of the Winnebago society itself. Just so, at a personal level, the witnessing of absurdity can help us to find release from its confines.

Every man in the Winnebago social order, notes Radin, was felt to possess a "Trickster unconscious which it was imperative for both the individual concerned and, even more so, for [the collectivity], to bring to consciousness lest it destroy him and those around him. No man can do this for himself. He must call his fellowmen and society to his aid. In the career of Trickster all this is depicted. There he sees his own instinctual and irrational self, unanchored, undirected, helpless, purposeless, knowing neither love, loyalty nor pity. Isolated, he cannot grow nor mature. He can do nothing with the two fundamental appetites, hunger and sex. Others, outsiders, must set proper limits to them." In itself, the life instinctual "leads inevitably to crime and the making of irrational demands. Both must end in tragedy. But how can man be warned against such an existence? In two ways, so it is . . . implied: by depicting the inexorable and tragic consequences that follow such a life and by holding it up to ridicule." [18]

---

18. Radin, THE WORLD OF PRIMITIVE MAN, p. 339.

18 THE ARTIST AS HERO IN THE CONTEMPORARY WESTERN WORLD

"Only as builders of the future, as knowing the present, will you understand it."

FRIEDRICH NIETZSCHE

"Ye hypocrites, ye can discern the face of the sky and of the earth; but how is it that ye do not discern this time? Yea, and why even of yourselves judge ye not what is right?"

ST. LUKE 12:56–57

"A truth lost long ages ago may be sought with confidence in the thousand years yet to come."

TSUNG PING

"Depend upon it, there is mythology now as there was in the time of Homer, only we do not perceive it, because we ourselves live in the very shadow of it, and because we all shrink from the full meridian light of truth."

MAX MÜLLER

That the images we admire today "should not have died along with the faiths they sponsored is one of the major mysteries of art. For we have not only realized that their forms were not due to clumsy attempts at imitation, but also that they mean far more to us than 'volumes arranged in a certain order.' Yet that very mystery has made clear what all these arts of the sacred have in common: an aspiration to the inapprehensible. True, they have undergone a metamorphosis. . . . But the very loss of that quality of the inapprehensible discloses the new significance they have acquired. . . . Our resuscitation of the arts of the past is gradually bringing to light — as against the elements that make for 'resemblance' in the work of art — that manifest or hidden quality which accounts for their basic dissimilitude from the thing seen, a dissimilitude that orients resemblances even when the artist's aim is nature-imitation. . . . The world of all that can be seen without art's help is confronted by the world of that which art alone enables us to see. A world whose successive reincarnations, making of every great artist a destroyer of that correlation of appearances which constitutes 'reality' and a revealer of a Truth once proclaimed though obsolete today, may well suggest that our deepest response to art is of a metaphysical order." [1]

ANDRÉ MALRAUX

"The student of art, if he is to do more than accumulate facts, must also sacrifice himself: the wider the scope of his study in time and space, the more must he cease to be a provincial, the more he must universalise himself, whatever may be his own temperament and training. He must assimilate whole cultures that seem strange to him, and must also be able to elevate his own levels of reference from those of observation to that of the vision of ideal forms. He must rather love than be curious about the subject of his study. It is just because so much is demanded that the study of 'art' can have a cultural value, that is to say may become a means of growth. How often our [institutions of learning] require of the student much less than this." [2]

ANANDA K. COOMARASWAMY

"The creative artist, whose mission it is to compensate for consciousness . . . is usually an isolated individual, a hero who must destroy the old in order to make possible the dawn of the new. . . . If he does not stop at the stage of representation of the cultural canon — and no truly great artist has ever done so — he finds himself alone. He is alone regardless of whether he is worshiped as an Olympian, whether he is an organist respected in a small circle, or whether he ends in deafness, poverty, or madness.

"In following the drive of the psychic substratum, the artist fulfills not only himself but also his epoch. In the original situation the artist . . . had to cleanse himself in order to achieve an exalted and detached transpersonal state, in which alone he could become the creative instrument of

---

1. Preface to Parrot, op. cit., p. L.
2. THE CHRISTIAN AND ORIENTAL OR TRUE PHILOSOPHY OF ART, Newport, Rhode Island: John Stevens, 1939, pp. 9–10.

the powers. In the original situation this ritual preparation was undertaken in accord with the collective. To the modern artist it happens involuntarily; an outsider in society, he stands alone, delivered over to the creative impulse in himself."

"The need of his times works inside the artist without his wanting it, seeing it, or understanding its true significance. In this sense he is close to the seer, the prophet, the mystic. And it is precisely when he does not represent the existing canon but transforms and overturns it that his function rises to the level of the sacral, for he then gives utterance to the authentic and direct revelation of the numinosum." [3]

ERICH NEUMANN

"The true genius nearly always intrudes and disturbs. He talks to a temporal world out of a world eternal. And thus he says the wrong things at the right time. Eternal truths are never true at any given moment in history. The process of transformation has to reassert itself in order to digest and assimilate the utterly unpractical things that the genius has produced from the storehouse of eternity. Yet the genius is the healer for his time, because anything he betrays of eternal truth is healing." [4]

CARL G. JUNG

"To find nature herself all her forms must be shattered."

MEISTER ECKHART

Is it not by way of the swifter eye of the artist that we become most acutely conscious of reality beyond, behind, and beneath appearance? Is it not the artist who — like our dreams — dissolves the pretenses that hide us from ourselves, disclosing both our self-serving fantasies and our unsuspected potentialities?

And then, since the artist, as the great illuminator, is always in advance of his time, he must be protected, so that he may work untrammeled, irrespective of whatever resistance or insensitivity initially confronts him. For, in due course, the gift he bestows upon a world impoverished without

---

3. "Art and Time," ART AND THE CREATIVE UNCONSCIOUS, translated by Ralph Manheim, Bollingen Series LXI, New York: Pantheon Books, 1959, pp. 94, 102–03, 97–98, 97.

4. "What India Can Teach Us," ASIA, February, 1939, p. 97.

98. MAN WITH A GUITAR
Oil painting by Georges Braque. French.
1911. Collection The Museum of Modern
Art, New York. Acquired through the
Lillie P. Bliss Bequest.

him, will necessarily be recognized and treasured for what it is. It would seem there is no alternative to this classic procedure.

The vision of the inner eye is no more static than the outer flow of life, nature abhorring lack of growth and change, even as it does a vacuum. Our sights shift: The earth is the center of the universe, and then it is not.

The infinitely subtle, singing line and unspoken doctrine of the artist startle us into sharper awareness — his revelation stemming as from some inextinguishable spring; from a bottomless source of positive faith, or a most delicate act of grace. It is, indeed, the very sense of wonder and affirmation communicated by the artist that causes him to be the hero.

The history of art is largely a saga of search, fulfillment, ossification, dissatisfaction, rebellion, and change; of revolution, denial, and renaissance; of being beguiled by order and tradition, and then hungering to experiment.

The history of art — whether by way of the visual, the literary, or any other medium — is a record of the revitalization of too rigidly established forms; of the seer's prophetic power to sharpen our insights, to lift the spirit of entire civilizations.

It is the artist, through his love and dedication, his passionate involvement; his courage to acknowledge, encounter, and transform what is demonic, who brings about our revivification. *But only if we are not, in turn, dogmatic about what has been achieved, or do not become blandly indifferent and antagonistic to still further metamorphosis.*

99. NO. 160b (IMPROVISATION 28)
Oil painting by Vasily Kandinsky. Russian.
1912. The Solomon R. Guggenheim Museum,
New York.

To consider but two recent points of departure in art: It is possible that, just as Cubism[5] succeeded most daringly in dissolving and dismantling previous ways of seeing, so the "abstract" vision of a Kandinsky helped to explode them. Indeed, the entire modern movement has affirmed the vitalizing notion that neither monolithic absolutism, nor bourgeois cluttering and inflexible attitudes could ever again imprison us. Which is but one of the reasons why totalitarian tyrants, on the one hand, and exponents of individual conservatism, on the other, have displayed such hostility to what has been truly creative in our time.

"Detaching themselves from the past, they see growing before them incessantly a track that proceeds out of themselves."

ST.-JOHN PERSE

---

5. Although Cézanne was the major precursor of Cubism, the work of Picasso — together with that of Braque — gave rise to popular use of the term. Because this section is devoted to more recent art than that by Cézanne, he is not represented. Moreover, since a Picasso appears elsewhere (Plate 102), only a Cubist painting by Braque is included in this section.

While Cubism (Plate 98), Abstraction (Plate 99), and other avant-garde art forms were evolving in both Europe and the United States, an American, the undogmatic John Marin, was also breaking accepted laws of painting in order to follow the dictates of his own vision. (He nonetheless had a strict sense about how the laws of nature operate and about how to construct his pictures, even while refusing to engage in either scientific or aesthetic discussions about what he did.)

The golden or sunlike core that blazes forth in the midst of Plate 100, is placed as it is not in order to prove some theory, but rather because Marin wished to bring the far near in his work, as an act of love. (Here the central point of focus is light itself.)

In creating as he did, whether through image or word, and despite having made no study of the myth of the hero — or of any other myth — Marin's intuition led him to be preoccupied precisely with the heroic principle in life.

100. LOWER MANHATTAN
Watercolor by John Marin. American.
1922. Collection The Museum of Modern
Art, New York. Acquired through the
Lillie P. Bliss Bequest.

As John Marin wrote: "Ever since life started — a battle ground existed — the battle ground of the spirits of light and those of darkness.

"To which band does one belong — no one knows — one only feels.
This much common horse sense tells us —
both sides claim us in part.

"What's one to do? How's one to tell?
Well if you glance along the top fence rail
you won't see the powers of evil astraddle the rail
— they're too positive.

"What's one to do how's one to tell —
No — You do —
And the *doers* haven't time to straddle fence rails.

"It seems those who do that worth the doing are possessed of good eyes —
alive eyes — warm eyes —
it seems they radiate a fire within outward.

"The places they inhabit have a light burning —
a light seen from near and far by those who need this light —
and this light sometimes dim — sometimes brilliant — *never out —*"

"And these forms used . . . have an exalted value in that they put in motion the Spirit, through the eye and approach the great Seeing, not as reminders of other seeings but in themselves. . . .

"And, last year's Auto is to the Now Auto, unsatisfying. So, in art product, last year's product cannot satisfy this year. So that we cannot fully satisfy, for the Future is forever encroaching, insistent.

"This seems to lead up to the fashioning of an art product. And it would seem, considering man as the highest nature product, that man in this fashioning would set about it, work, as nature, his creator, has set about it and worked, obeying the same laws, which he does, is forced to do. Lapses are death notices. . . .

"As time goes on, always a future village to meet the future, ready for the action of its age, free, clean cut, ready for the swift, the slow, the stop, at will."

"To live through our ladder climbings and our tumblings, be this our toast." [6]

---

6. THE SELECTED WRITINGS OF JOHN MARIN, edited by Dorothy Norman, New York: Pellegrini and Cudahy, 1949, pp. 157–58, 76–77, 220.

101. UNEMPLOYED, MADRID
Photograph by Henri Cartier-Bresson.
French. 1933. Original in Collection
Dorothy Norman, New York.

"For me photography is an affirmation of life, in all its contradictions.

"The decision to make a picture comes from the heart that shouts yes, yes, yes.

"Photography is a means of discovering the world in visual terms, of questioning and never receiving a permanent answer.

"It is essential to feel neither superior nor inferior to what one is watching in one's view-finder.

"In selecting what to photograph there can be no preconceived idea, fumbling, ulterior motive or missed moment. The image should speak for itself (a caption serving only to respect the context).

"Photography is nothing if it does not express total involvement, if it does not reflect one's own deepest instincts and intuitions. What is important is to be in a state of tension or meditation, but never relaxation.

"One photographs for oneself, for one's subject, and always with a sense of responsibility. Sharing is the greatest joy.

"Fortunately there are still those who encourage individuality, confirming that others also accept life and say yes, yes, yes."

A statement sent to the author by Cartier-Bresson.

"In the multitude of people is the king's honor: but in the want of people is the destruction of the prince."

PROVERBS 14:28

"We see the rift between those who do violence and those to whom violence is done . . . running not merely through every nation, but also through every group in a nation, and even through every soul. Only in times of great crisis does the hidden rift in a people become apparent."

MARTIN BUBER

Picasso made the first sketches for *Guernica* less than a week after Nazi Germany's bombing of the Spanish Basque town of the same name. In the study reproduced (Plate 102), we see a defenceless human figure with

102. COMPOSITION STUDY
FOR GUERNICA
Pencil sketch by Pablo Picasso. Spanish.
1937. On extended loan to The Museum of
Modern Art, New York, from the artist,
Picasso.

severed head; a stricken horse; a woman and bull confronting one another. A weak but outstretched light provides the sole illumination in the midst of war and devastation.

Picasso has been quoted as saying that when he painted his *Guernica,* whereas the bull represented brutality for him, the horse typified the people; that, in his view, no distinction could be made between fascism and its inevitable corollaries of darkness and brutality, death and destruction — here symbolized by the bull.[7]

Picasso also has said that his bull is simply a bull, his horse a horse. Still others have claimed that his bull personifies the people of Spain — meaning the Loyalist cause — and, alternately, the threat of fascism. Yet, what we see — beyond all need for further interpretation — is a stark portrait in which victor and victimized are inevitably engulfed in a single, disastrous holocaust.

Picasso wrote in 1937: "The Spanish struggle is the fight of reaction against the people, against freedom. My whole life as an artist has been nothing more than a continuous struggle against reaction and the death of art. . . . In the panel on which I am working which I shall call *Guernica* . . . I clearly express my abhorrence of the military caste which has sunk Spain in an ocean of pain and death." [8]

> *"And he looked for judgment, but behold oppression; for righteousness, but behold a cry."*
>
> ISAIAH 5:7

Without conscious intent, Alfred Stieglitz, too, spoke in the great heroic tradition: "How is it possible," he asked, "to conceive of black without white? Why reject either the one or the other, since both exist? I feel the duality of world forces forever at work. Yet it is when conflict hovers about a point — a focal point — and light is in the ascendency, that I am moved. It is then that I feel the urge to photograph." (Plate 103.)

---

7. See "Picasso Explains," Pfc. Jerome Seckler, NEW MASSES, March 13, 1945, pp. 5–6.

8. As quoted in PICASSO: FIFTY YEARS OF HIS ART, Alfred H. Barr, Jr., New York: The Museum of Modern Art, 1946, p. 202.

103. EQUIVALENT
Photograph by Alfred Stieglitz.
American. 1930. Original in
Collection Dorothy Norman,
New York.

"To see the moment," Stieglitz said, "is to liberate the moment."

"It is just because the truly creative artist puts down his own experience, that it will not have been said in exactly the same manner before. It is for the same reason that, inexorably, it will be in the great tradition." [9]

"What I tell you in darkness, that speak ye in light."

ST. MATTHEW 10:27

In the art of Jackson Pollock, the mask is heroically removed or, perhaps more accurately, an interior world, generally hidden, is revealed, unadorned. Pollock once told me he often felt like "a clam without a shell." To be sure, lyricism also pervaded his work, but what was relentlessly agonizing for him was fearlessly acknowledged. As a result, the beholder may also be released from dependence on subterfuge; from the temptation to disguise his own vulnerability — to evade inner conflict and chaos. In anguish, as in ecstasy, what was projected in the mature pictures broke a new path — Pollock's own. (Plate 104.)

---

9. From Stieglitz conversations with the author.

104. NO. 10
Enamel on canvas by Jackson Pollock.
American. 1951. Collection Alfonso
Ossorio, New York.

Alfonso Ossorio has written: "The attention focused on [Pollock's] immediate qualities — the unconventional materials and method of working, the scale and immediate splendor of much of his work — has left largely untouched the forces that compel him to work in the manner that he does. Why the tension and complexity of line, the violently interwoven movement so closely knit as almost to induce the static quality of perpetual motion, the careful preservation of the picture's surface plane linked with an intricately rich interplay upon the canvas, the rupture with traditional compositional devices that produces, momentarily, the sense that the picture could be continued indefinitely in any direction?

"His painting confronts us with a visual concept organically evolved from a belief in the unity that underlies the phenomena among which we live. Void and solid, human action and inertia, are metamorphosed and refined into the energy that sustains them and is their common denominator. An ocean's tides and a personal nightmare, the bursting of a bubble and the communal clamor for a victim are as inextricably meshed in the corruscation and darkness of his work as they are in actuality. His forms and textures germinate, climax, and decline, coalesce and dissolve across the canvas. The picture surface, with no depth of recognizable space or sequence of known time, gives us the never ending present. We are presented with a visualization of that remorseless consolation — in the end is the beginning.

"New visions demand new techniques: Pollock's use of unexpected materials and scales are the direct result of his concepts and of the organic intensity with which he works, an intensity that involves, in its complete identification of the artist with his work, a denial of the accident.

"The . . . group of paintings [to which No. 10 belongs] is done with an austerity of means that underlines their protean character: thin paint and raw canvas are the vehicles for images full of the compulsion of dreams and the orderliness of myth. Black and white are the sleep and waking of a world where the freedom of private agony and release finds its discipline in the communal basis of these tensions. Forms and images dissolve and re-form into new organisms; like Proteus they must be caught unawares, asleep. They demand of the viewer an alertness and a total involvement before releasing any answer to the questions posed. . . . They are filled with the . . . combination of strength, sensitivity, and exultant acceptance. Remote from anecdote or propaganda, stripped of immediate material appeal, they both reawaken in us the sense of personal struggle and its collective roots and recall to us the too easily forgotten fact that 'what is without is within.' " [10]

105. BIRD EATERS
Lithograph by Jean Dubuffet. French. 1944. From *Matière et Mémoire*, Paris, 1945, pl. 20.

> *"The way in this world is like the edge of a blade. On this side is the underworld, and on that side is the underworld, and the way of life lies between."*

MARTIN BUBER

Dubuffet portrays what we choose so often to deny and ignore, but on which we live. What he depicts is possibly so shattering not because of our need to eat in order to live, but rather because he indicates that a certain balance in the world is in danger of being disturbed by our wanton refusal to see what we do in the name of "life." Perhaps the lithograph (Plate

---

10. From the exhibition catalogue, JACKSON POLLOCK 1951, Betty Parsons Gallery, New York, 1951.

105) was created, instinctively, to unveil our self-delusion; to jolt us into reverencing the mystery of life itself; to penetrate our everyday, falsely comforting evaluations of ourselves. (But then, does not myth, in all of its myriad manifestations, lead us to the very same goal?)

Dubuffet makes pictures of the earth that say to us: It is not necessary to gaze at the sky, look under your feet; you need not travel, rather regard the inside of your hat.

———————————◀◆▶———————————

"One evening an actor asked me to write a play for an all-black cast. But what exactly is a black? First of all, what's his color?"

JEAN GENET

"I have always believed that a nation is answerable for its traitors as well as for its heroes. But so is a civilization, and the civilization of the white man in particular is surely as answerable for its perversions as for its glories."

ALBERT CAMUS

From Richard Wright's autobiographical Black Boy: *Of the period during Wright's youth, when he felt the driving necessity to leave the South, where he had spent his boyhood:* "I held my life in my mind, in my consciousness each day, feeling at times that I would stumble and drop it, spill it forever. . . . My days and nights were one long, quiet, continuously contained dream of terror, tension, and anxiety. I wondered how long I could bear it. . . .

"The shocks of southern living had rendered my personality tender and swollen, tense and volatile, and my flight was more a shunning of external and internal dangers than an attempt to embrace what I felt I wanted. . . .

"The white South had never known me — never known what I thought, what I felt. The white South said that I had a 'place' in life. Well, I had never felt my 'place'; or, rather, my deepest instincts had always made me reject the 'place' to which the white South had assigned me. It had never occurred to me that I was in any way an inferior being. And no word that I had ever heard fall from the lips of southern white men had ever made me really doubt the worth of my own humanity. . . . I had struggled to contain my seething anger. . . . But in what . . . ways had the South allowed me to be natural, to be real, to be myself, except in rejection, rebellion, and aggression?

"Not only had the southern whites not known me, but, more important still, as I had lived in the South I had not had the chance to learn who I was. The pressure of southern living kept me from being the kind of person that I might have been. I had been what my surroundings had demanded, what my family — conforming to the dictates of the whites above them — had exacted of me, and what the whites had said that I must be. Never being fully able to be myself, I had slowly learned that the South could recognize but a part of a man, could accept but a fragment of his personality, and all the rest — the best and deepest things of heart and mind — were tossed away in blind ignorance and hate.

"I was leaving the South to fling myself into the unknown, to meet other situations that would perhaps elicit from me other responses. And if I could meet enough of a different life, then, perhaps, gradually and slowly I might learn who I was, what I might be. I was not leaving the South to forget the South, but so that some day I might understand it, might come to know what its rigors had done to me, to its children. . . .

"So, in leaving, I was taking a part of the South to transplant in alien soil, to see if it could grow differently, if it could drink of new and cool rains, bend in strange winds, respond to the warmth of other suns, and, perhaps to bloom. . . . And if that miracle ever happened, then I would know that there was yet hope in that southern swamp of despair and violence, that light could emerge even out of the blackest of the southern night. I would know that the South too could overcome its fear, its hate, its cowardice, its heritage of guilt and blood, its burden of anxiety and compulsive cruelty.

"With ever watchful eyes and bearing scars, visible and invisible, I headed North, full of a hazy notion that life could be lived with dignity, that the personalities of others should not be violated, that men should be able to confront other men without fear or shame, and that if men were lucky in their living on earth they might win some redeeming meaning for their having struggled and suffered here beneath the stars." [11]

11. BLACK BOY, Richard Wright, New York: Harper & Bros., 1945, pp. 222, 226–28.

Plaint Into Psalm: How seldom do we risk all in the manner of a Richard Wright. How often do we wait until total catastrophe threatens, before we take action upon which we should long since have embarked. How frequently do we confront the world with our massively sorrowful plaints, unaccompanied by a single constructive deed, either in our own behalf, or that of others.

It is said, again and again, that we are alienated. From ourselves. From others. From the place in which we live, and the work that we do. We yearn for some paradisial utopia, ostensibly possessed of exalted justice, peace, and exemplary piety; of stability, purpose, tradition, and an absence of automation. It is only now, sounds the refrain in our forlorn and anxiety-ridden era of freedom, that we are strangers — unable to communicate with one another, pitilessly displaced — exiled from a state of perpetual bliss.

Bereft of identity, our psyches malfunction. We persecute and are persecuted. Overwhelmed by the cruelty of migrations, our relationships are disrupted. We are impotent in the face of crisis. We are so conditioned that we can experience only malaise — a feeling of emptiness, futility, guilt. We are delinquent, apathetic, lacking in dignity. Since love is absent from our lives, whatever we do is devoid of fulfillment.

There is a violent hitting out. We are haunted by the question of what might assist us: Non-violence, equality of opportunity, a less permissive state, a freshly authoritative church; the return of orthodoxy, traditionalism, the comfort of joint families? Psychiatry, hand-looms; a microscopically planned society (but by whom); artificially induced ecstasy, hallucination; astrology, magic?

Although diverse forms of suffering must be transcended in each age and place, it is doubtful whether the priests, kings, or holy men, the temples, cathedrals, rituals, the methods of production and distribution — indeed the entire social order of any other era — could have provided final answers to our plight.

To be sure there is, even now, recourse to sacred mantras, formulae, sects; to seemingly all-encompassing political platforms, intended obligingly to obliterate — with a sweeping gesture — whatever struggle, distress, or sense of loss we may undergo. But is it true that, in any epoch, there is an inevitable someone, or something, possessed of the supreme power blandly to resolve our every problem for us?

Why, it must be asked, when one of the major revolutions of our time has had to do, above all, with gaining liberation from constricting authority — as from excess of special privilege — should there be so large a chorus in our midst: *Waiting for Lefty, Waiting for Nothing, Waiting for Godot, Waiting for God?* Why must there be mere dependence, docility, or nihilism, on the one hand, or brutality, degradation, and blind fury on the other? For what do we wait, when the responsibility to behave in positive fashion lies within ourselves?

A price must be paid for every advance, as for every retrogression. So that what is of primary importance is to be clear about the nature of our task; to perform it, and not be deluded into believing that anything we achieve can ever be flawless. It is possible neither to plunge backward into an all-protective womb nor to proceed into a world utterly free of conflict.

We must eternally, fearlessly, question every value. We must question ourselves. But to succumb to the celebration of mere negation — to the cult of nothingness — is not the health of life-giving protest, but rather the banality, the illness, of negation itself.

One cannot for a moment suggest that our world is innocent of inflicting torture and destruction; of engaging in barbaric acts of oppression, depravity, murder. But what we lack increasingly is a sense of history. What we possess in excessive abundance is overintellectualized, abstract self-pity, blinding nostalgia, and misleading utopianism. War, tyranny, prejudice, dictatorship — the horror of inquisitions — have existed in the past, even as they do today. Which means only that the vaster their threat, the more intensive must be our opposing struggle.

We fail often to recall that ours is perhaps the first era during which the burden of what has been called the élite, falls relentlessly upon each of us. This is both a privilege and our greatest challenge. We have fought for the privilege. We must meet the challenge.

Nietzsche has said that God is dead. But now, of a sudden, his words are in danger of being understood in disturbingly literal fashion. Yes, Nietzsche asserted that God is dead. Yet does the phrase not succeed in helping to wipe the slate clean, so that out of the depths of each of us it may be possible to experience, as though for the first time, what the word God means, without restraint of preconception?

Of course we must attempt, with our every fiber, to create a world in which there will be the least possible anxiety and sense of alienation. *To help prevent such abominations from proliferating, wherever we are. To love. To have compassion for — to aid — to be one with — all who are afflicted, persecuted, dispossessed, endangered, or searching.* But not to mistake our opposition to what we abhor as being the whole of life. Neither to retreat, nor to become disoriented ourselves, in imitation of negation, but rather to affirm, to utilize our own untapped strength to the limit of our capacity.

To discover that life's meaning is life itself. To participate, with dedication, in the process of our own transformation, for only so can we possibly have significance for others.

No, the protective arms of another day or place are not outstretched to embrace and guard us. But then neither, we suspect, were they there for those who came before. Our predecessors survived — even as they created — in spite of every vicissitude. Just as our own land in its modern phase has been evolved primarily by the alienated, the displaced — their very achievement, despite all shortcomings, remaining cruelly unsung.

Whatever our difficulties, how dare we simply wait and lament? Or permit the opportunity to penetrate our own resources — trying though this may be — to go unheeded, unheralded? Is it not, in truth, our major task to metamorphose the hollowness of plaint, into the rich fullness of psalm? And then to bring the ennobling, caressing meaning of psalm over into life itself? It has been done before.

———————◆▶———————

There is the artist's affirmation of those who proceed against all odds — as reflected in the writing of Samuel Beckett: "I don't know, that's all words, never wake, all words, there's nothing else, you must go on, that's all I know, they're going to stop, I know that well, I can feel it, they're going to abandon me, it will be the silence, for a moment, a good few moments, or it will be mine, the lasting one, that didn't last, that still lasts, it will be I, you must go on, I can't go on, you must go on, I'll go on, you must say words, as long as there are any, until they find me, until they say me, strange pain, strange sin, you must go on, perhaps it's done already, perhaps they have said me already, perhaps they have carried me to the threshold of my story, before the door that opens on my story, that would surprise me, if it opens, it will be I, it will be the silence, where I am, I don't know, I'll never know, in the silence you don't know, you must go on, I can't go on, I'll go on." [12]

Of modern poetry: "It begs no favours of the times. Dedicated to its goal and free from all ideology, it knows itself to be the equal of life, which needs no self-justification. In one embrace, as in one great living strophe, it gathers to its present all the past and the future, the human and the superhuman, planetary space and total space. Its alleged obscurity is due, not to its own nature, which is to enlighten, but to the darkness which it explores, and must explore: the dark of the soul herself and the dark of the mystery which envelops human existence."

"Out of the poetic need, which is one of the spirit, all the religions have been born, and by the poetic grace the divine spark is kept eternally alight within the human flint. When the mythologies founder, it is in poetry that the divine finds its refuge, perhaps its relay stage. As, in the antique procession, the Bearers of bread were succeeded by the Bearers of torches, so now, in the social order and the immediacies of life it is the poetic image which rekindles the high passion of mankind in its quest for light. . . .

"Refusing to divorce art from life or love from knowledge, it is action, it is passion, it is power, a perpetual renewal that extends the boundaries. Love is its vital flame, independence is its law, and its domain is everywhere, an anticipation. It never wishes to be absence, nor refusal." [13]

ST.-JOHN PERSE

---

12. THE UNNAMABLE, written in French and translated into English by Samuel Beckett, New York: Grove Press, 1958, pp. 178–79.

13. "ON POETRY," translated by W. H. Auden, *Two Addresses,* Bollingen Series LXXXVI, New York: Pantheon Books, 1966, pp. 11–13.

19 EAST-WEST, WEST-EAST: *THE THINKER, MIROKU*

Nowhere, perhaps, are the purportedly dominant visions of East and West more clearly projected than in the dynamic figure of Rodin's *Thinker* and the calm and composed Japanese *Miroku*. (Plates 106–107.)

> *"Nature gives me my model, life and thought; the nostrils breathe, the heart beats, the lungs inhale, the being thinks, and feels, has pains and joys, ambitions, passions and emotions. These I must express. What makes my* Thinker *think is that he thinks not only with his brain, with his knitted brow, his distended nostrils and compressed lips, but with every muscle of his arms, back and legs, with his clenched fist and gripping toes."*

> *"The main thing is to feel emotion, to love, to hope, to quiver, to live."*

AUGUSTE RODIN

106. THE THINKER
   Bronze statue by Auguste Rodin. French.
   1880.

107. MIROKU
   Wood statue. Japanese. 7th century.
   Koryuji Temple, Kyoto.

"Rather abide at the center of your being; for the more you leave it, the less you learn."

LAO TZU

20 THE TEN OXHERDING PICTURES OF ZEN BUDDHISM..."ZEN IN THE ART OF ARCHERY"

"No man shall ever know
what is true blessedness
Till oneness overwhelm
and swallow separateness."

ANGELUS SILESIUS

"On action alone be thy interest,
Never on its fruits;
Let not the fruits of action be thy motive,
Nor be thy attachment to inaction."

BHAGAVAD GITA

To be convinced that what we name East and West represent opposite poles of vision is to find that no such extreme or rigid distinction is tenable. Whereas, initially, the famous Ten Oxherding Pictures appear to represent a totally Eastern concept, a more careful consideration of their meaning reveals how they express a profoundly universal view of life.

Kaku-an was neither the first nor the only artist to "illustrate by means of pictures stages of Zen discipline, for in his general preface to the pictures," as Dr. D. T. Suzuki has noted, "he refers to another Zen master called Seikyo (Ching-chu), probably a contemporary of his, who made use of the ox to explain his Zen teaching. But in Seikyo's case the gradual development of . . . Zen life was indicated by a progressive whitening of the animal, ending in the disappearance of the whole being. There were in this [series] only five pictures, instead of ten as by Kaku-an. Kaku-an thought this was somewhat misleading because of an empty circle being made the goal of Zen discipline. Some might take mere emptiness as all important and final. Hence his . . . 'Ten Oxherding Pictures' as we have them now." [1] (Plates 108–117.)

---

1. MANUAL OF ZEN BUDDHISM, Daisetz T. Suzuki, London: Rider and Company, 1956, pp. 127–28. (The Japanese term Zen stems from the Chinese transliteration *ch'an-na*, which in turn derives from the earlier Sanskrit *dhyana*.)

"The beast has never gone astray, and what is the use of searching for him? The reason why the oxherd is not on intimate terms with him is because the oxherd himself has violated his own inmost nature. The beast is lost, for the oxherd has himself been led out of the way through his deluding senses. Desire for gain and fear of loss burn like fire; ideas of right and wrong shoot up like a phalanx. Alone in the wilderness, lost in the jungle, the boy is searching, searching! Exhausted and in despair, he knows not where to go."

108. SEARCHING FOR THE OX
First of the Ten Oxherding Pictures, by Kaku-an Shi-en. Chinese. Sung dynasty, 960–1279.

"By inquiring into the doctrines, he has come to understand something, he has found the traces. He now knows that the objective world is a reflection of the Self. Yet, he is unable to distinguish what is good from what is not, his mind is still confused as to truth and falsehood. As he has not yet entered the gate, he is provisionally said to have noticed the traces."

109. SEEING THE TRACES

"The boy finds the way by the sound he hears; he sees thereby into the origin of things, and all his senses are in harmonious order. In all his activities, it is manifestly present .[It is there though not distinguishable as an individual entity.] When the eye is properly directed, he will find that it is no other than himself."

110. SEEING THE OX

"Long lost in the wilderness, the boy has at last found the ox and his hands are on him. But, owing to the overwhelming pressure of the outside world, the ox is hard to keep under control. The wild nature is still unruly, and altogether refuses to be broken. If the oxherd wishes to see the ox completely in harmony with himself, he has surely to use the whip freely. With the energy of his whole being, the boy has at last taken hold of the ox: But how wild his will, how ungovernable his power!"

111. CATCHING THE OX

"When a thought moves, another follows, and then another — an endless train of thoughts is thus awakened. Through enlightenment all this turns into truth; but falsehood asserts itself when confusion prevails. Things oppress us not because of an objective world, but because of a self-deceiving mind. The boy is not to separate himself with his whip and tether, lest the animal should wander away into a world of defilements; when the ox is properly tended to, he will grow pure and docile; without a chain, nothing binding, he will by himself follow the oxherd."

112. HERDING THE OX

"The struggle is over; the man is no more concerned with gain and loss. Saddling himself on the ox's back, his eyes are fixed on things not of the earth, earthy. Even if he is called, he will not turn his head; however enticed he will no more be kept back."

113. COMING HOME ON
THE OX'S BACK

"When you know that what you need is not the snare or set-net but the hare or fish, it is like gold separated from the dross. The one ray of light serene and penetrating shines even before days of creation. Riding on the animal, he is at last back in his home, where lo! the ox is no more; the man alone sits serenely. Though the red sun is high up he is still quietly dreaming, his whip and rope idly lying."

114. THE OX FORGOTTEN,
LEAVING THE MAN ALONE

"All confusion is set aside, and serenity alone prevails; even the idea of holiness does not obtain. He does not linger about where the Buddha is, and as to where there is no Buddha he speedily passes by. When there exists no form of dualism, even a thousand-eyed one fails to detect a loophole. Who can ever survey the vastness of heaven?"

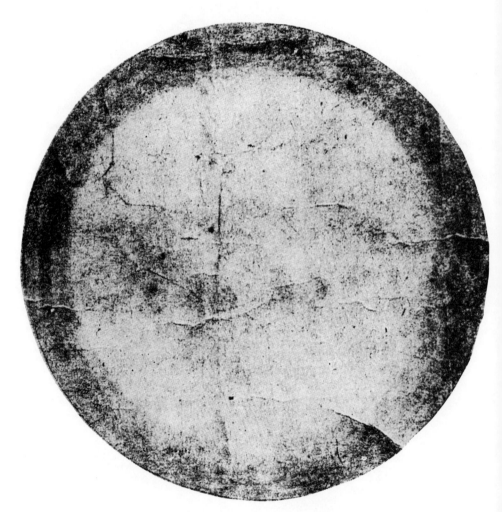

115. THE OX AND THE MAN
BOTH GONE OUT OF SIGHT

"The man watches the growth of things, while himself abiding in immovable serenity. Sitting alone, he observes things undergoing changes. To return to the Origin, to be back at the Source — already a false step this! Far better it is to stay at home, blind and deaf, and without much ado; sitting in the hut, he takes no cognisance of things outside, behold the streams flowing — whither nobody knows; and the flowers vividly red — for whom are they?"

116. RETURNING TO THE ORIGIN,
BACK TO THE SOURCE

"His thatched cottage gate is closed, and even the wisest know him not. No glimpses of his inner life are to be caught; for he goes on his own way without following the steps of the ancient sages. Carrying a gourd [symbol of emptiness] he goes out into the market, leaning against a staff he comes home. [No extra property he has, for he knows that the desire to possess is the curse of human life.] Bare-chested and bare-footed, he comes out into the market-place. There is no need for the miraculous power of the gods, for he touches, and lo! the dead trees are in full bloom." [2]

---

2. Ibid., pp. 129–34.

There can be no illusion that the oxherder should dominate the ox. The last three pictures must be viewed simultaneously: Only when a sense of non-dualism has been achieved — a feeling of harmony with oneself, with what one does, with the outer world — is one truly prepared to perform acts of any significance.

The figure shown at the end of the series holds in his ever-full sack that which may now be given freely, endlessly.

In a symbolical sense, to come to terms with the ox, as to slay a tyrant or dragon, is to develop one's own attributes in positive fashion; to release one's fullest creative potential. Not until such ends are attained can we grow beyond the limited aspects of the ego,[3] beyond the need to make merely willful and self-serving decisions.

———————◆▬—————

From Herrigel's *Zen in the Art of Archery* — a Contemporary Experience: [In conjunction with learning archery from a Zen master in Japan]: "I could not prevent my concentration from flagging at the very moment when the shot ought to come. Waiting at the point of highest tension not only became so tiring that the tension relaxed, but so agonizing that I was constantly wrenched out of my self-immersion and had to direct my attention to discharging the shot. 'Stop thinking about the shot!' the Master called out. 'That way it is bound to fail.' 'I can't help it,' I answered, 'the tension gets too painful.'

" 'You only feel it because you haven't really let go of yourself.' . . .

"In spite of everything I could do or did not do, I was unable to wait until the shot 'fell.' As before, I had no alternative but to loose it on purpose. And this obstinate failure depressed me all the more since I had already passed my third year of instruction. . . .

"We spent our summer holidays by the sea. . . . We had taken our bows with us as the most important part of our equipment. Day out and day in I concentrated on loosing the shot. This had become an *idée fixe,* which caused me to forget more and more the Master's warning that we

---

3. Because the integration of splintered or otherwise disturbed personalities is one of the major aims of the psychiatric or psychoanalytic process, it is often said that a patient's "ego" must be built up, so that he may properly function. When the word "ego" is employed in non-psychiatric fashion, it is generally associated with those obsessively preoccupied with themselves and their self-interest. (No effort has been made in this volume to utilize or define "ego" in specifically Freudian, Jungian, or any other technical terms.)

should not practice anything except self-detaching immersion. Turning all the possibilities over in my mind, I came to the conclusion that the fault could not lie where the Master suspected it: in lack of purposelessness and egolessness, but in the fact that the fingers of the right hand gripped the thumb too tight. The longer I had to wait for the shot, the more convulsively I pressed them together without thinking. It was at this point, I told myself, that I must set to work. And ere long I had found a simple and obvious solution to this problem. If, after drawing the bow, I cautiously eased the pressure of the fingers on the thumb, the moment came when the thumb, no longer held fast, was torn out of position as if spontaneously: in this way a lightning loose could be made and the shot would obviously 'fall like snow from a bamboo leaf'. . . .

"I was able to convince myself very quickly that I must be on the right track. Almost every shot went off smoothly and unexpectedly, to my way of thinking. Naturally I did not overlook the reverse side of this triumph: the precision work of the right hand demanded my full attention. But I comforted myself with the hope that this technical solution would gradually become so habitual that it would require no further notice from me, and that the day would come when, thanks to it, I would be in a position to loose the shot, self-obliviously and unconsciously, at the moment of highest tension, and that in this case the technical ability would spiritualize itself. Waxing more and more confident in this conviction I silenced the protest that rose up in me, ignored the contrary counsels of my wife, and went away with the satisfying feeling of having taken a decisive step forward.

"The very first shot I let off after the recommencement of the lessons was, to my mind, a brilliant success. The loose was smooth, unexpected. The Master looked at me for a while and then said hesitantly, like one who can scarcely believe his eyes: 'Once again, please!' My second shot seemed to me even better than the first. The Master stepped up to me without a word, took the bow from my hand, and sat down on a cushion, his back towards me. I knew what that meant, and withdrew.

"The next day Mr. [K.] informed me that the Master declined to instruct me any further because I had tried to cheat him. Horrified beyond measure by this interpretation of my behavior, I explained to Mr. [K.] why, in order to avoid marking time forever, I had hit upon this method of loosing the shot. On his interceding for me, the Master was finally prepared to give in, but made the continuation of the lessons conditional upon my express promise never to offend again against the spirit of the 'Great Doctrine.'

"If profound shame had not cured me, the Master's behavior would certainly have done so. He did not mention the incident by so much as a word, but only said quite quietly: 'You see what comes of not being able to wait without purpose in the state of highest tension. You cannot even learn to do this without continually asking yourself: Shall I be able to manage it? Wait patiently, and see what comes — and how it comes!'

"I pointed out to the Master that I was already in my fourth year and that my stay in Japan was limited.

" 'The way to the goal is not to be measured! Of what importance are weeks, months, years?'

" 'But what if I have to break off half way?' I asked.

" 'Once you have grown truly egoless you can break off at any time. Keep on practicing that.'

"And so we began again from the very beginning, as if everything I had learned hitherto had become useless. But the waiting at the point of highest tension was no more successful than before, as if it were impossible for me to get out of the rut.

"One day I asked the Master: 'How can the shot be loosed if "I" do not do it?'

" ' "It" shoots,' he replied.

" 'I have heard you say that several times before, so let me put it another way: How can I wait self-obliviously for the shot if "I" am no longer there?'

" ' "It" waits at the highest tension.'

" 'And who or what is this "It"?'

" 'Once you have understood that, you will have no further need of me. And if I tried to give you a clue at the cost of your own experience, I would be the worst of teachers and would deserve to be sacked! So let's stop talking about it and go on practicing.'

"Weeks went by without my advancing a step. At the same time I discovered that this did not disturb me in the least. Had I grown tired of the whole business? Whether I learned the art or not, whether I experienced what the Master meant by 'It' or not, whether I found the way to Zen or not — all this suddenly seemed to have become so remote, so indifferent, that it no longer troubled me. Several times I made up my mind to confide in the Master, but when I stood before him I lost courage; I was convinced that I would never hear anything but the monotonous answer: 'Don't ask, practice!' So I stopped asking, and would have liked to stop practicing, too, had not the Master held me inexorably in his grip. I lived from one day to the next, did my professional work as best I might, and in the end ceased to bemoan the fact that all my efforts of the last few years had become meaningless.

"Then, one day, after a shot, the Master made a deep bow and broke off the lesson. 'Just then "It" shot!' he cried, as I stared at him bewildered. And when I at last understood what he meant I couldn't suppress a sudden whoop of delight.

" 'What I have said,' the Master told me severely, 'was not praise, only a statement that ought not to touch you. Nor was my bow meant for you, for you are entirely innocent of this shot. You remained this time absolutely self-oblivious and without purpose in the highest tension, so that the shot fell from you like a ripe fruit. Now go on practicing as if nothing had happened.'

"Only after a considerable time did more right shots occasionally come off, which the Master signalized by a deep bow. How it happened that they loosed themselves without my doing anything, how it came about that my tightly closed right hand suddenly flew back wide open, I could not explain then and I cannot explain today. The fact remains that it did happen, and that alone is important." [4]

---

4. ZEN IN THE ART OF ARCHERY, Eugen Herrigel, translated by R. F. C. Hull, New York: Pantheon Books, 1953, pp. 72–78. The shot was rightly loosed without Herrigel having been aware of it, only because the time was ripe for this to occur. So, also, in the tale of Snow-White (see end of Chapter 15), the poisoned half of the apple was effortlessly dislodged, as a result of a seeming "accident" that could not have taken place in meaningful fashion until just that moment, and in just such unplanned manner. There is a Japanese saying: "Just this this."

21 BEYOND COMBAT... FURTHER REFLECTIONS ON THE RELATIONSHIP BETWEEN EAST AND WEST

"Let others systematise indifference and let them expel charity from history. I shall never understand how anyone can in the narration of human errors and suffering, not take the side of weakness against oppressive force and of poverty against the drunken pride of opulence."

LOUIS BLANC

Of Psalm 12 of the Old Testament: "God says that seeing the oppression of the poor, and hearing the sighing of the needy, He will 'now' arise. With this 'now' there breaks out in the midst of extreme trouble the manifestation of a salvation which is not just bound to come some time, but is always present and needs only to become effective. This 'now' is the decisive prophetic category. The 'day of the Lord,' on which the enthroned One 'arises,' and for terror and for rapture reveals his kingdom, which was the hidden meaning of creation from the beginning, is, in the power of the prophetic vision, this very present day. The Psalmists, who here as often prove themselves to be the heirs of this vision, know that the 'arising' means both judgement and 'the freeing of all the oppressed of the earth' (Ps. 76, 10). Our Psalm is specially emphatic that this judgement and this freeing are not two events, but one."

MARTIN BUBER

No conflict is shown between St. Jerome and the lion in Plate 118, but rather a feeling of compassion for the wounded creature. Jerome resembles the Oxherder (see Chapter 20) who, having achieved his own integration, is enabled to offer his overflowing gift to those who seek— much as Krishna, in the image that follows, protects his fellow-beings from the demon Aghasura.

"Jerome, a man learned in the holy scriptures, left the life of cities and went into the desert where 'he suffered for Christ's sake.' He slept on the bare earth, 'fellow unto scorpions and wild beasts.' He was often tempted by thoughts of 'the carols of maidens and the embracements' of the flesh, so that he beat his breast and prayed the Lord for peace. At last, after 'many weepings and tears' it seemed to him that he 'was among the company of angels' and thus was his penance done." [1]

With regard to the painting of Jerome healing a lion: "One day, as evening was drawing on, and Jerome sat with [his] brethren to hear the sacred lessons, suddenly a lion came limping into the monastery. At the sight of him all the other monks fled, but Jerome went forward to meet him as a host his guest. The lion then showed . . . his wounded foot, whereupon [Jerome] called the brothers and ordered them to wash the lion's feet and to dress his wound with care. When they did this, they found that the lion's pads were wounded by thorns. By their care, however, the foot was healed, and the lion, losing all his wildness, lived among them as a tame beast." [2]

1. THE BELLES HEURES OF JEAN, DUKE OF BERRY, PRINCE OF FRANCE, New York: The Metropolitan Museum of Art, 1958, description of Plate 19.

2. de Voragine, op. cit., p. 589.

118. SAINT JEROME
IN THE DESERT
Painting by Rogier van der Weyden. Flemish.
c. 1450. The Detroit Institute of Arts.

119. KRISHNA KILLING
AGHASURA
Painting, Mewar School. Indian. Early 18th
century. Collection Stella Kramrisch,
Philadelphia.

Krishna, through his heroic powers, saved those whom the fierce demon Aghasura (at times called Ugrasura) would otherwise have devoured. (Plate 119.)

The demon Aghasura beheld Krishna and others[3] who, "filled with love came out in great delight taking more than a thousand calves before them" in the forest. Aghasura was "unable to bear seeing their delightful" sport.

Having resolved to slay Krishna, his friends, and the calves, and having assumed the form of a huge snake, the wily demon planned to devour his victims "with an expanded mouth like unto the cave of a mountain." His lower lip extended to the earth, his upper one to the clouds. His teeth "were like the summits of a mountain." The interior of his mouth was "like darkness," and his "tongue was the road thereof." His breath was the dreadful wind. His "eyes looked as hot as the forest fire."

Krishna's companions, mistaking Aghasura's identity, and "looking at the beautiful face of Krishna" instead, clapped their hands, smiling, and entered the mouth of the demon. Krishna's friends and their calves were not in truth devoured, however, for the monster was awaiting Krishna himself who, meanwhile, was "surprised and stricken with agony" because of what was taking place. Then, deciding how his adversary could be demolished, and those in danger saved, Krishna entered Aghasura's mouth, speedily increasing his own form. When the demon's throat was obstructed, his eyes burst out of their sockets, and he "began to run about hither and thither." The wind inside his body "issued out, riving" his head. Krishna, on the contrary, recovering, raised his friends and their calves with a look, finally coming forth from Aghasura's mouth with his companions.

---

3. See THE SRIMAD-BHAGABATAM, Vol. IV, pp. 49–51.

22 THE RUNG AND
THE JOURNEY

Unification: "*Just as all worlds, the good and the evil, are comprised in the Divine Presence, so they were comprised in Moses. When God spoke to Moses for the first time, he did not answer: 'Here I am,' because he was stricken with wonder: how can unification come to pass? For when God revealed himself in the thornbush, that is to say, in evil, in the lowest rung, all the wells of fire gushed forth from the summit down to the depths — yet the thornbush did not burn; evil was not consumed. How could this be? But God called a second time: 'Moses!' And then the lowest and the highest rung linked within Moses himself, and he said: 'Here I am.'*"

Signs: "*This whole world is a cloak for the lowest rung of holiness, for its feet, as it were. As it is written: 'And the earth is my footstool.' God limits the godliness he has in infinity, and narrows it down to the focus of the material world in which man exists. And there he assigns every man his thought and word and deed according to the day, the place, and the person.*"

Let Everyone Cry out to God: "*Let everyone cry out to God and lift his heart up to him, as if he were hanging by a hair, and a tempest were raging to the very heart of heaven, and he were at a loss for what to do, and there were hardly time to cry out. It is a time when no counsel, indeed, can help a man and he has no refuge*

120. **MOSES AND THE
   BURNING BUSH**
Etching, with watercolor. American. 1827.
Collection Dorothy Norman, New York.

save to remain in his loneliness and lift his eyes and his heart up to
God, and cry out to him. And this should be done at all times, for
in the world a man is in great danger."

"When man is tried, all the rungs and all holiness are taken from
him. Stripped of everything he has attained, he stands face to face
with God who is putting him to the test." [1]

MARTIN BUBER

"For the kingdom of heaven is as a man travelling into a far coun-
try."

ST. MATTHEW 25:14

Jacob "dreamed, and behold a ladder set up on the earth, and the top of it reached to heaven: and behold the angels of God ascending and descending on it. . . . And Jacob awaked out of his sleep, and he said, Surely the Lord is in this place; and I knew it not. And he was afraid, and said, How dreadful is this place! this is none other but the house of God, and this is the gate of heaven." [2] (Plate 121.)

---

1. TEN RUNGS, pp. 91, 23, 27, 72.
2. GENESIS 28:12,16–17.

121. JACOB'S LADDER
Illumination from book of Old Testament
illustrations. Ms. 638, folio 4. French.
c. 1250. The Pierpont Morgan Library,
New York.

The miniature (Plate 122) relates to a prose romance[3] in which, at the end of Lancelot's journey to the prison of Guenevere, he "came to a river across which lay the castle where the queen was held."

The waters were "as swift and raging . . . black and turgid" — as fierce and terrible — as though they comprised "the devil's stream." The river was, in fact, "so dangerous and bottomless that anything falling into it would be as completely lost as if it fell into the salt sea." The bridge, which spanned the waters, was different from any other bridge, in that it consisted "of a polished, gleaming sword."

Two lions, writes Margaret Scherer, seemed "to guard the further end" of the bridge. Lancelot removed "the armor from his hands and feet to [secure] a firmer grasp of the blade," and thus passed "over with great pain and agony, being wounded in the hands, knees, and feet. But even this suffering" was sweet to him, for Love, who conducted and led him on, assuaged and relieved his pain. "Creeping on his hands, feet, and knees," he proceeded until he reached the other side of the bridge. He then remembered the lions, "but they were nowhere to be seen."

Similar phenomena occur frequently in myth. When the hero reaches a certain point in his quest, he no longer permits himself to be deflected. Hitherto formidable problems and obstacles consequently disappear or, as it is sometimes said, the gods intercede to bring aid.

In the myth of Eros and Psyche, when the latter must enter the nether-world — one of her final labors — she is warned to take a honey cake in each of her hands; to throw one to the hideous dog Cerberus upon entering the gate, the other when leaving. Under no circumstances should she

---

3. This account is based on Scherer, op. cit., pp. 53–54.

22. LANCELOT CROSSING THE
SWORD BRIDGE
From manuscript illumination. French.
c. 1310. The Pierpont Morgan Library,
New York.

permit either of the cakes to slip out of her hands, else she will be forever imprisoned in the Land of the Shades. When Psyche summons the courage to undertake the dreadful journey, she goes along a dark road until she reaches the gloomy twilight of the underworld. Presently she meets a lame man driving a lame, heavily laden ass. He holds up a burden falling from the ass, pleading with Psyche in a piteous voice to give him a piece of rope, so that he may attach the burden with it. It is difficult for the tender-hearted Psyche to refuse, but she cannot acquiesce unless she disregards the warning not to drop her honey cakes. She passes on without replying, whereupon the man and the ass vanish.[4]

Although, at first glance, Psyche's attitude may seem cold and insensitive, the very fact that the one requesting assistance immediately disappears proves the paramount importance of Psyche's own mission, with which nothing must be allowed to interfere. In like manner, Lancelot need no longer encounter the lions guarding the further end of the bridge he crosses, as described above, once he has traversed the treacherous span. In the case of Psyche, she has learned to discriminate; in that of Lancelot, he has conquered his fear.

The anguish caused by ignoring what arouses our compassion can be quite as great as that created by relinquishing what is most precious to us.

The task of the hero is infinite and complex. His initiation into successive phases of life — *his rites of passage* — are not to be hurried. His voyage, which is never-ending, dare not be interrupted. It must continue in the ever-present now. Let there be a turning back, and the fate of Orpheus and Eurydice, or of Lot's wife, will inevitably result. If the sacred commands are broken — as when Psyche looks upon Eros, or Elsa asks the name of Lohengrin, or Adam and Eve eat of the forbidden fruit — a most searing bereavement is suffered; most arduous labors are assigned, in order that growth toward more profound awareness will take place.

Failure to move onward, even for what may seem the highest of motives, is prohibited. Thus the Buddha, himself, when he hesitates to put into motion the Wheel of the Law — thinking it will lead to misunder-

---

4. See MYTHS OF HELLAS, C. Witt, translated by Frances Younghusband, London: Longmans, Green, and Co., 1915, pp. 240–41.

standing — is told by the gods that if he does not do so, the world will be lost.[5] Christ, too, in spite of knowing that He will be betrayed, has no choice but to enact His magnificently selfless, sacrificial role.

The desert, wilderness, wasteland — the valley of the shadow of death — must be endured; the impassable rivers and seas must be safely forded. The hero is cast into the pit, abyss, chasm, cavern, ark, and tomb. But only in order to transcend them, reborn, redeemed.

There are the numberless tenuous bridges to be crossed; the endless succession of ladders to ascend and descend; the clashing rocks and active doors between which we must pass with lightning speed. There are the floating islands to be transformed into firm ground, the twisted paths to be straightened, the ways that are closed to be opened, the darkness to be made light.

The hero-deed is an incessant tying of the knots that embrace, encompass, complete; the fashioning of the ropes to which we can hold fast; the weaving of the tissue that alone gives form and substance to our lives. But we dare not become wrongly dependent upon the fabric made by others, since unless we ourselves ultimately establish what sustains, we shall be bound, rather than liberated.

The thread of the spirit is most exceedingly fragile. The way to be traveled is as delicately modeled as the sharpest razor's edge. Thus we are released or enslaved during our pilgrimage — whether upon mountain heights or within direst depths — in direct proportion to how clearly we comprehend what is demanded of us; how fully we come to know who we are, and act in accordance with whatever wisdom we may gain.[6]

In India, there are "places of pilgrimage" beside the waters. "The purifying, fertilizing element" of water "being present, its current which is the river of life can be forded in inner realisation and the pilgrim can cross over to the other shore. The place of pilgrimage is the end of the journey to the Centre; but it is not itself the goal and only the means for crossing over to the Centre." [7]

---

5. See Coomaraswamy, HINDUISM AND BUDDHISM, p. 54.

6. I am indebted to the writing of both Dona Luisa and Ananda K. Coomaraswamy for various of the insights contained in the above sequence.

7. THE HINDU TEMPLE, Stella Kramrisch, Calcutta: University of Calcutta, 1946, Vol. I, p. 3.

Ithaca

"When you start on your journey to Ithaca,
then pray that the road is long,
full of adventure, full of knowledge.
Do not fear the Lestrygonians
and the Cyclopes and the angry Poseidon.
You will never meet such as these on your path,
if your thoughts remain lofty, if a fine
emotion touches your body and your spirit.
You will never meet the Lestrygonians,
the Cyclopes and the fierce Poseidon,
if you do not carry them within your soul,
if your soul does not raise them up before you.

"Then pray that the road is long,
That the summer mornings are many,
that you will enter ports seen for the first time
with such pleasure, with such joy!
Stop at Phoenician markets,
and purchase fine merchandise,
mother-of-pearl and corals, amber and ebony,
and pleasurable perfumes of all kinds,
buy as many pleasurable perfumes as you can;
visit hosts of Egyptian cities,
to learn and learn from those who have knowledge.

"Always keep Ithaca fixed in your mind.
To arrive there is your ultimate goal.
But do not hurry the voyage at all.
It is better to let it last for long years;
and even to anchor at the isle when you are old,
rich with all that you have gained on the way,
not expecting that Ithaca will offer you riches.

"Ithaca has given you the beautiful voyage.
Without her you would never have taken the road.
But she has nothing more to give you.

"And if you find her poor, Ithaca has not defrauded you.
With the great wisdom you have gained, with so much experience,
you must surely have understood by then what Ithacas mean." [8]

C. P. CAVAFY

---

8. Copyright, 1949, by Rae Dalven. Reprinted from THE COMPLETE POEMS OF CAVAFY, translated by Rae Dalven, by permission of Harcourt, Brace & World, Inc., New York, pp. 36–37.

Gilgamesh: Later Assyrian and Babylonian versions of the Sumerian *Epic of Gilgamesh* delineate the heroic quest in most subtle manner.

Gilgamesh,[9] born two-thirds god and one-third human, is described as wise and all-seeing in the first instance. He reigns over Uruk, whose foundations, it is said, were laid by the Seven Sages who brought civilization to seven of the oldest cities of the land. But it is Gilgamesh, himself, who builds there a great sanctuary — dwelling of Ishtar, goddess of love.

When the illustrious ruler subsequently becomes arrogant, plaguing his subjects in overbearing manner, the latter implore the gods to bring to earth one who can match the by-now-stormy heart of Gilgamesh, so that there may be peace in Uruk. Whereupon the valiant and shaggy-haired Enkidu is created to be the double of, and to contend with, the too-bold king.

Even as the ruthless acts of Gilgamesh must be curbed, so it is necessary to raise Enkidu — born to feed with the gazelles on grass and to jostle with wild beasts — to human stature.

Before the two heroic figures encounter one another, Gilgamesh reveals to his mother, the wise Ninsun, certain dreams he has had that greatly

---

9. The following summary of various incidents described in the EPIC OF GILGAMESH is based on Akkadian texts translated by E. A. Speiser, in ANCIENT NEAR EASTERN TEXTS RELATING TO THE OLD TESTAMENT, edited by James B. Pritchard, Princeton: Princeton University Press, 1955, pp. 73 ff.

The epic is divided into twelve tablets. "All but a few of the Akkadian texts come from the library of Ashurbanipal at Nineveh. . . . The Gilgamesh Epic is known also from versions which antedate the first millennium B.C. From the middle of the second millennium have come down fragments of an Akkadian recension current in the Hittite Empire, and the same Bogazkoy archives have yielded also important fragments of a Hittite translation, as well as a fragment of a Hurrian rendering. . . . From the first half of the second millennium we possess representative portions of the Old Babylonian version of the epic, which pertains to Tablets I–III, and X. That this version was itself a copy of an earlier text is suggested by the internal evidence of the material. The original date of composition of the Akkadian work has to be placed at the turn of the second millennium, if not slightly earlier.

"The connection between the Epic of Gilgamesh as we know it in its Akkadian form, and its various Sumerian analogues, has been clarified in recent years. . . . It has been demonstrated that Tablet XII is not of a piece with the other eleven tablets of the poem, but is instead a literal translation from the Sumerian. The epic proper, on the other hand, while utilizing certain motifs . . . featured in Sumerian poems, does so largely in the course of developing a central theme that has no Sumerian prototype. In other words, the first eleven tablets of the Akkadian poem of Gilgamesh constitute an instance of creative borrowing which, substantially, amounts to an independent creation." (Ibid., pp. 72–73.)

The term Akkadian "is now generally applied to the Semitic language spoken in the countries commonly known as Assyria and Babylonia; Assyrian and Babylonian, the terms formerly used to designate this language, are the names of the two best-known dialects of the [Akkadian] language." ("Sumerian Mythology," Samuel Noah Kramer, MEMOIRS OF THE AMERICAN PHILOSOPHICAL SOCIETY, Philadelphia, Vol. XXI, 1944, p. 107n^3.)

√ trouble him. In each of them rivals appear he fears will be too mighty for him. He is nonetheless drawn to them as to a woman.

When Gilgamesh describes what he subconsciously dreads, yet desires, his mother replies as in the name of all goddesses who give birth to the √ hero, that she herself has created the problems he must resolve. Moreover, the demons Gilgamesh envisions resemble various dragons of myth that stand guard over treasure of difficult access sought by the hero, but which he is not yet fully prepared to attain.

√ Both Gilgamesh's dreams, and what his mother tells him, reflect his { own still unresolved conflicts — conflicts symbolized by such a labyrinthine and terrifying face as that of Humbaba.[10]

Ninsun explains to her son that what has been so horrifying to him prefigures not at all the emergence of a destructive being, but rather a "stout comrade" who will rescue a friend. For the moment, through the ✗ very act of bringing his dreams into the light of day, the source of Gilgamesh's torment disappears.

II.

When Enkidu reaches Uruk, and the subjects of Gilgamesh recount the misdeeds of their unconscionable ruler, it is hoped that the "animal-man" will succeed in taming the king. Ironically, Enkidu, who, in the process of becoming humanized, has just had his initial relationship with woman — a "harlot-lass" — bars the gate to Gilgamesh when, in the night, the latter approaches Ishhara (a form of the goddess Ishtar), whose "bed is laid out." Whereupon the two men grapple with one another, "holding fast like bulls." They shatter the doorpost. The wall shakes. But then, even as Gilgamesh's terror had vanished when he understood his dreams, so now, as he bends his knee before Enkidu, his fury abates. Thenceforth, as has been foretold, the being brought to earth to diminish the pride of the great √ hero — and whom the psyche of Gilgamesh has feared — becomes his beloved and staunch companion.

After the friendship of Enkidu and Gilgamesh is warmly established,

---

10. Huwawa, in the Old Babylonian version, is Humbaba in the Assyrian recension. (See Plate 68 in Chapter 12.)

the latter determines to undertake an expedition against the monstrous Humbaba, who resides in the Cedar Forest to guard it at the behest of the storm god, Enlil. Enkidu strongly disapproves of Gilgamesh's plan.

Again, as in his dreams already recounted, Gilgamesh is eager to perform an act he is not yet prepared to accomplish. Although, unlike Ninsun, Enkidu sighs and weeps,[11] Gilgamesh must nonetheless attempt, in typically heroic fashion, to gain the treasure on which his heart is set, at whatever the risk. He must overcome his fears and resolve his gnawing conflicts, if he is to develop in positive manner.

Enkidu cautions Gilgamesh about what he has himself discovered while roaming the hills with wild beasts, namely that the forest in which the fierce Humbaba resides extends for ten thousand leagues. Ignoring this fact, as well as Enkidu's further admonitions about the invincibility of the monster, and about his very breath being death, Gilgamesh remains intent upon "tangling with" Humbaba, saying to Enkidu: "[The cedar] — its mountain I would scale!"

From Gilgamesh's viewpoint, his desire to slay Humbaba involves ridding the land of evil. From the perspective of the gods, Humbaba has been appointed to safeguard the Cedar Forest, which is a terror to mortals.

As he sets forth on his perilous journey to confront Humbaba, Gilgamesh is advised not to trust merely his own strength. He is urged to rely, instead, upon Enkidu's going before him, as a means of protection.

When finally all opposition abates — including that of Enkidu — the two friends approach the gate of the forest guarded by Humbaba's watchman. Once again, rather than being pleased with his comrade's venture, Enkidu objects to it. Yet, as he opens the gate, it is his own hand that prophetically becomes limp.

Gilgamesh implores his companion not to fear death, adding that even if the resolute fall, still they will "have made a name" for themselves.

When the two comrades arrive at the forest — at the green mountain

---

11. In view of the findings of contemporary psychoanalysis and psychiatry, it is significant that, whereas the incidents about which Gilgamesh first dreams are consistently frightening to him — but are interpreted in propitious manner by his mother, who has created the obstacles to be surmounted — his friend, Enkidu, who sets none of the problems with which he must contend, discourages Gilgamesh from embarking upon the exploits the latter hopes to carry out. Clearly Ninsun and Enkidu represent antithetical, yet nonetheless interdependent, projections of Gilgamesh's own psyche.

— their words are silenced. They gaze upon "the height of the cedars . . . the entrance to the forest." They behold both the path upon which Humbaba is wont to walk, and "the cedar mountain, abode of the gods — throne-seat" of one of the many aspects of Ishtar. Whereupon Gilgamesh again dreams.

III.

Mountain gorges appear in the dreams of Gilgamesh. A mountain topples. The fairest man in the land pulls the great hero from under the massive weight, gives him water to drink, quiets his heart, and sets his feet upon the ground.

Is it because Gilgamesh is at last truly prepared to embark on his quest that his dreams are now promising, and even Enkidu interprets what has been envisioned in favorable light? Or is it just because what is foreshadowed seems propitious, that Gilgamesh must beware? (Noting that the mountain Gilgamesh has glimpsed is Humbaba, Enkidu predicts that, together, he and his comrade will seize the monstrous figure and destroy him.)

After the two friends dig a well in the depths, before the sun god, Shamash, Gilgamesh ascends the mountain he has aspired to climb. But then there is a still further dream — this time a terrifying one — in which a cold shower passes over. Startled, Gilgamesh cries out to Enkidu: "My friend, didst thou not call me? . . . Didst thou not touch me? . . . Did not some god go by? Why is my flesh numb?"

In a subsequent vision the heavens shriek, the earth booms, daylight fails, darkness comes. Lightning flashes, a flame shoots upward, death is rained from the heavens. The glow vanishes, the fire goes out, and all that has fallen is turned to ash.

IV.

When Gilgamesh finally fells the cedar with a mighty axe, Humbaba hears the noise and becomes angry. He demands to know who has slighted what is grown in his mountains; who "has felled the cedar?" But, from heaven, the god Shamash addresses Gilgamesh and Enkidu: "Draw near. ✓ Fear you not." [12]

In answer to Gilgamesh's prayer, the gods send mighty winds against Humbaba, so that he is unable to move either forward or backward. When the fierce figure's resistance ultimately ceases, he asks to be released by Gilgamesh, acknowledging the king as his master, and promising to be a servant to him. Enkidu warns Gilgamesh not to pay heed to Humbaba's words. Whereupon the head of the demon is "cut down."

V.

Gilgamesh, who garbs himself freshly and magnificently, after the successful battle against Humbaba, is an object of such radiant beauty that the goddess of love — Ishtar — glancing upon him, beseeches him to become her husband, promising lavish rewards. Refusing to be tempted by her advances, Gilgamesh recounts how faithlessly she has behaved toward former lovers. Enraged at his rejection and insults, Ishtar mounts to the sky, imploring that the Bull of Heaven be created, in order to smite Gilgamesh in revenge.

When the Bull of Heaven descends to earth, killing hundreds of men, Enkidu seizes it by the horns. Gilgamesh and he slay the Bull, tearing out its heart. They place it before Shamash, paying homage to the god. Although Ishtar continues to curse Gilgamesh for his treatment of her, when the people of Uruk gather to gaze upon their mighty ruler and his companion Enkidu, they call Gilgamesh the "most splendid among the heroes."

After a celebration in the palace, Enkidu describes a dream he has had to Gilgamesh, in which the gods have convened because the two friends have slain Humbaba and the Bull of Heaven. Although one of the gods proclaims that he who has stripped the mountains of the cedar must die, Enlil declares it is Enkidu, rather than Gilgamesh, who must perish.

---

12. Here, as in the case of various other tablets, a fragment is mutilated. As E. A. Speiser indicates, matters are not going well for the two friends. It is then that Gilgamesh weeps, and prays to Shamash.

As Enkidu falls ill, Gilgamesh — tears streaming down his cheeks — cries out: "O my brother, my dear brother! Me they would clear at the expense of my brother!"

Enkidu has another unfavorable dream, and then his suffering increases. Lying stricken on his bed for a number of days, he reviews his life, noting regretfully, "Not like one fallen in battle shall I die. For I feared the battle. My friend, he who is slain in battle is blessed. But as for me. . . ." Despite his self-doubt, the death of Enkidu has momentous consequences: It arouses the most profound compassion within Gilgamesh, even as it awakens him to the full knowledge that he too will die.

VI.

Gilgamesh, who was first all-wise, and then destructively overbearing, has at last become warmly human, because of the loss of his beloved comrade. And, even as Enkidu originally journeyed over steppes and through forests with animals, now that he is no more, the proud ruler of Uruk, himself, sets forth, also to roam far and wide. But whereas Enkidu, during his wanderings, had been elevated to the stature of man, Gilgamesh aims to attain something far more extraordinary: eternal life. His goal is to find Utnapishtim, the Mesopotamian hero of the Flood — the Sumerian Ziusudra, the Greek Xisouthros — possessor of the secret of immortality.

Despite being advised concerning the difficulty of his quest, Gilgamesh proceeds through dense darkness, toward the rising and then the setting of the sun. He is told to go forth into the mountains to find what he seeks, even though he can see nothing either ahead or behind. Dawn finally breaks when he has proceeded eleven leagues. The sky becomes bright as he reaches the end of the twelfth. He thereupon emerges into a grove of stones, where the "carnelian bears its fruit." There are vines good to look at, as is the lush fruit and the foliage of the lapis.

The god Shamash, however, is distraught. He asks Gilgamesh whither he roves, warning: "The life thou pursuest thou shalt not find."

Having wept and lamented for seven days and nights over the death of Enkidu, Gilgamesh asks Shamash whether he must himself also ultimately lay his head in the heart of the earth and sleep through all the years? "Let mine eyes behold the sun," pleads Gilgamesh, so "that I may have my fill of the light! Darkness withdraws when there is enough light. May one who indeed is dead behold yet the radiance of the sun!"

Continuing to roam the steppe like a hunter, Gilgamesh finally encounters an ale-wife,[13] who addresses him: "When the gods created mankind, Death for mankind they set aside, Life in their own hands retaining. Thou, Gilgamesh, let full be thy belly, Make thou merry by day and by night. Of each day make thou a feast of rejoicing, Day and night dance thou and play! Let thy garments be sparkling fresh, Thy head be washed; bathe thou in water. Pay heed to the little one that holds on to thy hand, Let thy spouse delight in thy bosom! For this is the task of (mankind)!"

As Gilgamesh wanders ever further afield, he is asked repeatedly why, if he has conquered Humbaba, has slain lions in mountain passes, and has succeeded in seizing and slaying the Bull of Heaven, his face is so sunken, his heart so sad, his features so worn. His reply is ever the same: There is woe within him. His face is like that of a wayfarer from afar, because his younger friend who had accompanied him on his various exploits, and had undergone so many hardships with him, has been overtaken by the fate of all mankind. "How can I be still?" asks Gilgamesh, now that the companion he loved has turned to clay: "Must I, too, like him," he inquires, "lay me down, not to rise again for ever and ever?"

It is the ale-wife who tells Gilgamesh to approach the boatman Urshanabi, and, if it seems suitable, to cross with him to Utnapishtim. If not, she adds, "draw thou back." After experiencing many difficulties, Gilgamesh and the boatman arrive at the Waters of Death.

His destination reached, Gilgamesh, hoping finally to learn the secret of immortality, inquires of Utnapishtim, "the Faraway," why one no different from himself has been permitted to join the Assembly of the gods.

Utnapishtim describes how he has forsworn worldly goods and kept his soul alive. He tells of having taken the seed of all living things aboard

13. It has been said that the term Siduri — the name of the ale-wife Gilgamesh encounters during his journey — is a "Hurrian term for 'young woman' used to describe Hebat, [still another] . . . form of Ishtar in the Hurrian texts." (ANCIENT NEAR EASTERN TEXTS RELATING TO THE OLD TESTAMENT, p. 89.)

the ship he had built, in order to weather the flood produced by the gods.[14]
He then helpfully instructs Gilgamesh not to lie down to sleep for six days
and seven nights. If Gilgamesh, it has been suggested, could "master sleep,
the twin brother of death," he might also master death itself.[15]

Although Gilgamesh fails to stay awake, Utnapishtim further yields to
the mighty hero's passionate desire to attain immortality, promising to
disclose a hidden thing, "a secret of the gods." Utnapishtim speaks of a
plant whose thorns will prick the hand, just as does the rose, but if Gilgamesh can obtain it, the hero will find new life.

Gilgamesh finally succeeds in discovering the plant. Yet, when he sees
"a well whose water" is cool, and goes to bathe in it, a serpent, snuffing the
fragrance of the plant, comes up from the water and carries off the treasure. Going back, the serpent sheds its skin — an act symbolical of rejuve-
nation. For Gilgamesh, however, the theft is so disastrous, he "sits down
and weeps." (Is it not possible, however, that he failed to remain awake,
and went to bathe in the cool waters, because life itself beckoned to him
more strongly than the plant he permitted to elude him?)

Having failed to attain his goal, Gilgamesh takes the hand of the boatman, Urshanabi, admitting at last that he should terminate his quest. Also
having failed to hold fast to the secret of immortality, he accepts the human condition, seeking no solace, but reentering his own realm, to pursue
the role that is his, if only he will carry it out responsibly.

At one level the epic ends dramatically, where it began. Yet it is a record, too, of extraordinary development.

Utnapishtim has attained immortality. But he is "faraway," and lies in-
dolent. It is implied that Gilgamesh, on the other hand, will continue to
function in the midst of life. More aware — with eyes opened — as a result of the complex experiences he has undergone — he ceases to be arrogant. He no longer questions the immutable laws of life.[16]

---

14. For full details about Utnapishtim and the Flood — which throws much light on the later Biblical account of
Noah and the Ark — see ibid., pp. 93–95.

15. THE GILGAMESH EPIC AND OLD TESTAMENT PARALLELS, Alexander Heidel, Chicago: The University of
Chicago Press, 1958, p. 9.

16. Since Tablet XII, which has to do with the netherworld, and with the reappearance of Enkidu, seems not to
be a direct continuation of the other eleven tablets, the episodes it describes have been omitted.

VII.

The *Epic of Gilgamesh* reflects a pulsating, rhythmic relationship between darkness and light, life and death, pride and humility. It by no means describes a merely straight and inanimate line, involving, as it does, movement, grandeur, victory, and defeat; flux, aspiration, and tragedy; struggle, paradox, affirmation. Gilgamesh contends with himself as with external forces that hamper his growth. He reaches the greatest of heights, only to fall into deepest despair. He performs deeds considered impossible of achievement, yet ultimately accepts the limits of man.

The heroic Gilgamesh mediates between heaven and earth. He holds our interest because he is a complete personage. He is sorrowful as well as joyous, both extrovert and introvert. As the epic opens, he is all-wise. Although he becomes crudely overbearing and irresponsible, in the end he attains wisdom once more.

Constantly searching, although he temporarily loses his way, Gilgamesh possesses the capacity to find it again, and to continue with his search. As his comprehension increases, he attempts to act in accordance with what he understands.

In the case of Gilgamesh and Enkidu, as in that of Eve and Adam, whereas the one moves toward what tempts, the other resists. Duality is implied, yet, just because of clash, contrast, and interdependence; antithesis, synthesis, and reversal, a sense of discrimination and relationship evolves.

From one point of view, although Enkidu is a projection of certain aspects of Gilgamesh, he must also tame and warn the hero. Enkidu is cautious and protective. Gilgamesh is the visionary — ever-striving. He advances fearlessly, despite the making of errors and being periodically frustrated in various of his quests.

Enkidu causes Gilgamesh to become aware it is not possible simply to ride roughshod over others; that merely to do everything one pleases, oneself, is to make the life of others a living hell.

Initially, Enkidu, a creature of great strength, is a companion of animals, as was Esau. Like Esau, too, he is covered with hair.

It is the very fact that Enkidu is born of clay that he can serve as a necessary counterfoil to the near-divinity, Gilgamesh. It is the task of Enkidu to rectify Gilgamesh's overweening pride, in a manner complementary to that in which the act of love transforms Enkidu. When the latter returns to the animals with whom he has lived, they take flight from him. He is no longer one of them. They recognize the difference between the way he was before his relationship with woman, and after.

Enkidu, like Adam, represents earth (Edom). Adam, too, evolves through his relationship with Eve. Like Enkidu, he loses his primal innocence — the Garden of Eden — although, in so doing, he also becomes human, thenceforth having to develop discrimination and consciousness.

Gilgamesh and Enkidu, like Isaac and Ishmael, Jacob and Esau, are brothers to one another, even as they oppose each other. The tale of Enkidu and Gilgamesh involves the interplay of primordial source and heroic search. We observe that conflict occurs between the two figures, just as does friendship. We have witnessed a destructive lust for power, yet constructive growth; brutality, yet forces that civilize.

No oversimplified battle between good and evil is waged in the *Epic of Gilgamesh*. Although victory for the ruler spells the reverse for his companion, it is only after Gilgamesh has seen Enkidu die — when he actually has experienced the death of his beloved friend — that the great hero feels compassion, as a result of bereavement. Fully comprehending, at last, that he too will die — but incapable of facing the fact — he labors to achieve immortality. Unable to retain its secret, he ultimately accepts death as inherent within life, thereby becoming heroically human.

Gilgamesh evolves, like each of us, both through love, and confronting the dark forces within and without; as a result of pain, struggle, anguish, and rising above them. When Gilgamesh goes to Utnapishtim to attain eternal life and fails, conflict finally subsides within him. It is then that he quite simply returns to the stronghold of Uruk, over which he rules. Whereupon he describes to the boatman, Urshanabi — who has taken him to and from Utnapishtim — how Uruk is divided into city, orchards, margin land, and the precinct of the Temple of Ishtar.

Uruk is a center of civilization in which law, order, the word, sagacity — constructive deeds — are valued. Because life must be fruitful and sustained, there are the orchards. And there is the margin land, too.

Finally, there is the precinct of the Temple of Ishtar. At the beginning of the epic, we are told that Gilgamesh has constructed a great sanctuary, dwelling of the goddess of love. But when, initially, he visits Ishtar, he goes to her in her form as Ishhara — a negative, because merely lustful, gesture on his part.

By the time he encounters Ishtar again, he has learned discrimination. His ability to withstand the temptations of the goddess represents the (death of illusion) the (transcending of mere lust,) the gaining of maturity. Similarly, the slaying of Humbaba typifies a mastery of fear.

Thus, at the epic's end, because the great hero has outgrown undisciplined desire, he rightfully indicates that the Temple of Ishtar is, in fact, a (sacred citadel of love.) As such, it is an essential part of the fourfold foundation of Uruk. Just as the city, itself, having been established by the Seven Sages — like all counterparts of what the gods created at the beginning — is a symbolical center of the world.

Despite having lost the secret of eternal life, Gilgamesh is nonetheless immortal. For when what is dross and imperfect in each of us fades from view, the positive remains. A sense of measure and of nourishing tradition is thereby contributed to those who remain behind: a new dimension of equilibrium, purpose, direction, form.

Even when we temporarily betray what is life-giving, our conscience ultimately warns us to rectify our error, else we perish. It is the hero who possesses the courage to listen — to alter his life in conformity with conscience. Although this rarely can take place in the first instance, there is a relentless imperative that it must ultimately occur as a result of experience, reversal, anguish, revelation.

> "Where Darkness and Light 'stand not distant from one another, but together in one another' [there are] the single track and 'strait way' that penetrate the cardinal 'point' on which the contraries turn; their unity is only to be reached by entering in there where they coincide: That is, in the last analysis, not any where or when, but within you; 'World's End is not to be found by walking. It is within this very fathom-long body that the pilgrimage must be made.'"

ANANDA K. COOMARASWAMY

123. JOHN THE BAPTIST
Altarpiece by Giovanni del Biondo. Italian. Last
third 14th century. Contini Collection,
Florence.

124. THE FEAST OF HEROD
Manuscript illumination from Gospel Book.
Ms. 13, folio 28 verso. German. 1250–1260.
Hofbibliothek, Aschaffenburg.

23 TRANSFORMATION: I

"Who can understand his errors? cleanse thou me from secret faults."

PSALMS 19:12

O n the opposite page, the life of the spirit is shown triumphant over temporal power, and also the reverse.

In the first instance (Plate 123) we see John the Baptist, precursor of Christ, standing upon Herod, whereas Plate 124 shows Herod in the ascendency. (The choice between John the Baptist and Herod is forever to be made by each of us — the dual forces representing life's eternally dual challenge.)

The altarpiece shows a recumbent Herod being trod upon by John the Baptist's talon-like feet and long, predacious nails.[1] The latter holds a cross staff and scroll. On the scroll is written "He treads upon Herod Antipas." St. Matthew (3:3) speaks of John the Baptist: "The voice of one crying in the wilderness, Prepare ye the way of the Lord, make his paths straight."

"Hail, all ye gods of the Temple of the Soul, who weigh heaven and earth in the balance."

PAPYRUS OF ANI

---

1. PAINTING IN FLORENCE AND SIENA AFTER THE BLACK DEATH, Millard Meiss, Princeton: Princeton University Press, 1951, p. 49.

Balancing of the Scales: It is at the midpoint in the netherworld that the crucial judgments are made — that a feather of truth is balanced against the heart, in order to ascertain whether *maat* or the right order (see Chapter 9), has indeed been achieved.

> *"A balance with the heart, symbolizing . . . conscience . . . in one scale, and the feather, emblematic of Right and Truth, in the other."*
>
> PAPYRUS OF ANI

> *"It is written: 'Justice, justice shalt thou follow.' For when a man believes that he is wholly just and need not strive further, then justice does not recognize him. You must follow justice and never stand still, and in your own eyes you must always be like a new-born child that has not yet achieved anything at all — for that is true justice."*
>
> MARTIN BUBER

> *"Jove lifts the golden balances that show*
> *The fates of mortal men and things below;*
> *Here each contending hero's lot he tries,*
> *And weighs with equal hand their destinies."*
>
> HOMER

24 TRANSFORMATION: II

"We have come full circle, not in an 'evolution of thought' but in our own understanding, from the position that the perfect celebration of rites is our task, to the position that the perfect performance of our tasks . . . is itself the celebration of the rite. Sacrifice, thus understood, is no longer a matter of doing specifically sacred things only on particular occasions, but of sacrificing (making sacred) *all we do and all we are."*

ANANDA K. COOMARASWAMY

"Sacred rites are an imitation — a union of the imitator with the deity imitated."

OTTO G. VON SIMSON

"The Myth," wrote Coomaraswamy, "is not a 'poetic invention' in the sense these words now bear: on the other hand, and just because of its universality, it can be told, and with equal authority, from many different points of view. . . . Myth [is] the penultimate truth, of which all experience is the temporal reflection. The mythical narrative is of timeless and placeless validity, true nowever and everywhere: just as in Christianity, 'In the beginning God created' and 'Through him all things were made,' regardless of the millennia that come between the dateable words, [which amounts] to saying that the creation took place at Christ's 'eternal birth.' 'In the beginning' . . . or rather 'at the summit,' means 'in the first cause': just as in our still told myths, 'once upon a time' does not mean 'once' alone but 'once for all.' . . .

"In this eternal beginning there is only the Supreme Identity of 'That One' . . . without differentiation of being from non-being, light from darkness, or separation of sky from earth. The All is for the present impounded in the first principle, which may be spoken of as the Person, Progenitor, Mountain, Tree, Dragon or endless Serpent. Related to this principle by filiation or younger brotherhood and *alter ego* rather than another principle, is the Dragon-slayer, born to supplant the Father and take possession of the kingdom, distributing its treasures to his followers. For if there is to be a world, the prison must be shattered and its potentialities liberated. This can be done either in accordance with the Father's will or against his will; he may 'choose death for his children's sake,' or it may be that the Gods impose the passion upon him, making him their sacrificial victim. These are not contradictory doctrines, but different ways of telling one and the same story." Thus "the Dragon-Father [is] no more diminished by what he exhales than he is increased by what is repossest. He is the Death, on whom our life depends; and to the question 'Is Death one, or many?' the answer is made that 'He is one as he is there, but many as he is in his children here.'" [1] For symbolical death, in the above sense is, after all, the prelude — in myth, as in life — to revivification, to rebirth at a deeper level.

Before what we name God formed anything else, He "made matter — *materia, matrix, mater* — as the maternal womb of the universe, for it is a principle in mythology that material is the feminine component and spirit the masculine, their respective symbols being water or earth and air or fire." [2]

We have noted, in passing, how the Great Mother operates in her Benign, as well as her Terrible aspects. We have placed special emphasis upon the latter form, in accordance with which the problems are set that the hero in man must resolve. At this point, however, it is essential to consider the Good Mother in greater detail; to contemplate how the Madonna of Christianity, for example, functions in the latter role only.

Although, in the early phases of Christianity, the Conception of the Virgin Mother was not deemed miraculous or immaculate, as was that of the Christ Child, the Roman Catholic view of this subject altered gradually, yet substantially, even before the Reformation.

Thus Roman Catholics came to look upon Our Lady as having been born spiritually devoid of the taint of original sin, even though she was conceived physically, of human parents. Hence, not being possessed of the guilt of Adam, the Son of God could become incarnate within her, an event viewed as predestined from the very first.

Since, in this context, the Madonna's soul is spoken of as innocent, pure, she was enabled to give birth to Christ — referred to as the God-man — through being impregnated by the Holy Spirit or Ghost, the latter often symbolized by the dove, or by rays of light.

---

1. Coomaraswamy, HINDUISM AND BUDDHISM, pp. 6–7.
2. Watts, op. cit., p. 46.

126. **VIRGIN AND CHILD
IN A CRESCENT**
Woodcut by Albrecht Dürer. German.
c. 1511. The Metropolitan Museum of Art, New
York. Gift of Junius S. Morgan, 1919.

The Madonna and apple are shown at left in Plate 127. At right is the Christ Child, holding a book: the Logos:[3] "In the beginning was the word." At one level, God is to be seen working through woman. Existence is expressed by way of woman. From another perspective, God incarnate — born of the Virgin Mother — is the Christ Child, personifying not only love, but also consciousness: the word — the Way. The Christ Child moves from the Mother Goddess into life, cutting the cords of dependence at His very birth.

---

3. Logos: *"Theol.* Christ, the divine word; used by St. John, and thence passing into theological use, under the influence of the philosophies of Plato and Philo Judaeus, as a name for the second person of the Trinity considered as the expression or incarnation of the Divine Reason, esp. as the mediatory between God and man." WEBSTER'S INTERNATIONAL DICTIONARY.

127. MADONNA AND CHILD
Polychromed wood statue from Seon Cloister.
Upper Bavarian Master. German. c. 1430.
Bayerisches Nationalmuseum, Munich.

128. CHRIST ON THE TREE OF
LIFE (THE INSTITUTION
OF THE ROSARY)
Painting by Alsatian Master. Alsatian. 3rd
quarter 15th century. Musée des Beaux Arts
de la Ville de Strasbourg.

The figures in Plate 128 radiate from Christ crucified. On one side depictions of the two St. Johns — John the Baptist, the precursor of Christ, and John, His beloved disciple — flank the portrayal of the Virgin Mary. On the opposite side we see St. Peter — the first Pope; the enactment of the Mass, and various saints.

"In early Christianity, the identification of the cross with the Saviour was so close, and so often was the cross idealized as a living tree, that there are many invocations of it as 'a divine tree, a noble tree, the likeness of which no earthly forest could produce.' Therefore crosses of conventionalized living vegetation were regarded as the particular symbol of Christ Himself, the divine source of life." [4]

"It is by no means without good and sufficient reasons that Jesus was called the 'Son of the carpenter,' for indeed there is a 'wood' of which the world is wrought by the Master Carpenter." [5]

The rebirth of Lazarus foreshadows the resurrection of Christ. It is John the Baptist who cries out in the wilderness. It is John the Baptist, too, who proclaims, "After me cometh a man which is preferred before me: for he was before me."

In the view of many Christian historians and philosophers, it is Christ who brings Adam back through the jaws of the dragon into Paradise. Even "as Moses lifted up the serpent in the wilderness, even so must the Son of man be lifted up." [6]

---

4. SIXTEEN ILLUSTRATIONS FROM AN EXHIBITION OF RELIGIOUS SYMBOLISM IN ILLUMINATED MANU-
SCRIPTS, New York: The Pierpont Morgan Library, 1944, unnumbered p.
5. "TWO PASSAGES IN DANTE'S *PARADISO,*" Ananda K. Coomaraswamy, SPECULUM, Vol. XI, No. 3, July,
1936, p. 329n^2.
6. ST. JOHN 1:15; 3:14.

*129. CRUCIFIXION, AND THE
SERPENT LIFTED UP
From thaler struck by goldsmith Hieronymus
Magdeburger of Annaberg. German. 1st
quarter 16th century.

130. R E S U R R E C T I O N
Fresco by Fra Angelico. Italian. Between
1438 and 1443. Museo San Marco, Florence.

"Jesus said unto them, Yet a little while is the light with you. Walk
while ye have the light, lest darkness come upon you: for he that walketh
in darkness knoweth not whither he goeth. While ye have light, believe in
the light, that ye may be the children of light." [7]

"And they shall scourge him, and put him to death: and the third day
he shall rise again. And they understood none of these things: and this
saying was hid from them, neither knew they the things which were
spoken." [8]

7. ST. JOHN 12:35–36.
8. ST. LUKE 18:33–34.

"And when they were come to the place, which is called Calvary, there they crucified him, and the malefactors, one on the right hand, and the other on the left.

"Then said Jesus, Father, forgive them; for they know not what they do."

"And it was about the sixth hour, and there was a darkness over all the earth until the ninth hour. And the sun was darkened, and the veil of the temple was rent in the midst. And when Jesus had cried with a loud voice, he said, Father, into thy hands I commend my spirit: and having said thus, he gave up the ghost."

"And they found the stone rolled away from the sepulchre. And they entered in, and found not the body of the Lord Jesus. And it came to pass, as they were much perplexed thereabout, behold, two men stood by them in shining garments: And as they were afraid, and bowed down their faces to the earth, they said unto them, Why seek ye the living among the dead? He is not here, but is risen: remember how he spake unto you when he was yet in Galilee." [9]

———————— ◆ ————————

"The two dragons knotted about the 'waist' of the . . . 'thunderbolt' " in the Bazaklik representation (Plate 131) divide "the upper from the lower range," which correspond, as Coomaraswamy has pointed out, to Vedic and Gnostic[10] forms that at once separate and connect heaven and earth.[11] The image we see resembles a tree, within which there are lotus forms, upon one of which the Bodhisattva is seated.

"That the ancient symbol of the Tree of Life . . . should . . . have been chosen to represent the Buddha is highly significant; for . . . every traditional symbol necessarily carries with it its original values, even when used or intended to be used in a more restricted sense. . . . The Tree of

---

9. ST. LUKE 23:33–34,44–46;24:2–6.

10. The words Vedic and Gnostic relate to knowledge. "Vedic" pertains to the body of sacred literature contained in four ancient Indian sacred books: the Rig, Yajur, Sama, and Atharva Vedas.

"Gnostic" was the name of certain heretical sects among early Christians who claimed they possessed esoteric knowledge of spiritual matters or mysteries. They interpreted sacred writings by means of a mystical philosophy.

11. "The Tree of Jesse and Oriental Parallels," Ananda K. Coomaraswamy, PARNASSUS, 1935, Vol. VII, No. 1, p. 18n^4.

Life, synonymous with all existence, all the worlds, all life, springs up, out, or down into space from its root in the navel centre of the Supreme Being."

"The World-tree . . . equally in and apart from its Buddhist application, is the procession of incessant life. [The tree] standing erect and midmost in the garden of life [extends] from Earth to Heaven, branching throughout Space (. . . 'space' [that] is 'within you')." [12]

---

12. Coomaraswamy, ELEMENTS OF BUDDHIST ICONOGRAPHY, pp. 7–8,11.

131. THE BODHISATTVA PADMAPANI, SIX-ARMED AND SUPPORTED BY A LOTUS
Painting. c. 9th century. Bazaklik, Murtuq, Turkistan.

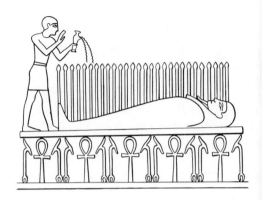

*132. THE CORPSE OF OSIRIS
SPROUTING GRAIN AND
WATERED BY A SERVANT
From bas-relief. Philae. Egyptian. Roman
period. c. 1st–3rd centuries.

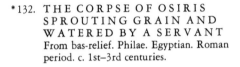

Remote though the origins of Osiris as a grain god may be, he was so identified and worshipped in ancient Egypt. He was not simply a god of death, but his resurrection symbolized the renewal of life and growth — in this instance typified by the sprouting of grain from his own grave.

Below the figure of Osiris are "Ankh" symbols, signifying life, flanked by forms named "Was Scepters" — the latter alluding to dominion.

"The ineffable mystery that [is] Osiris, though always dying in the grain, always revives."

HENRI FRANKFORT

"Except a corn of wheat fall into the ground and die, it abideth alone: but if it die, it bringeth forth much fruit. He that loveth his life shall lose it; and he that hateth his life in this world shall keep it unto life eternal." [13] (Plate 133.)

The phoenix — to the Chinese, the vermilion bird — was, at times, represented in ancient Egypt as a symbol of rebirth — as "He who comes to life through himself." In the *Book of the Dead,* the deceased says: "I enter as a hawk, I come out as a phoenix in the morning." [14] (Plate 134.)

---

13. ST. JOHN 12:24–25.

14. See Chapter 13 of the Egyptian BOOK OF THE DEAD, as quoted in THE SHRINES OF TUT-ANKH-AMON, translated by Alexandre Piankoff, edited by N. Rambova, Bollingen Series XL, New York: Pantheon Books, 1955, p. 21*n*[41].

*133. GRIFFIN ON WHEAT SHEAF
WITH A SPEAR IN ITS MOUTH
From gold coin. Greek. 315–300 B.C.
Panticapaeum.

134. PHOENIX
Pottery tile. Chinese. Han dynasty, 206 B.C.–
221 A.D. The Cleveland Museum of Art.
Gift of Dr. Vladimir G. Simkhovitch.

135. K A R T T I K E Y A
Bas-relief. Indian. c. early 7th century. Cave
No. 1. Exterior. Badami, India. Photograph
by Gunvor Moitessier. Original in Collection
Dorothy Norman, New York.

There is an ancient Indian myth relating to the god Karttikeya (Plate 135), who rides on his vehicle, the peacock. If we consider but a single aspect of the various accounts of Karttikeya and the demon Taraka that have come down to us, what is suggested is so hauntingly provocative that, did it not exist, there would be a temptation to invent it.

It is told that there once existed a demon Taraka, whom none could succeed in destroying. Since it became absolutely essential that he be vanquished, a problem of unparalleled seriousness arose. Who was to fell him?

When the monster demanded that he be made invulnerable, Brahma, the all-pervading spirit of the universe, granted his wish, but with limitations. The great god explained how no beings endowed with bodies "are exempt from death. Choose therefore your death," he declared. "Let it be by the hand of the one you fear the least." To which Taraka replied he would choose to perish by the hand of an infant seven days old, thinking to himself, "What infant of seven days could kill me?" He then set forth to conquer the world, driving the gods from their thrones and realms. Because of the boon bestowed upon him by Brahma, none he encountered could withstand him.

Taraka thenceforth "established his tyrannical empire . . . even presuming to release the gods after he had overthrown them." "Go where you please!" he exclaimed. " 'The universe is your prison. You cannot escape; you cannot oppose my will.' Indra, the king, and all the other deities were roaming over the surface of the earth like vagrant beggars, or like destitute monarchs in exile, while impudent Taraka sat on high, on Indra's throne.

"Filled with despair, the gods betook themselves in impotent wrath to Brahma, begging his assistance and advice," but he replied that the being to destroy " 'Taraka does not yet exist; for what infant possesses strength enough to kill this demon? What parents, moreover, should be potent enough to generate such an infant-hero? None but the Great Goddess [Uma] could bear the child; no male but the Great God, Shiva . . . has, through his timeless austerities, stored up the boundless energies needed to beget such a being.' The gods, therefore, began to concentrate on the bringing of this divine couple together, and it was a long task, beset with difficulties, disappointments, even catastrophes."

When Shiva finally "condescended" to become the lover and husband of the Goddess Uma (also named Parvati) — that is, when the two higher planes of intelligence or consciousness were to be united — it was possible for the miraculous child, Karttikeya, or new, fiery energy to be conceived. Although the gods had wished this great event to occur, they finally became fearful lest the child to be born might shatter the world "by its very coming into being." Hence they "sent the fire-god Agni to receive Shiva's seed in his fiery mouth." Because Agni could not retain its glowing essence, "it fell to the ground, where it turned into a golden lake with golden lotuses." When Parvati drank from the waters, "she conceived her child, Skanda Karttikeya." [15]

So it was that Karttikeya was miraculously born, and when seven days old, vanquished Taraka: Karttikeya, the ever-chaste one, symbol of intactness, the eternally virginal, the forever young, who rides upon his peacock, typifying the yogic principle of independence.

So it is, too, that once everything upon which we have relied in the past fails to bring light out of darkness, it is the equivalent of Karttikeya we must bring to life — a new being capable of replacing whatever tyrant threatens our well-being. Equally important is the fact that even the way in which change is to be brought about must transcend all that has occurred before, one of man's most extraordinary qualities consisting of his power to regenerate himself in the face of the most severe disruptions and unpredictable disasters.

The new-born Karttikeyas of the world must eternally proceed with their hitherto unwaged struggles. Which is to suggest that we must continue our own search with unceasing courage; that we must, without surcease, both confront and transmute the diabolical Tarakas within ourselves. And who is to say that Taraka is anything other than a form of Vritra who — as was shown at the very outset — was intent upon thwarting the release of the world's creative energies, including what is life-enhancing within each of us?

We began our discourse at dawn, with the god Indra; with the Dioskouroi and the Aswins — the latter representing the twofold force that

---

15. Zimmer, THE ART OF INDIAN ASIA, Vol. I, pp. 118, 284.

activates and vitalizes. Whereas now we have encountered the menacing Taraka — Tara, itself, meaning star. Is it not even possible that the very reason Taraka initially became a demon was that he permitted the star within his name to sink into darkness and to remain there? For if the life principle becomes weak and deficient, disintegration and extinction threaten. Hence Taraka was in danger of obliterating all light, until Karttikeya appeared with his power to rekindle and release it — to bring night over into the new day: the task of each of the heroes. And, even though "the springs of life" are ever beyond comprehension — "are a secret and have always remained so"— it seems entirely fitting that their mystery should be described as "the Supreme Secret," [16] still another name of the valiant, revivifying Karttikeya.

"Zeus, disguised as a mortal, had a secret love affair with Semele ('moon'), daughter of King Cadmus of Thebes. . . . Jealous Hera, disguising herself as an old neighbour, advised Semele, then already six months with child, to make her mysterious lover a request: that he would no longer deceive her, but reveal himself in his true nature and form. How, otherwise, could she know that he was not a monster? Semele followed this advice and, when Zeus refused her plea, denied him further access to her bed. Then in anger, he appeared as thunder and lightning, and she was consumed. But Hermes saved her six-months son; sewed him up inside Zeus's thigh, to mature there for three months longer; and, in due course of time, delivered him." [17] Which is why Dionysos is often called the "twice-born" (Plate 136), or "the child of the double door."

---

16. Agrawala, op. cit., p. 5.
17. Graves, op. cit., Vol. I, p. 56.

*136. THE BIRTH OF DIONYSOS
From bas-relief. Greek. c. 1st century B.C.
Monumenti Musei e Gallerie Pontificie,
Vatican City.

The eternal hero — each of whose battles but leads to the next. (Plate 137.)

"The Sacrifice reflects the Myth; but like all reflections, inverts it. What had been a process of generation and division becomes now one of regeneration and composition. . . . To sacrifice is to be born, and it can be said, 'As yet unborn, forsooth, is the man who does not sacrifice.'"

ANANDA K. COOMARASWAMY

"The dark takes form in the heart of the white and reveals it."

RABINDRANATH TAGORE

137. RIDER SLAYING DRAGON
Stone relief. Italian. 9th century. Aversa.
Photograph by Bulloz.

Without Beginning or End: Because chaos does not end once and for all, any more than does creation, we find it often difficult to accept certain paradoxical situations that occur relentlessly: Were there no Vritra, there would be no Indra, quite as clearly as the reverse is true. Without Seth there would be no Horus; without Devadatta, no Buddha; without Satan, no Christ. Thus, although darkness must ever be combatted in favor of light, we must learn to function in the midst of the conflict between them, even as we must recognize what is negative within ourselves.

The god Indra's striking down of the serpent Vritra is a prototype of one of the essential acts to be performed by each of us. Unless an equivalent of the clash between these two great powers is perennially re-enacted, there can be no life worth the living.

Although, in the form of Sesha (mentioned in Chapter 14), the serpent means literally, and is, what is left over, Vritra is synonymous with drought. Hence, if we combine the two concepts, we find that, just as what is termed *at the very first* need not necessarily be thought of as literally *in the beginning,* so, when we speak of Vritra having been opposed by Indra — because holding back the waters would interfere with creation — drought *already* existed.

We have referred to the birth of the hero, yet his coming is ever proph-esied, and takes place just because tyrannical, oppressive powers *already* threaten mankind. Kadmos founds a citadel *as at the very inception of the world,* in imitation of what the gods did then, although, before he can accomplish his great task, he must slay an *already* existent dragon. More-over, when we are told that he, and no one else, may confront it, this must be so because the dragon exemplifies an aspect of Kadmos, himself, that he alone can transform (quite as much as it personifies a pernicious force in the outer world). Thus the goal of each of the heroes — like that of the god Indra — is inevitably to transcend what *already threatens.*

In certain traditional societies not even the simplest house can be built without every operation involved in its making serving as a rite — a reli-gious or devotional one — one that, as Coomaraswamy has described it, is again "a mimesis of what was done 'in the beginning.' " [18]

In India the symbolically "all-supporting Serpent" was pegged below

---

18. Coomaraswamy, SYMBOLISM OF THE DOME, p. 19.

the floor of each such structure — a custom that originated because the earth was viewed as insecure; as quaking like a lotus leaf, a gale "tossing it hither and thither."

"The architect," Coomaraswamy explains, "who drives down his peg into the head of the Serpent [underground], is doing what was done by the Gods in the beginning, what was done for example . . . by Indra when 'he smote the Serpent in his lair' . . . and what has been . . . and is done by every solar hero and Messiah when he transfixes the Dragon and treads him underfoot." [19] And were there no serpent underground, who is to say there would be an edifice rising toward the sky?

We began by alluding to Indra; to the thunderbolt; to lightning and the serpent — powers that serve to awaken us at varying levels. At this point, however, we find "It is by means of the sacrifice, the incantation, [the] reduction of potentiality to act, that the livid scaly snakeskin must be cast, and a sunny skin revealed; it is as a streak of serpentine lightning that the Wayfarer returns to the source from which he came forth, for which source and now goal no other symbol than that of lightning is adequate." [20] In other words, that which is awakened has become one with the awakener.

And, just because the basic theme of this volume has no beginning or end, what Stella Kramrisch has written is also of moment: The "residue is that which remains . . . when everything else has come to a conclusion. If something is complete in itself, perfection, nothing is left over, there is an end of it. If there is a remainder there is no end to it. So the remainder is the germ and material cause for what subsists." [21]

The necessity to transfix the serpent underground is quite as essential as to build the edifice rising above it, or to transform the "remainder." For what, after all, is the awakener, the awakened, or even the obstacle to awakening — the hero, or that which would thwart him? Each is an integral part of the mysteriously challenging, yet ever releasing process, without which human life lacks all form, all hope, all grandeur — *without beginning or end.*

19. Ibid., pp. 21–22.
20. Ibid., p. 43n^{51}.
21. Kramrisch, THE HINDU TEMPLE, Vol. I, p. 45.

As a result of the performing of the sacrifice: "We who were at war with ourselves are now reintegrated and where there had been a conflict of wills there is now unanimity. The reconciliation of conflicting powers for which the Sacrifice continually provides is also their marriage. There are more ways than one of 'killing' a Dragon. The Dragon-slayer's bolt [is] in fact a shaft of light — 'light the progenitive power.' It is the battle of love that has been won when the Dragon 'expires.' 'What is eaten is called by the eater's name and not its own.' "

"In reality, Slayer and Dragon, sacrificer and victim are of one mind behind the scenes, where there is no polarity of contraries. . . . The Dragon-slayer is *our Friend;* the Dragon must be pacified and made *a friend of.*"

ANANDA K. COOMARASWAMY

"The worst catastrophes of history are but seasonal rhythms in a vaster cycle of repetitions and renewals. The Furies who cross the stage, torches high, do but throw light upon one moment in the immense plot as it unfolds itself through time. Growing civilizations do not perish from the pangs of one autumn; they merely shed their leaves. Inertia is the only mortal danger. Poet is he who breaks for us the bonds of habit.

"In this way, in spite of himself, the poet also is tied to historical events. Nothing in the drama of his times is alien to him."

ST.-JOHN PERSE

"Such as men themselves are, such will God Himself seem to them to be."

JOHN SMITH, THE PLATONIST

"The way of truth is like a great road. . . . Do you go home and search for it and you will have an abundance of teachers."

MENCIUS

"Make your own Bible. Select and collect all the words and sentences that in all your reading have been to you like the blast of triumph out of Shakspear, Seneca, Moses, John and Paul."

RALPH WALDO EMERSON

It has been said that Devadatta, struck anew by the wonder of the Buddha, spoke to him: "My Lord, there never has been nor will be a Buddha like you." To which the Buddha replied: "Devadatta, have you known the Buddhas of the past?" "No, My Lord." "Perhaps you know the Buddhas that are to be?" "No, My Lord." "Then, perhaps you know me better than I know myself." "No, My Lord." "Then, oh Devadatta, how vain and empty are your words."

TRADITIONAL

"When a man grows aware of a new way in which to serve God, he should carry it around with him secretly, and without uttering it, for nine months, as though he were pregnant with it, and let others know of it only at the end of that time, as though it were a birth."

MARTIN BUBER

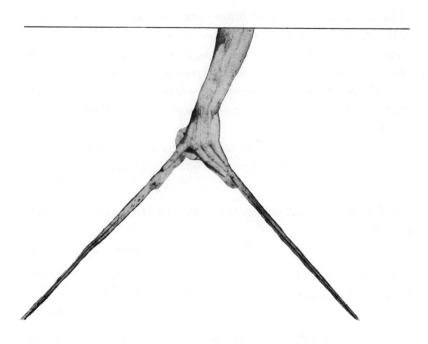

INDEX

Proper Names, Authors, Artists, Sacred Books, Places
(Numerals pertaining to illustrations are set in italics.)

ABOUT THE AUTHOR

Born in Philadelphia in 1905, Dorothy Norman moved to New York in 1925 and began a distinguished career as editor, publisher, columnist, writer, and photographer. From 1937 to 1948 she was editor and publisher of *Twice a Year* and simultaneously, from 1942 to 1949, wrote a regular column, "A World to Live In," for the *New York Post*. She has contributed innumerable poems, reviews, articles, and photographs to various publications in the United States and abroad. Her book *The Heroic Encounter* grew out of the widely heralded Exhibition of Symbolical Art, which Mrs. Norman conceived and prepared, and she chose the captions for the Museum of Modern Art's famous Family of Man photographic exhibition. Mrs. Norman was closely associated with Alfred Stieglitz from 1927 until his death, and wrote *Alfred Stieglitz — Introduction to an American Seer*, a tribute to the dean of American photographers. She is also the author of *Nehru — The First Sixty Years*; *Selected Writings of John Marin*; *America and Alfred Stieglitz*; *Indira Gandhi: Letters to an American Friend*; *Dualities*; and *Encounters — A Memoir*. Dorothy Norman lives in New York and is presently at work on a second collection of memoirs.